C.S. Lewis

"It may seem difficult to imagine that we could have a new take on C.S. Lewis's life when so much has been written – but this book is just that, thoroughly researched, wide-ranging, sympathetic, telling Lewis's story through the development of his greatest friendships, and so allowing us to see him not as a solitary genius but as someone whose brilliance was always being honed and clarified in conversation and letter-writing and plain human affection. This is a fine contribution to our understanding of a great man and a great disciple."
– **Rowan Williams**, Cambridge

"For many readers, C.S. Lewis books are like old friends – by turn wise, comforting, amusing, thought-provoking, and occasionally annoying. This is not surprising, because Lewis knew how to make and keep friends. This is a book about a man steeped in friendships: academic, literary, spiritual, and emotional. Colin Duriez's engaging and perceptive biography introduces us to C.S. Lewis's many friends – from childhood companions to the late-won love of his life – and in meeting them, we have a uniquely intimate encounter with the man himself."
– **Brian Sibley**, author of Shadowlands

In memory of David Porter
1945–2005

C.S. Lewis

=== *A biography of friendship* ===

COLIN DURIEZ

Published by Lion Books
an imprint of
Lion Hudson plc
Wilkinson House, Jordan Hill Road,
Oxford OX2 8DR, England
www.lionhudson.com/lion

ISBN 978 0 7459 5587 2
e-ISBN 978 0 7459 5725 8

First edition 2013

Picture Acknowledgments

p. i (top and bottom); p. iii (centre and
bottom); p. v (centre left); p. viii (top right):
Used by permission of The Marion E. Wade
Centre, Wheaton College, Wheaton, IL

p. ii (top left, top right, and bottom):
© Northern Ireland Tourist Board 2010

p. vi: © AmandaLewis/iStockphoto.com
All other images: © Colin Duriez

Text Acknowledgments

Every effort has been made to trace the
original copyright holders where required.
In some cases this has proved impossible.
We shall be happy to correct any such
omissions in future editions.

pp. 15, 17, 27, 30, 38, 39, 150, 151, 191:
Extracts from The Diaries of Warren Lewis
copyright © The Marion E. Wade Center,
Wheaton College, Wheaton Illinois.

pp. 16, 31, 42, 48, 77, 91, 95–96, 108, 115,
120, 121, 125, 135–36, 177: Extracts from
Surprised by Joy by C. S. Lewis copyright
© C. S. Lewis Pte. Ltd. 1955; pp. 22–23:
Extract from Boxen by C. S. Lewis copyright
© C. S. Lewis Pte. Ltd. 1985; p. 29: Extract
from The Magician's Nephew by C. S. Lewis
copyright © C. S. Lewis Pte. Ltd. 1955;
p. 68: Extract from Dymer by C. S. Lewis
copyright © C. S. Lewis Pte. Ltd. 1926;

pp. 160–61: Extracts from The Allegory of Love
by C. S. Lewis copyright © C. S. Lewis Pte.
Ltd. 1936; pp. 165–66: Extract from That
Hideous Strength by C. S. Lewis copyright ©
C. S. Lewis Pte. Ltd. 1945; p. 167: Extract
from The Abolition of Man by C. S. Lewis
copyright © C. S. Lewis Pte. Ltd. 1943,
1946, 1978. Reprinted by permission of The
C. S. Lewis Company.

pp. 42, 90, 92–93: Extracts from Owen
Barfield on C. S. Lewis edited by G. B.
Tennyson copyright © Owen Barfield, 2006.
Originally published by The Barfield Press;
pp. 88, 217: Extracts from Light on C. S. Lewis
edited by Jocelyn Gibb, 1965. Originally
published by Geoffrey Bles. Reprinted by
permission of Owen Barfield.

pp. 43, 69, 116, 125, 134, 145, 162,
181, 212, 222: Extracts from C. S. Lewis:
A Biography by Roger Lancelyn Green and
Walter Hooper copyright © Green and
Hooper, 1988. Reprinted by permission of
HarperCollins Publishers Ltd.

pp. 43, 77, 80: Extracts from C. S. Lewis:
A Biography by A. N. Wilson copyright ©
A. N. Wilson, 2005. Reprinted by permission
of Aitken Alexander.

pp. 92, 185: Extracts from C. S. Lewis at the
Breakfast Table and Other Reminiscences edited
by James T. Como copyright © James T.
Como, 1980. Originally published by Simon
and Schuster, reprinted by permission of
James T. Como.

p. 156: Extract from "Against the Stream:
C. S. Lewis and the Literary Scene" by Harry
Blamires in Journal of the Irish Christian Study
Centre copyright © Harry Blamires, 1983.
Reprinted by permission of Harry Blamires.

pp. 161–62: Extract from The Place of the Lion
by Charles Williams copyright © Charles
Williams, 1931; p. 176: Extract from The
House by the Stable by Charles Williams
copyright © Charles Williams. Reprinted by
permission of David Higham.

p. 167: Extract from Voyages to the Moon
by Marjorie Hope Nicolson copyright ©
Marjorie Hope Nicolson, 1948. Sourced
from Simon and Schuster.

A catalogue record for this book is available
from the British Library

Printed and bound in the UK, September
2013, LH26

Contents

Preface

An Oxford student of C.S. Lewis's told J.R.R. Tolkien that he found his new tutor interesting. Tolkien responded: "Interesting? Yes, he's certainly that. You'll never get to the bottom of him."

There is a proverb in a number of languages that goes like this: "Tell me who your friends are, and I'll tell you who you are." You can learn a great deal about people by their friends – the company they keep – and nowhere is this more true than in the case of C.S. Lewis, the remarkable academic, author, popularizer of faith, and creator of Narnia.

Throughout Lewis's life, key relationships mattered deeply to him, from his early days in the north of Ireland and his schooldays in England, as a teenager in the trenches of the First World War, and then later in Oxford. The friendships he cultivated throughout his life proved to be vital, influencing his thoughts, his beliefs, and his writings.

My biography of Lewis focuses on some of his most important friendships, including members of the literary group associated with him, the Inklings. Along with the places and events of his life, as well as his writings, these friendships help us to understand just who C.S. Lewis was. What did Arthur Greeves, for instance, a lifelong friend from his adolescence, bring to him? How did J.R.R. Tolkien, and the other members of the now famous Inklings, shape him? Why, in his early twenties, did he share a home with a single mother twice his age, Janie Moore, looking after her for so many years until her death? And why did he choose to marry so late? What of the relationship with his alcoholic and gifted brother, who joined his unusual household?

C.S. Lewis was, in many ways, a remarkable enigma, as Tolkien intimated to the student. He guarded his inner life, yet attracted his readers by his friendly, warm, and open tone. Even in his erudite scholarship, the reader feels they are being treated as an equal with whom Lewis's insights into ancient poets and writers are being shared. Lewis appears to assume you are a fellow learner, but wears his knowledge lightly. He does not intimidate, but draws you in. As the narrator of the Narnian stories, his voice is simply like that of a kindly uncle.

An atheist for much of his formative early life, Lewis became one of the most well known of modern popularizers of the Christian faith. Yet the scope of his varied books is not limited by age, creed, or nationality. He wrote books for children as well as for students and scholars, and successfully explored new genres such as science fiction and fantasy for adults. He breathed new life into the traditional world of theological writing, with his best-selling *The Screwtape Letters,* which put him on the cover of *Time* magazine after the Second World War, signalling an extraordinary impact upon America that has lasted to this day. Works of his literary scholarship are still in print half a century after his death, and he is a household name in the British Isles, mainly through his *The Chronicles of Narnia.*

My book is not aimed at the scholar, but the general reader who may have read a Narnia book or two, or perhaps *The Screwtape Letters*. Some readers may have dipped into his popular theology, such as *Mere Christianity*, or the record of his bereavement in losing his wife, *A Grief Observed*. Others may have seen the film *Shadowlands*, or an adaptation of a Narnia story.

Though my book aims first of all to tell the story of Lewis's life, and the part played in it by his friends, it draws upon the latest scholarship (suitably digested) and unpublished material housed at The Marion E. Wade Center, Wheaton College, Illinois, USA, and at the Bodleian Library, Oxford.

The Marion E. Wade Center in particular holds extensive writings by Warren Hamilton Lewis (known as Warnie), bequeathed by him to its archives, and oral history interviews from those who knew Lewis and have since died. The centre shares copies of W.H. Lewis's manuscripts with the Bodleian. Scholars and others knowledgeable of C.S. Lewis to whom I'm indebted are too numerous to mention, but I must especially acknowledge previous biographers Roger Lancelyn Green, Walter Hooper, A.N. Wilson, George Sayer, Alan Jacobs, Douglas Gresham, and others writing from an Ulster context (David Bleakley, Ronald W. Bresland, and Derick Bingham). There are those too who wrote of Lewis's relationship with Joy Davidman (Brian Sibley, Douglas Gresham, Don W. King, and Lyle Dorsett) and the Inklings (Humphrey Carpenter and Diana Glyer). David C. Downing's *The Most Reluctant Convert* was also invaluable, as was K.J. Gilchrist's *A Morning After War*.

A special note of thanks must be given to Bruce L. Edwards for allowing me to adapt sections from my chapter in volume one of *C.S. Lewis: Life, Works, and Legacy* (Praeger Publishers), and to the Paulist Press for similarly giving permission to adapt material from my book *Tolkien and C.S. Lewis: The Gift of Friendship*. Always at my side was my *The C.S. Lewis Chronicles* (BlueBridge) – I must thank the publisher of that, my friend Jan Guerth, for persuading me to compile it some years ago. It helped me immensely in finding my way through the tangled terrain of the chronology of Lewis's life; he went through three conversions (to atheism, then theism, then Christianity), an enormous number of house moves, and much else. I also must mention the help of my publisher, particularly Ali Hull, Jessica Tinker, Margaret Milton, Sheila Jacobs, Miranda Lever, Jude May, Leisa Nugent, and Rhoda Hardie.

A note is needed about naming. With Clive Staples Lewis, I tend to call him Jack (the name he adopted when very young, and by which he was thereafter known by family and close friends) when writing about his childhood and teenage years, and usually Lewis after that. His family also called him "Jacks". With his brother, Warren Hamilton Lewis, I use the name by which he was almost universally known – Warnie.

An important preparation for writing this biography was my student years in the seventies at the University of Ulster, Coleraine, in Northern Ireland. I stayed in various digs in Portrush, Portstewart, Downhill, and Castlerock. As I explored the north Antrim coast, the articles and other pieces on C.S. Lewis I was writing, and talks I was giving at that time, helped me to discover Lewis's close childhood association with that area and other parts of Ulster. I found I had already explored Cair Paravel, to give just one instance, in the Narnia stories; actually, it was Dunluce Castle, its ruins towering over the cliffs near sandy beaches in one direction and the Giant's Causeway in another. Over the years I revisited that area often, and other parts of the north of Ireland.

During a conference in Belfast in 1998 marking the centenary of Lewis's birth, a highlight was being shown around Little Lea, his childhood home, which remains a private residence. The whole experience was enhanced by friends I made in Ulster, such as John and Rosalind Gillespie. There is no doubt that the north of Ireland, along with County Donegal, shared the same status in Lewis's affection as Oxford: places in which he felt most at home.

Colin Duriez
Keswick, December 2012

1

A Northern Irish Childhood

Lessons of the day, given by their governess, Annie Harper, were long over. The weather had improved since then. Two small boys were returning home from a walk when the younger noticed a rainbow. His face alight with excitement, he pointed it out to his older brother, Warnie (Warren). The younger was convinced that the rainbow ended by their house.

Running nearer, the two saw that the shining arc seemed indeed to touch the ground in the middle of the path from the gate to the front door.

Always persuasive, the youthful C.S. Lewis convinced his older brother that they must dig there for the crock of gold. Jack, as he insisted on being called, reminded Warnie of stories their nurse, Lizzie Endicott, had told them about buried pots of gold at the end of rainbows. It was characteristic of the younger boy that he could convince the older, and also act on what gripped his imagination. When their cousin Claire Lewis sometimes visited, Warnie did not need persuading to join his brother and Claire in the large oak wardrobe carved by their grandfather. There, as they sat on its floor, Jack would tell Warnie and Claire (who was Warnie's age) stories of his own. In the gloom, Claire recalled years later, she and Warnie would listen silently "while Jacks told us his tales of adventure".[1]

Soon the two brothers were energetically digging up the garden path. The dense shrubbery hid their digging from watchful eyes in the house. As the dusk deepened, the boys had yet to uncover the treasure. Finally, they were forced to obey the summons for tea from the house.

It was not long before the front door was flung open and their dishevelled father burst in. In the twilight, smart-suited Albert Lewis had stumbled into the substantial hole in the path, the contents of his briefcase tumbling out. In his fury, Albert refused to listen to Jack's explanation, perfectly reasonable to the young boy, or to his older brother. Assuming his solicitor's role as if he were in a police court, but not measuring his anger, Albert accused his sons of deliberately creating a booby trap for him. Nothing would convince him otherwise. Their sentence is not recorded.

Clive Staples Lewis was born on 29 November 1898, on the wealthy fringes of Belfast in the north of Ireland, the second son of successful city solicitor Albert, and Florence (Flora), the daughter of a clergyman. His brother, Warnie, was three and a half years older than him. Belfast in 1898 and into the twentieth century was humming as a burgeoning industrial city. At its heart was one of the world's greatest shipyards. It was proud to have the largest gantry in the British Isles and launched the biggest ship, the *Oceanic*, and later its sister, the short-lived *Titanic*. As the leading city economy in Ireland, Belfast's prosperity grew, and privileged families, including the Lewises, prospered with it.

Jack's father was the son of an evangelical Welshman and engineer, Richard Lewis, who had settled in Ireland and been a partner in a shipping company in the nearby docks. Jack's mother, Flora, was considered to have the more cultured breeding, because of her aristocratic and highly intelligent mother, Mary Warren. Flora came from County Cork in the south of Ireland and, unusually for a woman at that time, was educated at Queen's University, Belfast (then the Royal University of Ireland), obtaining First Class honours in algebra, geometry, and logic. She sensibly avoided her mother's eccentric lifestyle. Jack Lewis remembered Flora as a "voracious reader of novels". She wrote short stories and other pieces, including "The Princess Rosetta", which was published in *The Household Journal* of 1889, and an accomplished parody of a sermon. Albert also had literary aspirations, including poetry writing, but it seems none of his verses were published.

As a growing and alert child, Jack soon noticed the contrast in their temperaments – Albert was passionate and emotionally unpredictable, while Flora was analytical and cool in her emotions. Sunny and stable, she was the young boy's dependable Atlantis (as Lewis later put it), a great island continent of peacefulness. Jack's early life was marked by the reassuring presence of his highly educated mother. Flora's personality is captured in letters she wrote to Albert (rarely) while he was away from home, or (often) while she was away on long summer vacations with their boys. When baby Jack was nearly eighteen months old, Albert had to be away in London on business for a while. She wrote of "Babbins": "If you ask where Daddy is, he says 'gone'." In another letter to Albert, in London, Flora mentions looking after "Babsie" and "Badgie" (Warnie) while suffering a headache. She tells Albert it had been a very stormy night, with hard rain. The next day her sister-in-law, Jack's Aunt Annie, had come around, bringing her second child, baby Ruth. Flora notes that "Clive is about, and was anxious to look at it, but objected to be asked to kiss it".[2]

Some months later in 1900, Flora took her sons, accompanied by their maid, for a long summer holiday in Ballycastle, on the north Antrim coast, where she relished the crisp air. Albert, as usual, remained behind, working. He hated any change in his routine, a trait that later would affect his relationship with his sons. Describing baby Jack to him in a letter, she observed, "Babsie is talking like anything. He astonished me this morning; Warren sniffled, and he turned around and said, 'Warnie wipe nose.'"

The precocious infant was not averse to creating words. Flora continued: "There are some nice girls in the house next to us who talk to him and Warren in the garden. Baby calls them the

'Joddies'." She remarked that Baby enjoyed the story of the three bears that Martha, the maid, was reading to Warren. It was some time after this that the toddler declared, pointing to himself, "He is Jacksie." Jacksie was later shortened to "Jacks" and then "Jack". Thereafter he refused to answer to any other name, according to Warnie. "Jack" turned out to be the name by which he was known to family and close friends throughout his life

Sometime probably in the following year, 1901, Warnie brought the lid of a biscuit tin into his younger brother's nursery. He had created a miniature garden or forest in the lid, from moss, twigs, and flowers. When he looked at it, Jack encountered beauty for the first time, an "incurably romantic" experience, or epiphany of what he called "joy", despite the crudity of the art.

> It made me aware of nature – not, indeed, as a storehouse of forms and colours but as something cool, dewy, fresh, exuberant. I do not think the impression was very important at the moment, but it soon became important in memory. As long as I live my imagination of Paradise will retain something of my brother's toy garden.[3]

Warnie was always to have a more heightened perception of the ordinary natural world than his brother, and one of the gifts to Jack of Warnie's friendship was to teach him to see more clearly the natural world. The experience of joy or longing that the adult C.S. Lewis speaks about, of which the toy garden was one of many pivotal examples, ran like a thread through his life, helping in his later return to belief in God and Christian faith from atheism in adulthood.

In June and July 1901, when Jack was two years old, he went on holiday with Flora, Warnie, and nurse/housemaid Lizzie Endicott to the small seaside resort of Castlerock, on the north coast of Ireland. Many years later, Lewis told his brother of his first experience of viewing the sea. In an unpublished memoir, Warren records that "when he first saw it he had not mastered perspective;

to him then, the horizon appeared only a few yards away, and so high above his head that the effect was like looking upwards at water streaming over a weir".[4] This amazing infant memory may perhaps have contributed to Lewis's beautiful imagining of the approach to Aslan's Country in *The Voyage of the "Dawn Treader"*, where the very world's end of Narnia is portrayed.

> It was if a wall stood up between them and the sky, a greenish-grey, trembling, shimmering wall. Then up came the sun, and at its first rising they saw it through the wall and it turned into wonderful rainbow colours. Then they knew that the wall was really a long, tall wave – a wave endlessly fixed in one place as you may often see at the edge of a waterfall.[5]

Beyond the unmoving wave, and behind the sun, the voyagers could glimpse the vastly tall, verdant mountains of Aslan's Country.

On showery days, Flora kept the boys near the railway station or the house in which they were staying, so as not to get caught in the rain. The station was as big an attraction as the beach, with the steam engines puffing through the small town and into the tunnel just by the station, heading in the direction of Downhill around the coast. Trains from the other way would dramatically emerge from the tunnel's darkness.

In one of her many letters, Flora told Albert that Baby had made friends with the stationmaster. The toddler went with her to pick up a newspaper, "and as soon as he saw him in the distance he called out, 'Hello, station master.'" Within a few weeks, Jack was insisting upon calling out, "Good morning Robert" every morning to the stationmaster, and getting a smile in return. Baby Jack continued to be "infatuated" with the steam trains stopping at Castlerock – Flora reported to Albert that if he saw a "siglan" down, he had to be taken back to the station.[6]

In another letter, Flora told a further railway tale about the toddler.

Here is a story to amuse the old people. I took him to buy
a [toy] engine, and the woman asked him if she should tie
a string to it for him. Baby just looked at her with great
contempt and said, "Baby doesn't see any string on the engines
what baby sees on the station." You never saw a woman so
taken aback as she was.[7]

The correspondence wasn't one-sided. A letter came for Flora
from Albert that included a poem. She expressed pleasure at it
in her reply, considering that it had real feeling in it, rather than
(as usual with Albert, she felt) being "written for the sake of the
verses". Poignantly – in the light of her early death a little over
seven years later – Flora wrote about their love:

I don't see that there is anything else to look to in this life for
comfort or happiness, at least for you and me. I don't think
either of us could ever find pleasure in outside things in which
the other had not a part; it is going to be so with us always,
isn't it dear?[8]

As the family prospered, it nevertheless took a great deal of time
for Flora to persuade her husband to move house from their
rented accommodation – he was pathologically averse to change,
as mentioned before. By 1905, however, the young family was able
to move to a larger, specially built house nearby, which they called
Little Lea.

The often eccentric construction of the house is not evident in an
estate agent's description over fifty years later, when structurally
it still resembled the original house (though the lack of proper
foundations presumably had been remedied by then).

Little Lea was advertised in 1957 as a "residence of distinction"
with about two acres of land, and continues:

This Well-Built Residence is situated in a secluded position
on the Circular Road, convenient to Campbell College and

Stormont, and is approached by two gravel drives.

The Grounds are tastefully laid out for ease of management in lawns, rose beds, rock gardens, &c.

Lounge Hall with Fireplace; 3 Reception-rooms; 4 Principal Bedrooms; 2 Secondary Bedrooms; Dressing-room; 2 Bathrooms; Kitchen (Esse cooker); Double Garage; Greenhouses. The Rooms are spacious and the excellent woodwork includes parquet flooring in the Principal Bedrooms and oak and maple floors in the Hall and Reception-rooms....

His new home was "almost a major character in my story", Lewis later wrote. The house was soon bursting with books, lodged into every conceivable space, even the attic. Jack was to explore unhindered, savouring books that were (he later said) suitable and unsuitable, but discovering authors connected by a hidden path that was to continue to run through his own writings. From the moment he could read, he gave his allegiance, he tells us, to books in which the horns of elfland could be heard – stories and poetry of romance, carrying tantalizing glimpses of other worlds, whether worlds of the spirit or imagined ones.[9]

The native stories told him by Lizzie Endicott reinforced this allegiance, rooted as they were, he tells us, in "the peasantry of County Down". County Down, in fact, was a fundamental source of the later land of Narnia. As well as explaining during a snowstorm that "the old woman in the sky was plucking her goose", the nurse told him folk and fairy tales of Ireland. The boy sat enraptured as she recounted stories of leprechauns and pots of buried gold, the sagas of Cuchulain, the champion of Ulster, and legends of the faery people and their immortal worlds, the Isle of Apples and Tir-na-nÓg, the Land of Youth.

Into this imaginative world of Lizzie Endicott's storytelling came Jack's discovery of the early Beatrix Potter books. Stories such as *The Tale of Benjamin Bunny* and *The Tale of Squirrel Nutkin* told of talking animals, and were accompanied by exquisite coloured illustrations. The stories were set in the Lake District in northern England. Squirrel Nutkin gave him a clear experience of beauty and what he later described as "the Idea of Autumn", which enchanted the young Lewis and connected with his growing sense of "sweet desire" or inconsolable longing, so important in his writings as an adult. Such an enchantment was also highlighted for him, and Warnie, by the outlook from their upstairs window in their house.

The site on which Little Lea was built had been chosen by Albert and Flora because of its view. The north side of the house looked down over fields to Belfast Lough, with the "long mountain line of the Antrim shore" beyond, while the south side faced the Holywood Hills, "greener, lower, and nearer" than the Antrim slopes. As the boys grew, they were able to walk and cycle around those Holywood Hills. Here Lewis's lifelong devotion to the countryside of County Down was shaped. From the hills one could see the expanse of Strangford Lough, gentle undulations of pasture land and woods, and, in the distance, the blue, majestic mountains of Mourne. Looking at these views afforded by the hills today, one seems to be looking southwards across Narnia to the mountains of Archenland in the dim distance, the Eastern Ocean to one's left.

Jack's new home was near to a suburb of Belfast called Dundonald, then a village. In later years, Warnie came across a description that evoked the view they loved. The description, in a novel by Agnes Romilly White called *Gape Row,* led him to think the place pictured was based around Dundonald: "Half-way up the hill they looked back and saw Slieve Donard peer over the shoulder of the Castlereagh Hills inquiringly, and at the summit, the long blue range of the Mourne Mountains huddled and linked together, came suddenly into view."[10]

The Lewis family was staunchly Church of Ireland (Anglican) and worshipped at nearby St Mark's, Dundela, where Lewis had been baptized as an infant, and Albert and Flora had married on 29 August 1894. Flora Lewis's father, Thomas Hamilton, was rector of the church, and tears came easily to his eyes as he preached. He and his aristocratic, clever wife lived in a cat-ridden rectory, which was rank with the animals' stench. In contrast to her husband's views, Mary Hamilton happily employed Roman Catholic servants and supported Home Rule for Ireland. The doorknocker of the rectory was a lion's head, which the future maker of Narnia must have used many times. The traditional symbol of St Mark, Christ's apostle, after whom the church was named, is the lion. Through the services, the young Lewis became familiar with the liturgy of *The Book of Common Prayer* and *Hymns Ancient and Modern*.

Jack had a number of uncles, aunts, and cousins living nearby. Flora had a sister and two brothers, one of whom, Augustus (known as Gussie), was a family favourite, as was his wife, Annie. Albert in turn had two sisters and three brothers, the nearest to his age being Richard, known as Dick. His father, Richard Lewis, lived with the family at Little Lea, having been widowed in 1903. In his youth, Jack, with Warnie, was gradually to develop a network of friends in the area, some of whom he kept in contact with throughout his life. But as children, they had no one nearby of their own age to befriend. Among his favourite relations was his mother's cousin and close friend, Mary, married to Sir William Quartus Ewart. Sir William was a wealthy Belfast linen manufacturer and one of the city's most prominent industrialists. The Ewarts represented the ideal of civilized life for the Lewis family. They lived in a large house called Glenmachan (called by C.S. Lewis Mountbracken in *Surprised by Joy*), less than a mile away from Little Lea, to which the brothers had an open invitation. The Ewarts' children were all much older than Warnie and Jack, but some still lived at home. Gundreda Ewart, ten years Jack's senior, was a favourite of his, and he later described her as "the most beautiful woman I have ever seen, perfect in shape and colour and voice and every movement", a view with which Warnie concurred.[11]

The frequent rain of Ireland's north was an important feature of Jack and Warnie's childhood. Parental wisdom of the time, edged with the fear of tuberculosis, was to keep children indoors during showers. Warnie and Jack made good use of such rainy times, reading, drawing, and writing. During this happy period of his early life, Lewis, fluent with pen and paintbrush, began illustrating and writing a cycle of junior stories about "chivalrous mice and rabbits who rode out in complete mail to kill not giants but cats". These stories, he later observed, were his attempt to bring together his two foremost literary pleasures, which were "dressed animals" and knights in armour. In collaboration with Warnie, who was also writing stories that created a world, Jack developed the stories into an "Animal-land" with a considerable history, known generically as Boxen. In order to include Warnie in its creation and shaping, features of the modern world, such as trains and steamships, had to be built in.

Boxen's land of talking animals is strikingly different from the later Narnian Chronicles, being both full of a child's view of adult preoccupations and, in Lewis's words, "prosaic", lacking wonder rather than reflecting his emerging imaginative interests. In fact, in many features, the Boxen stories reflect the social history of early twentieth-century Belfast in its preoccupation with the issues of Home Rule versus Union with Britain and other adult concerns. Unlike *The Chronicles of Narnia*, therefore, the main focus is on this world, even though Boxen has talking animals.

Some of the dialogue reveals Jack's ear for the speech patterns around him, as in this extract from "The Sailor: A Study, Volume II" about events leading up to a railway strike.

> The foremost villain, who held a lamp, which revealed his fierce and bearded face, exclaimed, "Ah, have done with your talkin' an' pother! Come to something! Do you mean to strike or do you nut?"
>
> "We do," cried a chorus of hoarse voices.
>
> "Aye, an' its right ye are! In the old days, the raily men did what work they liked, & none more. Were they any better than we?"

"No!" came the chorus.

"No," repeated the speaker, refreshing himself from a heavy jug. "A thousan' times – No! An' we will nut do it, either. This new stashun master, has a wrong noshun. He takes his men fer beasts of the field! An' will we stan' it?"

"No!" thundered the others.

"Then strike! Let him know he cant do without us! Do we mind work?" – the chorus seemed disposed to return an affirmative but the orator continued – "No! But we mind tyranny [sic]!!"[12]

At one stage the youthful author made a list of his writings:

Building of the Promenade (a tale)

Man Against Man (a novel)

Town (an essay)

Relief of Murry (a history)

Bunny (a paper)

Home Rule (an essay)

My Life (a journal)

In 1905, at the age of nine, Warnie departed for Wynyard School in Watford, north of London, an event that deepened Jack's isolation from children his own age. Albert took a great deal of time deciding where to send his older son. An English boarding school was deemed socially superior to a local Irish one. After much deliberation, he chose a school that seemed to fit his criteria, but which in reality was in decline, its headmaster slowly descending into insanity.

Warnie said goodbye to Jack on 10 May, less than three weeks after the family's move into Little Lea. Thereafter they only had the school holidays in which to share each other's company, though they wrote to each other frequently, Warnie eager to learn of Jack's latest activities, such as his explorations of the fascinating attic areas of the large new house. The boys had been given the "little end room", which gave them privacy and a haven of solitude, and which they would remember all their lives. In an early draft of his autobiography, *Surprised by Joy*, Lewis noted that the years he lived in the new house before his mother's illness were "very solitary", with Warnie away for most of the year. He added that he "loved solitude", but not after dark – an allusion to nightmares, perhaps, to which he was prone.[13]

In a jotting among his unpublished papers, Lewis reflects that he is unable to make up his mind whether his childhood was all but "supernaturally happy" or all but "supernaturally miserable", quoting William Wordsworth's line, "Heaven lay about me in my infancy" – but adding after it "and Hell".[14] The darkest moment in his life was to be the death of his mother, but there were many happy occasions before then. In the year following Warnie's exile to Wynyard School, 1906, a late part of the summer holiday was spent once again in Castlerock, on the north coast.

On 15 September, some weeks into the holiday, Flora wrote to Albert of a trip with Jack and Warnie to Dunluce Castle the day before.

> We went to Portrush again yesterday; they wanted to go to Dunluce and to the white rocks where there is a cave to be seen. We had a very nice day and they enjoyed it. The bridge you have to cross at Dunluce is quite a dangerous place without any climbing; it was there that Mr. Lanyon was killed. I did not like going over it at all, and I would not have taken the boys if I had remembered what it was like; however they were not nervous about it, so it was not so bad.

This excursion is notable because with subsequent visits remembered in adulthood, it is a likely source for Cair Paravel, the seat of kings and queens in Narnia that is found in ruins in *Prince Caspian*. The plausible source is not literal, but its setting is imaginatively transformed in the Narnia tales. Dunluce Castle has well-preserved ruins, and is perched high on a cliff top by the Atlantic, with sandy beaches at the White Rocks not far distant between it and the resort of Portrush.

Nine years after the visit described by Flora, Jack recorded his memories in a letter to a Belfast friend, Arthur Greeves, who had written while staying in or near Portrush:

> I... certainly wish I could have been with you; I have some vague memories of the cliffs round there and of Dunluce Castle, and some memories which are not at all vague of the same coast a little further on at Castlerock where we used to go in the old days. Don't you love a windy day at a place like that? Waves make one kind of music on rocks and another on sand and I don't know which of the two I would rather have.[15]

Near the end of *The Lion, the Witch and the Wardrobe,* Lewis describes the Narnian castle in a way that particularly evokes Dunluce Castle.

> The castle of Cair Paravel on its little hill towered up above them; before them were the sands, with rocks and little pools of salt water, and seaweed, and the smell of the sea and long miles of bluish-green waves breaking for ever and ever on the beach. And oh, the cry of the sea-gulls! Have you heard it? Can you remember?[16]

Life for Jack continued in its happy but solitary way; Warnie's end of term returns from school were awaited with long anticipation. They could resume their activities, such as cycling in the hills nearby, or collaborating in creating more of the adventures of Boxen. There was a holiday in the seaside town of Berneval in northern France, to improve their French. At the end of 1907, Jack, who was reading far ahead of his years, attempted an account of his life.

In "My Life. By Jacks Lewis, 1907" the nine-year-old wrote:

> Papy of course is the master of the house, and a man in whom you can see strong Lewis features, bad temper, very sensible, nice wen not in a temper. Mamy is like most middle-aged ladys, stout, brown hair, spectaciles, knitting her chief industry etc., etc.

Jack adds that he is "like most boys of 9 and I am like Papy, bad temper, thick lips, thin and generaly weraing a jersy."[17]

He also recorded that he had told Maude (Scott), the housemaid, and Mat (Martha the cook) that he was a "home-ruler", that is, a supporter of independence from Britain.

Early in 1908, Flora's health suddenly began to cause great concern, requiring immediate medical advice. Albert Lewis noted in his pocket diary early in February, 1908: "[Drs] Campbell and Leslie, 1st. Consultation at Little Lea." On 11 February, Flora urgently wrote to Warnie, away at school in Watford, that she was to have an operation later that week, on the Friday. In fact, she underwent major cancer surgery at home under chloroform. Albert recorded: "Operation on Flora lasted from 10 till 12 o'c. Drs. Campbell, Leslie, and Fielden, a nurse. Horrible operation."

Despite the disruption of life, however, Jack's intellectual growth continued. In a tiny Letts's diary, he simply noted on 5 March that he had read *Paradise Lost* and made "reflections thereon". This is one of the greatest poems in English, an epic in twelve books by John Milton that daunts even sixth form pupils. Over the years, it was to be a major influence on Lewis, both in his future scholarship and fiction.

Flora's illness meant that Albert's father, Richard Lewis, was no longer able to stay at Little Lea, but was looked after by another relative. A little over a month later, on 24 March, Albert wrote in his diary: "My father had a stroke this night." Just over a week later, on 2 April, he died, five years after losing his wife, Martha. Albert's mother-in-law, Mary Hamilton, had been sitting with him. Albert noted: "My father died at 1 o'c today, Mary and the nurse alone being present."

As part of her long convalescence, in late May Flora took Jack with her for a break in Larne, a harbour town north of Belfast Lough, close by Islandmagee. From the house at which they stayed, Flora noted reassuringly to Albert,

> Jacks has a great time watching the boats, there is a pair of opera glasses here that he looks out at them with.... Jacks and nurse were over on Island Magee today, I think Jacks thought the ferry the best part of the trip.[18]

The boy believed that his mother was doing well at Larne, but Warnie observed many years later, "... alas, it was only the final bright flame from the dying candle."[19]

Away at boarding school, Warnie frequently asked for news of his mother, sensing Albert's hesitation to upset him. In a letter in early June he asked his father: "From your letters you don't seem to think she is likely to live. Do tell me plainly next time you write." The last letter preserved from Flora was written to Warnie on 15 June. Composing it was a struggle.

> I am sorry not to have been able to write to you regularly this term, but I find I am really not well enough to do so. I have been feeling very poorly lately and writing tires me very much. But I must write today to wish you a happy birthday. (Warnie was thirteen on 16 June)

A few days later, Albert wrote painfully to Badge, as he called Warnie: "My dear son, it may be that God in His mercy has decided that you will have no person in the future to turn to but me."[20] It was sent on 24 June, from his solicitor's office at 83, Royal Avenue, Belfast. He also communicated with Wynyard School around this time.

In early July, Warnie returned home, before term ended, because of Flora's decline. All Albert, Warnie, and Jack could do now was await the inevitable. In August, a few days before her death, she gave a Bible to each of her sons. Albert recorded some of Flora's last words in one of his notebooks:

In the middle of the night of the 21st. August while at times she was wandering and at other times perfectly possessed, I spoke to her (not by any means for the first time – nor was it the first time by any means that a conversation on heavenly things had taken place between us – sometimes begun by her, sometimes by me), of the goodness of God. Like a flash she said, "What have we done for Him?" May I never forget that![21]

Two days later, on Sunday 23 August, she died. It was Albert's forty-fifth birthday. On his Shakespearean calendar for that date, the inscription ran: "Men must endure their going hence." Neither son forgot those words, and fifty-five years later Warnie was to have them written on his brother's gravestone.

Albert was soon hit by a further grief. Less than two weeks later he jotted in his diary, on 3 September: "Poor dear Joe died at 7 o'c this evg." Joseph was one of Albert's older brothers, born just a few years before him in 1856.

When his mother became seriously ill with cancer, Jack found it natural to pray for her recovery. Even after she died he fervently hoped for a miracle, but the corpse he was forced to view removed this hope. War was to confirm his view that the dead look more animal than human; that the ugliest man alive looks beautiful in comparison. In fact, that sight, and the subsequent funeral, fuelled his nightmares. The endless flowers, coffin, hearse, black dress, and other accoutrements of the rituals, he much later wrote, plentifully served to add furniture to his appalling dreams.[22]

Before that, the process of his mother's decline had filled him with fear, not eased by his father's uncontrolled emotions. Lewis's memories of this dark period are eloquently captured in Digory's story in *The Magician's Nephew*.

Digory... went softly into his Mother's room. And there she lay, as he had seen her lie so many other times, propped up on the pillows, with a thin, pale face that would make you cry to look at it. Digory took the Apple of Life out of his pocket.... The brightness of the Apple threw strange lights on the ceiling.... And the smell of the Apple of Youth was as if there was a window in the room that opened on Heaven....

"You will eat it, won't you? Please," said Digory.[23]

Albert Lewis did not realize that during Flora's decline, he was losing not only his wife but also his sons. In *Surprised by Joy,* Lewis observed:

We were coming, my brother and I, to rely more and more exclusively on each other for all that made life bearable; to have confidence only in each other.... Everything that had made the house a home had failed us; everything except one another. We drew daily closer together (that was the good result) – two frightened urchins huddled for warmth in a bleak world.

With his mother's death, only sea and islands were left, he said; Atlantis had sunk. Nearly fifty years later, he wrote: "All settled happiness, all that was tranquil and reliable, disappeared from my life."

A mere four weeks after Flora died, Jack rode in a horse-drawn taxi with Warnie to Donegall Quay in Belfast to catch the night ferry over the rough Irish Sea to Fleetwood, in Lancashire. To Jack, England was a foreign country. They were on their way to Wynyard School, which Jack was to call a concentration camp and Belsen.

2

Schooldays and Arthur Greeves: Watford, Belfast, and Malvern

Lewis was to spend five academic years in private schools, from that autumn, 1908. Far from providing the superior education that Albert had hoped for, Wynyard did the opposite. As Warnie Lewis explained in later years:

> ... the school was slack and inefficient, and the time-table, if such it could be called, ridiculous. When not saying lessons, the boys spent the whole of school working out sums on slates; of this endless arithmetic there was little or no supervision. Of the remaining subjects, English and Latin consisted, the first solely and the second mainly, of grammar. History was a ceaseless circuit of the late Middle Ages; Geography was a meaningless list of rivers, towns, imports and exports.[1]

When he and Jack arrived in Watford, Warnie was already worldly-wise over its cruel regime. Jack was to be haunted by his time there throughout his life, much more than his brother, probably because he was to be exposed to more of its days of final decline. Lewis dwelt upon Belsen in a large section of *Surprised by Joy*; a telling observation in it only begins to capture the brutality of the school: "The only stimulating element in the teaching," he wrote, "consisted of a few well-used canes which hung on the green iron chimney-piece of the single school-room." Jack found the regime there difficult to endure, learning little to satisfy his hungry mind. Like the loss of their mother, the suffering caused by a headmaster on the verge of insanity in a tiny school brought the two brothers even closer together.

In later years, Warnie, with a historian's eye, traced the beginning of the decline back to at least 1901, reasoning that the school must once have been of high quality. It had in former days been responsible for many scholarships to universities. The head, Reverend Robert Capron (dubbed Oldie by the boys), at one point had descended into such a rage that he viciously attacked a boy called "Punch" Hickmott. Such was the severity of the beating that his parents took the headmaster to the high court, exposing the scandal of his abuse and brutality. There was an out-of-court settlement.

Though Albert apparently had researched thoroughly which school to send his children to, he was unaware of this legal action against Wynyard School, even though Warnie was able to uncover it years later. Lewis gave a vivid instance of Capron's gratuitous, often casual cruelty in *Surprised by Joy*. The head teacher had favourite victims, boys Jack eventually realized had something in common – they were of lower social classes, revealed by accent or father's occupation. Capron constantly beat one victim. Lewis wrote in his autobiography: "I have seen Oldie make that child bend down at one end of the school room and then take a run of the room's length at each stroke..."[2] Though he feared the anger of his father, there was no comparison with the insane rages of Capron. The combined effect of those two adults led him to a distrust of uninhibited, raw emotion and irrational anger.

Shortly into the term, Warnie incurred the fickle wrath of the brutal headmaster. On 29 September, a Tuesday, he wrote home:

I have stood this sort of thing for three years and I cannot stand it any longer. Please let us leave at once....You have never refused me anything Papy and I know you won't refuse me this – that I may leave Wynyard. Jacks wants to too.

Jack also wrote to his father at about the same time, recounting a trivial event that led to Capron cursing Warnie behind his back, and pleaded, "Please may we not leave on Saturday? We simply *cannot* wait in this hole till the end of term."[3] Albert had no idea of the true situation, and refused their plea. He tended to translate everything said to him by his sons into his own perception of a situation. Jack's aunt, Annie, did however visit the boys on the Saturday that weekend, taking them on a trip to the Franco-British exhibition in nearby London. She tried to do what she could to help care for the motherless boys.

The massive exhibition celebrated a new accord between Britain and France, and among its many spectacles was an elaborate working Irish village, featuring 150 Irish girls (coleens) demonstrating colonial life and local industry, complete with donkeys and spinning wheels, Celtic round tower and an ancient church ruin. Jack conceded to Albert in a letter postmarked 3 October that they were getting on much better following her time with them. It seems that she reassured them. However, Warnie was sick on that Saturday night of the trip, and was unable to attend church the next day with the other pupils, which perhaps was a psychosomatic upset.

The church that Capron, who was ordained into the Church of England, forced the boys to attend twice every Sunday was high church, unlike the familiar St Mark's in Dundela. This jarred on both Jack and Warnie, because of their Ulster Protestant background. But while the unfamiliar rituals were an abomination to them, Lewis confessed in *Surprised by Joy* that the services may have considerably affected his faith at this time. He heard, he said, the essential doctrines of Christianity taught by people who actually believed them.

In 1909, at the end of the summer term, Warnie was released from the concentration camp. He was bound for the prestigious Malvern College, Worcestershire (called Wyvern by Lewis in his autobiography), the following term. Meanwhile, Jack had to endure another year at Wynyard before it was forced to close because of declining numbers. Capron wrote to Albert Lewis on 27 April 1910, informing him that he was "giving up school work". Jack spent his last day at Wynyard on 12 July.

Robert Capron was to briefly blight the lives of others before he was committed to an asylum. He was entrusted with the care of a small church at Radwell, near Hitchin, being inducted on 13 June that year. There he became violent towards members of the choir, and the churchwardens. He was quickly restrained and then certified as insane. Over a year later, on 18 November 1911, he died in Camberwell House Asylum, Peckham Road, south London, unable to recognize those who knew him.

In September 1910, Lewis was enrolled by his father at Campbell College, just one mile from Little Lea. Here he was a boarder, being allowed home on Sundays. The college "had been founded with the express purpose of giving Ulster boys all the advantages of a public school education without the trouble of crossing the Irish Sea". Because of its noise and constant movement, Lewis later described it as "very like living permanently in a large railway station". He found it hard to settle there; he was no fan of bustling corporate life, with no chance of solitude. Jack only remained until November, when Albert withdrew him after he developed serious breathing problems. These difficulties were not helped by the fact that Jack by now was, like his brother, a habitual and secret smoker. In fact, in the spring of the following year, Warnie gathered up his courage and asked Albert's permission to smoke.

After the failure of the Campbell College experiment, Jack was sent to Malvern, in January 1911. The town was a famous health resort, especially for those with lung problems. Because of his age (he was still only twelve) Jack was enrolled as a student at Cherbourg House (which he referred to in *Surprised by Joy* as

Chartres, presumably after the elegant medieval cathedral, to hide its identity, but keeping a French theme). This preparatory school was perched on the steep slopes above Malvern College, where Warnie was enrolled as a student. Jack remained in the regency-style house until June 1913. He later observed that his education truly began here. Not least, he soon found his footing in Latin and English. Cherbourg House was made up of around twenty boys between the ages of eight and thirteen. He was pleased to discover that they had hot water in the mornings, unlike in Wynyard School and Campbell College. His penchant for storytelling amused the other boys, and made him popular.

When Jack arrived back in Belfast from the summer term after travelling by train and then overnight boat from Malvern, Albert was relieved to find him looking much better than when he had left for the new school six months before. On 29 July 1911, he wrote to Warnie:

> Jacks arrived on Tuesday morning in good health and good spirits. Of course it will be rather lonely for him until you arrive. However, he does a bit of drawing and reading and writing and "biking", and so gets in the day.

In the summer holidays that year, Albert took his sons to Dunbar in Scotland for a joint vacation with their uncle Dick Lewis, Aunt Agnes, and their cousins Eileen and Leonard. It was during August, in which there was a record heat wave, with temperatures up to an astonishing 36°C (97°F) at times, leading to thousands of deaths.

Dunbar is a small coastal resort about thirty miles east of Edinburgh, with rocky shores, a fishing harbour, some sandy coves, and a nearby bay with a long beach called Tynninghame Sands. The party had booked into what they expected to be a hotel, but turned out to be a rough-and-ready public house. Here the meals were memorably unappetizing and the accommodation uncomfortable. Albert bluntly described the place as "a dirty pot-house". His temper had deteriorated steadily since departing from Little Lea. At the hotel, wrote Warnie many years later, "he relapsed into a sullen despair, broken only by violent exhibitions of ill-temper".

Jack, in a letter to a friend that he never completed, described the room that he and Warnie shared. It had a double bed that was so uncomfortable that each night he and Warnie would toss a coin to determine who was going to sleep in the bed and who on the floor. It was the *loser*, he revealed, who had the bed.

In *Surprised by Joy* we learn how Jack lost his faith during his terms at Cherbourg school, which had much to do with esoteric religious interests of the matron, Miss Cowie, who may have been a theosophist or similar. Despite the immaturity or naivety of her spiritual seekings, and what Lewis later described as her selflessness, she helped to give him an unhealthy taste for the occult, a "spiritual lust" that was to bedevil him for a long time. He retained a deep and enduring affection for her.

Other reasons conspired to make him drop his faith with the greatest relief. A legalistic preoccupation with prayer at this time had made it a painful penance. In addition, a tenacious pessimism had evolved from his clumsiness with his hands, his mother's death, the black cloud of Wynyard School, and his father's unconcealed fears, usually without foundation, such as of bankruptcy. An alluring sexuality too was awakened at this time of puberty by the beauty of his dancing mistress. She was, he later confessed, the first woman he lusted after, though he could remember no deliberate provocation on her part. Ironically, the matron, who was kind and caring, was dismissed by the school partly because of her special affection for the motherless boy, and because she took Jack's side when he protested about the school's censorship policy on letters home.[4] Her sacking deprived Jack of much-needed care and attention.

In the December of 1911, Jack was suddenly overwhelmed by the return of the experience he called "Joy", the sweet, inconsolable longing, that he had first felt as an infant when he saw Warnie's toy garden in his nursery. It resulted from reading the

Christmas issue of *The Bookman*, which had a coloured supplement reproducing several of Arthur Rackham's illustrations to *Siegfried and the Twilight of the Gods*. The title and the illustration combined to evoke his desire for northern worlds. At the same time he remembered reading an account of the death of Balder from northern mythology:

Balder the Beautiful,
God of the summer sun,
Fairest of all the Gods![5]

Siegfried belonged to the same world as the god who died. This soon led Jack to begin writing a play, *Loki Bound*, a poetic tragedy about the Norse gods. (Loki was the god whose malice was responsible for Balder's death.)

Jack would struggle to find the best name for this human desire or longing, eventually settling on Joy as a technical name for it. He also in his writings tried a variety of images to capture the longing, such as the sight of remote mountains or a distant line of hills, the quality of northernness, or the idea of a basic homelessness that we feel, with our real home being elsewhere. Tenaciously, through his period of atheism, then exploration of alternative views, he tried to follow the path that the longing seemed to be leading him along. Years later the quest would be resolved for him, allowing him to conclude: "Most people, if they had really learned to look into their own hearts, would know that they do want, and want acutely, something that cannot be had in this world."[6]

Soon after the return of Jack's experience of longing, or Joy, there was an important event in Warnie's life. He began to keep a diary. There would be gaps in the instalments but he determinedly kept it up, using the model of diarists he loved, such as Samuel Pepys. By the end of his life, he had written more than a million and a quarter words, filling twenty-three handwritten volumes, much concerning his brother. They have proved to be a central source of our knowledge of Lewis's life.[7] In the early days of his diary-keeping, in cold February 1912, Warnie recorded skating on Newpool in Malvern. It was, he wrote, his first attempt, and not nearly as hard as he had expected. Jack was with him and, according to Warnie, also picked up skating "quite well". The two of them spent most of that day skating together. Another early entry, in the next month, noted Warnie's confirmation ceremony. Like Jack, he was, however, to lose his Christian faith for many years.

At the end of the summer term at Cherbourg House, 1913, Jack sat his examinations for entry to Malvern College. These were taken over several days. He was ill, with a high temperature, and therefore had to take them while in bed at school. Many years later, after his brother's death, Warnie reflected: "I am inclined to rate his winning of a scholarship under these circumstances as the greatest academic triumph of his career." The papers Jack sat included Latin and Greek grammar, and Latin prose and verses. There was the essay paper, his forte. Jack also took a general paper, which included history and geography, Scripture and English. Later he did a French paper, with difficulty, and finally a paper on arithmetic and algebra.

As the school term ended, Jack's first published poem appeared in the school magazine. It was called "*Quam Bene Saturno*" in the style of Tibullus, a minor Latin poet, and gave an early indication of his interest in the planets and the gods traditionally associated with them.

That same term, Warnie prematurely ended his education at Malvern College, as he was expelled for smoking and other pranks. Albert decided to send him to a tutor to complete his education. Once again, Jack was to be deprived of his older brother's company for most of the year. Warnie had already decided, that term when war seemed far away, to join the Royal Army Service Corps (RASC) as a career, a decision that probably saved his life. Throughout the entire years of the First World War, as he served in France and Belgium, he was not thrown into the front line trenches.

In September 1913, Warnie began private studies with his father's former teacher, William Thompson Kirkpatrick, in Gastons cottage, Bookham in Surrey, a tutor who would soon play an integral role in Jack's intellectual development. The purpose of Warnie's studies in the rural town was to cram for the entrance exam to the Royal Military Academy at Sandhurst, on the nearby borders of Surrey and Berkshire, less than thirty miles to the west.

Meanwhile, Jack entered Malvern College at the same time, with a classical scholarship. He was only to stay at the college for an unhappy year, until the following June. He found life here uncongenial, heavily detailed in *Surprised by Joy*. He found some escape from the drudgery of his daily round and a great deal of satisfaction working on *Loki Bound*. The main contrast he created in his play is between Loki's sad wisdom and Thor's brutal orthodoxy. Thor, in reality, symbolizes the Bloods of Malvern College – the ruling older boys so criticized in *Surprised by Joy* (published over forty years later). Loki appears to be a projection of Jack's own struggles.

When Lewis was writing *Surprised by Joy,* Warnie protested about his brother's portrayal of Malvern College.[8] In particular, he thought Jack's account of immorality among the older boys inaccurate. Homosexuality was more apparent than real, he believed. This was confirmed for Warnie when he later compared notes at Sandhurst with lads from public schools around the country. He of course knew many of "the brutes of prefects" Jack had characterized in *Surprised by Joy*, and had a very different view of them.

When writing *Surprised by Joy,* his brother read out a chapter about Malvern College to the Inklings, a group of his friends. Warnie responded with "great emphasis and vigour", remembered an Inklings member who was present, objecting that the account was unfair to the school and should not be published. Lewis obstinately said something like, "I'm going to."[9] Nevertheless, Warnie in later life was searingly critical of the public school system as he had experienced it, and of its impact upon his outstandingly brilliant brother:

… the main function of the Public School in those days was to produce a standardized article. With two or three notable exceptions they were factories turning out the spare parts and replacements needed to keep imperial and commercial machinery functioning efficiently, and obviously it was essential that the new part should be identical with the worn-out one. But no polishing, filing, or grinding could have made Jack a cog in any machine, and he was lucky to leave Wyvern [Malvern] before the process had done him any lasting damage.[10]

In November, Warnie took the army entrance exam, receiving very high marks (he was twenty-first out of 201 candidates), meaning that his tutorage with Kirkpatrick was now over. He planned it so that his return to Ireland, and Little Lea, would be via Malvern, so that he and Jack could travel most of the way back together for Christmas. This enabled him to attend a House Supper (the schoolboys were divided into several houses). There he noticed his brother's deep unhappiness. That House Supper, he recorded, was "a noisy and cheerful function, of which I can remember only one thing – Jack's gloom and boredom… glaringly obvious to all, not calculated to increase his popularity with the House".

It was not true, however, that Jack had no friends. A fellow pupil, Hardman (later Air Chief Marshal Sir Donald Hardman) recalled a very different Jack: "I can remember going with him for long walks on Sundays when he was in the gayest of moods. Story telling and mimicking people." He also remembered, "When I knew him, I can only describe him as a riotously amusing atheist."[11] Hardman was shocked to find him in later life the author of *The Screwtape Letters*.

As well as the benefit of friends at his school, Jack could not but be pleased by his father's Christmas gift to him of *The Rhinegold and the Valkyries*, a companion volume to *Siegfried and the Twilight of the Gods*. Though he and his father had an often fraught relationship, this gift touched the heart of Jack's love for the north and everything associated with it.

Jack returned to Malvern College for the spring term. He appreciated discoveries that he was making in his English class under the teaching of Smugy (Harry Wakelyn Smith). One exercise, to write a poem asking a friend to stay at the most beautiful place you know, gave him the chance to describe Castlerock in some detail. In mid-March, however, he wrote to his father that school life, with its attendant bullying and fagging, was getting harder to bear and more severe as the term progressed. He begged Albert to take him out of the college as soon as possible.

In *Surprised by Joy,* Lewis was to sum up his state at this time as being "tired, dog-tired, cab-horse tired, tired (almost) like a child in a factory". Albert took Jack seriously on this occasion – he constantly worried about his son. He confided in Warnie, in a letter:

> He is very uncomfortable at Malvern… He is not popular with the prefects apparently, and gets more than a fair share of the fagging and bullying. In a word, the thing is a failure and must be ended. His letters make me unhappy…. I suppose the best thing I can do is to send him to "Kirk" [W.T. Kirkpatrick] after next term.

When Jack arrived at Little Lea for the Easter holiday, still full of unhappiness over Malvern, Albert continued to correspond with Warnie about what to do, and the possibility of Jack going to Kirkpatrick. In one such letter, Albert confessed

> … that knowing Jacks's mind and character, I am not greatly surprised to find him and a Public School unsuited to one another. In saying that I blame neither the one nor the other. He is simply out of his proper environment, and would possibly wither and decay rather than grow if kept in such surroundings…. What is to be done? For a boy like Jacks to spend the next three or four years alone with an old man like Kirk is almost certain to strengthen the very faults that are strongest in his disposition. He will make no acquaintances.

He will see few people and he will grow more into a hermit than ever. The position is a difficult one and gives me many anxious hours.[12]

Over that Easter holiday, however, a new chapter opened in Jack's life. In the Strandtown and Belmont area in which he lived, he mixed with his many cousins and relations. But now he also started make friends in the community. These would be first-name friends, rather than the circles of friends he was later to make in Oxford, who were normally called by their surnames.

One person that he had hitherto ignored was a boy some years older than him, about the same age as Warnie. Arthur Greeves lived nearly opposite in one of the large, spread-out houses on Circular Road. He was ill (as he often was) and had invited Jack to visit. Arthur had unsuccessfully in the past tried to befriend him and Warnie. Usually, Jack would ignore such an invitation, but was feeling more cheerful at the prospect of leaving Malvern College. Albert had finally decided to send him to Kirk.

Jack was soon crossing the tree-lined road, walking up it past the extensive grounds of a distant property belonging to a linen merchant called James Taylor, and then turning into a short drive to Arthur's front door. Writing years later, Lewis takes up the story:

I found Arthur sitting up in bed. On the table beside him lay a copy of *Myths of the Norsemen*.
"Do *you* like that?" said I.
"Do *you* like that?" said he.

Jack very quickly realized that Arthur shared his window onto the world. Not only did they both like the book, they both appreciated the very same parts of the book. As they talked, and even nearly shouted in excitement at times, they discovered that their common interests and enjoyments extended far beyond that book. Indeed, these seemed to range the world of each other's hearts. They were what are often called soulmates. Usually, this term refers to a long-standing friendship or relationship, but in the case of Jack and Arthur, it was an immediate recognition. Reflecting on their friendship years after Lewis's death, another lifelong friend, Owen Barfield, said: "His friendship with Arthur Greeves… was based entirely on their seeing things from the same angle rather than on their having the same sort of minds."[13] In *Surprised by Joy,* Lewis characterized his meeting with Arthur like this: "Many thousands of people have had the experience of finding the first friend, and it is none the less a wonder; as great a wonder… as first love, or even a greater."[14]

Arthur was the youngest of five children, and attended Campbell College nearby. He was tall and thin, had a burgeoning gift as a painter, and was intelligent but not scholarly in any way. Someone who knew him well described him as a "complex character".[15] He suffered from a "bad heart", and was frequently ill. His physical maladies, which continued throughout his life, were echoed in his emotional life. Arthur could appear diffident, but this expressed a deep-rooted lack of self-confidence that was to blight his life. In many ways, he was to become dependent upon his friendship with Lewis. His father, Joseph, was the director of a company of flax spinners, and his American mother, Mary (née Gribbon), came from Brooklyn, New York.

His family in earlier generations had been Quakers, but had become Brethren. This old Christian denomination is very varied, but the Greeveses practised a relatively new version associated with the nineteenth-century Calvinist J.N. Darby and the Plymouth Brethren. Joseph Greeves, in fact, was so rigid and authoritarian in his observance that he was to alienate all his children, and is likely to have contributed to Arthur's wandering spirituality in his adult years. At their first meeting, Arthur was a Christian and Jack an atheist. They were to be friends for fifty years, and Lewis was to correspond with him more than with any other person. His letters to Arthur make up a substantial proportion of the three large volumes of Lewis's *Collected Letters*.

A.N. Wilson, a Lewis biographer, astutely illuminated the significance of Arthur on Lewis's development, both for his character and his writings. "It was in writing to Greeves," Wilson remarks,

> that he decided, very often, the sort of person he wanted to be. We could very definitely say that if it had not been for Arthur Greeves, many of Lewis's most distinctive and imaginatively successful books would not have been written. The letters were a dress rehearsal for that intimate and fluent manner which was to make Lewis such a successful author.... In the letters to Greeves, he learnt to write for an audience.[16]

Arthur thus became part of his network of friends established from his youth in Strandtown and Belmont. These also included Janie (Jane) McNeill (daughter of the head teacher at Campbell College), and the cousins who had become friends in the desolation of his mother's always-present absence. In his correspondence with Arthur, Lewis called Janie "Chanie" because of her accent. The Belfast friends were relatively ordinary, if well-heeled, but people of "substance". Lewis might well have used this term of them, meaning they were not superficial and somehow weightless, as he had used the term of some Belfast people in a fragment from an unfinished novel (called the "Easely Fragment" by scholars).

When Lewis reflected years later in 1935 on his long friendship with Arthur Greeves, he tried to pinpoint the substantial quality in him that he found so attractive.

> I could give concepts, logic, facts, arguments, but he had feelings to offer, feelings which most mysteriously – for he was always very inarticulate – he taught me to share. Hence, in our commerce, I dealt in superficies, but he in solids. I learned charity from him but failed, for all my efforts, to teach him arrogance in return.[17]

In Jack's last term at Malvern College, he discovered the poems and plays of W.B. Yeats in the school library (known by the boys as the Grundy). It was now natural for him to report that very day to Arthur in one of his frequent letters that Yeats wrote with "rare spirit and beauty" of their Irish mythology. His works, Jack said, had the eerie and strange quality that he and Arthur loved; what he would later call "romance" in literature, which provided a glimpse of other worlds. In the same letter, Jack lyrically recalled their common memories of County Down, which he was missing: he pictured the prospect of Belfast Lough and the distant Cave Hill from beside the Shepherd's Hut, the sun's rise over the Holywood Hills, and the refreshing tranquillity of early morning. He wrote of these insights, emotions, and experiences with a confidence that Arthur would share them.

3

"The Great Knock": Bookham, Surrey

The day after war broke out, while home at Little Lea on leave visiting Jack and his father, Warnie Lewis was abruptly recalled to Sandhurst, his period of military training having been sharply curtailed from two years to nine months. On 4 August 1914, Germany had invaded Belgium, and Britain declared war on the invader. Within hours, five superpowers were at war – the Austro-Hungarians, the Germans, the Russians, the French, and the British divided into two formidable alignments. Less than two weeks later, the British Expeditionary Force landed in France, which Britain had promised to defend. The following month, Jack began his studies with W. T. Kirkpatrick in Bookham, knowing that Warnie was likely soon to be in France. Bookham was an apt name for a place that proved to be so congenial to the bookish Jack.

Jack Lewis was only fifteen when the First World War began. He was to reach the trenches of northern France around his nineteenth birthday. During this period of the war, he remained a convinced atheist of sorts; a rather solitary person. His letters to his new-found soulmate, Arthur Greeves, provide valuable insight into his life, development, and particularly his early thinking, stimulated by his tutor. Arthur also read widely, though no one ever would keep up with Jack in his reading, either as a boy or an adult. In his abilities in music and art, however, Arthur outshone Jack.

Mr Kirkpatrick was Lewis's tutor from September 1914 to March 1917 and was nicknamed by him "the Great Knock" because of the impact of his stringent logical mind on the teenager.

Kirkpatrick, a retired Irish headmaster, lived with his wife, Louisa, in a picturesque cottage named Gastons, in the rural village of Bookham in Surrey, where Lewis lodged happily during the tutorage. Surrounding Bookham were many mainly deciduous woods already displaying rich autumn colours. Lewis grew to hold a great affection for Kirkpatrick, describing him as the person who came closer to being "a purely logical entity" than anyone else he had ever met.

Kirkpatrick's method was to combine language study with first-hand experience of major works; he would guide the brilliant boy in German, French, Italian, Latin, and classical Greek. His rationalism and atheism were to reinforce Lewis's own beliefs at that time, though he did not force these on his charge and, indeed, insisted that he attended the parish church, St Nicholas, out of respect for Jack's father.[1] Kirkpatrick had a Presbyterian background, steeped in liberal theology, and thought he could subject all belief, including his own, to impersonal, logical scrutiny. In a sense, he was a Presbyterian atheist, to the extent of always putting on his Sunday best on the first day of the week. Albert had been a pupil of Kirkpatrick's when he was headmaster of Lurgan College, in County Armagh, in the north of Ireland, a position from which he had retired fifteen years earlier.

The month following the outbreak of war, Lewis began his studies with the Great Knock, soon responding to his tutor's intellectual rigour. Almost immediately, he was presented with the ancient Greek poet Homer, whom he had not previously read. Kirkpatrick's strategy was to read aloud twenty lines or so of the Greek, and then translate. This would go on with a few explanations for another 100 lines or thereabouts. Then he would leave the boy to go over the lines he had covered with the aid of a dictionary, and to make as much sense of it as he could. Utilizing his phenomenal memory, the fifteen year-old had no difficulty in retaining every word as he looked up its meaning. Soon Jack was able to understand what he read without translating it – that is, actually starting to think in Greek. What he was to call the music of Homer became a very part of him.

Not wanting Jack to turn into a dull boy, Louisa Kirkpatrick often played piano music to him in the evenings, much to his delight. Chopin, Beethoven, Grieg, and many other old favourites helped him to feel at home and to relax. Recording his new experiences of life with the Kirkpatricks, Jack wrote to Arthur that now he had tried it for a week, he was already convinced that he was going to have the time of his life – and so it turned out to be for the next two and a half years.

Near the end of September, Warnie was commissioned as a second lieutenant in the Royal Army Service Corps, and on 4 November 1914 he crossed over to France, to a base in Le Havre. Lewis's rural haven was not untouched by events in France and Belgium. He noted in a letter to his father that an excess of "war fever" was raging around the Bookham neighbourhood. Soon the village people prepared a cottage for Belgian refugees – with the rapid German push into that country, tens of thousands of refugees had poured into England.

When a Belgian family of seven was installed in the cottage, Mrs Kirkpatrick and the teenager visited them. Fortunately the mother was able to speak French, so that the educated ladies of the village were able to converse with her. Lewis tried out his schoolboy French, with the help of a stilted phrase book. Among the refugee family was a girl who seemed about his age for whom he soon developed a crush, the development of which he shared in his letters to Arthur in sometimes embroidered detail. The "brown girl" of his story *The Pilgrim's Regress* (1933) may owe something to his sexual fantasies about her at this time.

As autumn deepened, Bookham was coated with a deep fall of snow. Regretting he wasn't able to see County Down in these wintery conditions, he wrote to Arthur of their effects in Surrey. Jack, in his simple delight, saw the early snow almost like (viewed from the vantage point of our hindsight) the winter-world of Narnia. A nearby pine wood, particularly, had white snow masses on trees and ground, forming a "beautiful sight". Jack almost expected, he wrote, a hasty "march of dwarfs" to pass. Many years later, Lewis remembered the origin of Narnia:

> The Lion [the Witch and the Wardrobe] all began with a
> picture of a Faun carrying an umbrella and parcels in a snowy
> wood. This picture had been in my mind since I was about
> sixteen. Then one day, when I was about forty, I said to myself:
> "Let's try to make a story about it."[2]

That pine woodland near Bookham may well have put this picture in his mind. His sixteenth birthday was a few days after his visit to the Narnia-like wood.

In deference to Albert, a few days after the week of snow, Jack returned early to Belfast, instead of going later in December for the Christmas holiday. The purpose was his confirmation, in Anglican practice, at St Mark's Church, the bells of which could be heard from Little Lea. On Sunday 6 December, to his later shame, Jack went through the rites of confirmation while disbelieving in the Christian faith. In *Surprised by Joy* he confessed:

> My relations to my father help to explain (I am not suggesting
> they excuse) one of the worst acts of my life. I allowed myself
> to be prepared for confirmation, and confirmed, and to make
> my first Communion, in total disbelief, acting a part, eating
> and drinking my own condemnation.[3]

Early in the New Year, while Jack was still at Little Lea, his tutor wrote a revealing comment to Albert about his pupil:

He was born with the literary temperament and we have
to face that fact with all it implies. This is not a case of early
precocity showing itself in rapid assimilation of knowledge
and followed by subsequent indifference or torpor. As I
said before, it is the maturity and originality of his literary
judgements which is so unusual and surprising. By an unerring
instinct he detects first rate quality in literary workmanship,
and the second rate does not interest him in any way.[4]

Over this long holiday it is likely that Jack confided to Arthur more
about his secret feelings for, and adolescent fantasies about, the
pretty Belgian refugee. In later years he was to tell Arthur that a
meeting he said he arranged with the Belgian girl (apparently for
a sexual assignment) was a fabrication.[5] This does not mean that
Jack never tried to meet up with her in a more natural way, and
perhaps failed.

The sharing, of course, was two-way, and Jack was gradually
to learn that Arthur's inclinations tended towards his own sex, a
discovery that left their friendship unchanged. During the long
break, Jack, as usual, continued to read voraciously, one of his
latest discoveries being Thomas Malory's *Morte D'Arthur*, which
opened up a new world for him. Soon after encountering Malory,
Jack began calling Arthur Galahad in his letters, referring to the
son of Launcelot and Elaine in *Morte D'Arthur*, whose purity allows
him to attain the Holy Grail. Jack may have called him this because
of his strict morality, as he describes Arthur's stance on things in a
later letter.[6]

In one of his letters to Arthur during the next year, Jack
revealed how much at that time he looked at reality, including
the reality of love, through the texts of books. While admitting
to having had no experience of love, he has something better:
acquaintance with great writers who have written on love. "We
see through their eyes," he wrote. This was an emphasis Lewis
kept throughout his life, but which he developed as the idea that
books, poems, and stories shape or even radically change our

perception of reality as we look through them, rather as we see through a pair of spectacles.[7]

Jack was not to return to Bookham until mid-January. Albert had made sure his son would be at home for a longer period than usual. Like many, he feared that the Germans might invade England at this time. Also there was aggressive activity by German submarines in the Irish Sea, which Jack had to cross whenever he was going to or from Belfast. The fear of enemy submarines was real, even if exaggerated. On 30 January 1915, just two weeks after Jack crossed to England, a submarine sank a collier, the *Kilcoan,* in a raid near Fleetwood. The *Kilcoan* had been designed by Jack's uncle Joseph Lewis, a fact that particularly upset Albert.[8] It may have been around this time that Albert began drinking heavily.

In early February 1915, Warnie had his first leave from France, which was just a week. Lewis was allowed by Kirkpatrick to visit his home in Little Lea in Belfast with his brother. This and other leave visits (such as a week in July that year) would have reminded Jack very much of the reality of the war, which he liked to think about as little as possible.

Some weeks later, the impact of the conflict would be forced upon Jack again. A serviceman, Gerald Smythe, who had recently lost an arm in battle, stayed at Gastons. He had only been up from his bed for a week, yet planned to return to the front the next week. Gerald had even learned to light his pipe with one hand, Lewis noted.[9] Gerald's example was likely to have been one of many factors that led to Lewis's eventual resolve to enlist and fight – as an Irish national, he knew that he was likely to be exempt from conscription, and therefore enlistment would be voluntary.

In June 1915 there was the first Zeppelin attack on London. When the airships bombed Waterloo station, Jack and the Kirkpatricks were able to see from Bookham electric flashes in the skies as a result of the bomb explosions. This was another unwelcome indication to Jack of the threats of modern warfare.

Later in the summer, a "theatrical lady", a young woman called Miss McMullen, was staying with the Kirkpatricks. Jack regarded her as one of those few whose society he preferred above his own, and tolerated her with ease. Miss McMullen employed Jack as a dummy for bandage practise, as she prepared for her part in the war. He was, in turn, treated for a broken arm, sprained ankle, and head wound. The war seemed to be encroaching into every part of Jack's life. Only two and a half years later, when still a teenager, he would be treated for real and major wounds.

Jack found that he was relishing the pattern of life at Gastons. In fact, in future years he was to regard this pattern as the ideal. A typical day would start with breakfast at 8 a.m., followed by a solitary walk until 9:15 a.m. Then, the next two hours would be devoted to reading Homer's *The Iliad* in the original language, or similar. After a short break at 11:15 a.m., Jack would work on Latin texts until 1 p.m., when lunch would be served. The afternoon was at his disposal until 5 p.m. He could read, or write, or wander the surrounding countryside. Then, between 5 p.m. and 7 p.m., he and Kirkpatrick would set to work again. After dinner, which was at 7.30 p.m., Jack would pursue a more relaxed course of English literature, mapped out by his tutor, which excluded novels (felt to be more suitable for leisure reading). This routine became for him the pattern of a "normal day".

He later wrote that "if I could please myself I would always live as I lived there".[10] Following this daily timetable, Jack got through an enormous amount of work and breadth of reading. In one report to Arthur, he revealed that he was reading *Prometheus Bound* (in Greek, "a red letter day in my life"), Aristotle, Horace, Keats, Ruskin, and Virginia Woolf. Also to Arthur he described himself as liking "sleeping late, good food & clothes etc as well as sonnets, & thunderstorms".

So life continued in Gastons, while war raged, and Warnie made periodic reappearances on short leaves. Jack had a holiday with Arthur (possibly with his older sister, Lily) in Portsalon in County Donegal, and returned there with him the following summer for another holiday.

The war, however, eventually could be set aside no more. In February 1916 a new Military Service Act came into force, bringing in conscription. It caused much discussion between Jack, Warnie, and Albert. It only partly clarified the situation of an Irishman such as Jack who was resident in Great Britain. Among those obliged to serve, the Act stated, were:

Every male British subject who, on the fifteenth day of August nineteen hundred and fifteen – (a) was ordinarily resident in Great Britain; and (b) had attained the age of eighteen years and had not attained the age of forty-one years; and (c) was unmarried or was a widower without children dependent on him.

Because he was an Irish resident, Lewis seemed to be excluded from the obligation as being among those who are "resident in Great Britain for the purpose only of their education or for some other purpose". However, as the issue of exemptions for Irishmen was debated nationally over many ensuing months, the teenager determined, contrary to the wishes of his father, that he would enlist even if remaining exempt from conscription. He decided on a strategy of trying to enter Oxford University, which, it gradually emerged, would enable him to join the Officers' Training Corps and get a commission as soon as his papers came through.[11]

On 4 March 1916, while having time off on a Saturday, Jack found a weathered copy of George MacDonald's *Phantastes* on Leatherhead station bookstall. It was in the popular Everyman Library edition. First published in 1858, *Phantastes* was MacDonald's first prose work of fiction. It begins:

I awoke one morning with the usual perplexity of mind which accompanies the return of consciousness. As I lay and looked through the eastern window of my room, a faint streak of peach-colour, dividing a cloud that just rose above the low swell of the horizon, announced the approach of the sun. As my thoughts, which a deep and apparently dreamless sleep had dissolved, began again to assume crystalline forms, the strange events of the foregoing night presented themselves anew to my wondering consciousness.

Anodos, the narrator, then recounts how his bedroom had metamorphosed into a woodland scene. He continues:

After washing as well as I could in the clear stream, I rose and looked around me. The tree under which I seemed to have lain all night was one of the advanced guard of a dense forest, towards which the rivulet ran. Faint traces of a footpath, much overgrown with grass and moss, and with here and there a pimpernel even, were discernible along the right bank. "This," thought I, "must surely be the path into Fairy Land, which the lady of last night promised I should so soon find." I crossed the rivulet, and accompanied it, keeping the footpath on its right bank, until it led me, as I expected, into the wood.

Anodos, whose name means aimless or pathless, has many encounters and adventures, the narrative unfolding with a dream-like logic rather than the normal pattern of a story. The effect conveys a mood and new emotional experience that instantly captivated Lewis. It is in this book that he encountered another magical wardrobe of sorts (the first was in E. Nesbit's story *The Aunt and Amabel*, which probably he had read some years earlier). This time it is a cupboard in the wall inside a mysterious hut in a forest clearing.

It seemed a common closet, with shelves on each hand, on which stood various little necessaries for the humble uses of a cottage. In one corner stood one or two brooms, in another a hatchet and other common tools; showing that it was in use every hour of the day for household purposes. But, as I looked, I saw that there were no shelves at the back, and that an empty space went in further; its termination appearing to be a faintly glimmering wall or curtain, somewhat less, however, than the width and height of the doorway where I stood. But, as I continued looking, for a few seconds, towards this faintly luminous limit, my eyes came into true relation with their object. All at once, with such a shiver as when one is suddenly conscious of the presence of another in a room where he has, for hours, considered himself alone, I saw that the seemingly luminous extremity was a sky, as of night, beheld through the long perspective of a narrow, dark passage, through what, or built of what, I could not tell. As I gazed, I clearly discerned two or three stars glimmering faintly in the distant blue.

This closet is a harbinger of the wardrobe in *The Lion, the Witch and the Wardrobe*, which is a portal into the magical world of Narnia.

Lewis tells us, many years later, that *Phantastes* powerfully "baptized" his imagination and impressed him with a deep sense of the holy, and the "bright shadow" it cast upon the real world, he said, transfigured all it touched. He acknowledged about MacDonald: "I have never concealed the fact that I regard him as my master; indeed, I fancy I have never written a book in which I did not quote from him."

Jack Lewis remained an atheist, but the baptism of his imagination, acknowledging the power of the holy and pure in the ordinary world, pitted his imaginative side against the intellectual, creating a tension that made him restless for fifteen or so years until he found a satisfactory resolution. That resolution then would work out in his writings in stresses and strains and triumphs for the remainder of his life.

Shortly after Jack's discovery of George MacDonald's writings, he and the Kirkpatrick household were horrified to learn that Lord Kitchener, British Secretary of State for War, had died with all the crew of the British cruiser the *Hampshire* when it was sunk by a German submarine. They wondered what this great loss would mean for the war. Worse news was to follow, as the late summer and autumn was dominated by news and rumours about the Battle of the Somme in northern France. Two of Lewis's future friends served in that conflict: J.R.R. Tolkien and H.V.D. "Hugo" Dyson. Dyson also fought in the much later battle of Passchendaele, where he was seriously wounded at Ypres shortly before the end of the war.

It is clear that Jack was continually aware of the events of the war, particularly in France. France for him was not an abstract concept; he and Warnie had shared a memorable holiday with their mother in 1907 in a French coastal town not far from some of the places made familiar by the war. The conflict, however, failed to erode his deep happiness under the tutorage of Kirkpatrick.

Arthur, whose Christian belief was an important part of his life and upbringing, had on some occasion asked the always secretive Jack about his religious views. In early October 1916, Jack replied that he believed in no religion, as there was no proof for any of them, and Christianity, philosophically speaking, was not even the best of them. Mythologies were simply human invention, whether they were of Loki or Christ, and belonged to the primitive stages of human development. This was not to deny that Jesus (whom he preferred to call Yeshua, regarding the name Jesus as a corruption) was a real historical person, unlike Loki, Balder, and other legends. Christ, however, was a mythological figure created by popular imagination from the man, Yeshua.

Jack regarded himself as being emancipated from superstition. We must try to be truthful, chaste, kindly, honest, and so on, but we owed these qualities to our dignity and humanity, not to imagined gods. A week or so later he admitted to a more or less agnostic position over the immortality of the human soul. He didn't know, one way or the other.

For the last part of 1916, Jack's thoughts and anxieties became focused upon passing his necessary examinations for entering an Oxford college. For him, everything was at stake, as he saw no alternative to an academic career, and it also provided a good entry into officer training, after establishing a future place in such a career. In December 1916, Lewis accordingly made his first trip to Oxford to take a scholarship examination. This took place between 5 and 9 December. Passed over by New College, he received a classical scholarship to University College, Oxford. A few days later *The Times* newspaper listed among the successful candidates, besides "Clive S. Lewis, University College", two who one day were to be among his closest friends – "Alfred C. Harwood, Christ Church" and "Arthur Owen Barfield, Wadham College". By that time, Britain had been at war with Germany for nearly two and a half years.

Lewis's success in gaining a scholarship at University College was a decisive moment for his future. The goal of an academic life now seemed achievable, though he still had his university-wide entrance examinations (Responsions) to take.[12] Lewis was well aware of his weakness in mathematics, a compulsory element.

Soon after arriving back with his private tutor, Lewis dropped the study of German in favour of Italian. The idea was to master it in seven weeks, so that he would have another language in case he failed the Oxford entrance examination and had to try for the Foreign Office for employment. The possibility of failure was not the only topic discussed in Gastons; the prospect of America coming into the war was becoming much more likely, increasing the likelihood of victory and the end of the conflict. (President Woodrow Wilson for the United States in fact declared war on Germany on 6 April 1917. Four days earlier, before a joint session of Congress, he had said: "The world must be made safe for democracy.")

The household at Gastons was now suffering increasingly from food rationing, and their daily topic of conversation was the impact upon shipping by German submarines. Particularly hard-hitting were the shortages of bread and potatoes.

Jack Lewis had turned eighteen near the end of 1916. The path before him was one of very basic and brief officer training based at Oxford University, and then posting to the battle front. His prospects of survival were poor, as the casualty rate among junior officers was high. The experience of war was to mould his basic ideas about the nature of the universe, and influence a central theme of his writings – a cosmic war between good and evil forming a larger context for human battles, whether strife within the individual human soul, or bloody conflicts between states. The Great War would shape much of his life.

4

Oxford and France: "This is What War is Like…"

In March 1917, eighteen-year-old Jack Lewis took Responsions but, as feared by his tutor, duly failed in mathematics, particularly algebra. In spite of failing the university entrance examination, he was allowed to come into residence at University College, in the Trinity or summer term. This allowed him to start his passage into the army by way of the University Officers' Training Corps. Though he had further algebra lessons, he was never to pass Responsions. By a freakish irony, Lewis – one of the most brilliant minds at Oxford – would have been barred from entering the university if it had not been for his eventual war service, ex-servicemen being exempted from having to pass the examination.

University College opens onto High Street, and claims to be the oldest Oxford college, founded in AD 1249. Its full name is The Master and Fellows of the College of the Great Hall of Oxford University. In its first centuries, when it was very small, the college only served fellows studying theology, and all its students were male until 1979.

One of its most famous students, the poet Shelley, was expelled from the college for atheism in 1811, the year he published *The Necessity of Atheism*. Lewis, also still an atheist when he entered the college, was officially a student without requirements of formal studies from late April until September 1917. Despite the impact of war everywhere, Lewis enjoyed a pleasant few months. He relished the library of the Oxford Union, punting on the River Cherwell, or swimming in it. He was very much aware of the general absence of undergraduates in Oxford, and other marks of war in the unusually quiet town. Most of his college building was taken up with serving as an army hospital. In one of his many letters to his father he commented on the troublesome Flying Corps cadets in Oxford, who, he said, like most people caught up in danger, eat, drink, and are merry, for tomorrow they die.[1]

Much of what we know of Lewis at this time is revealed in weekly letters to Arthur Greeves, who remained living in his family home in Bernagh, in Strandtown, Belfast. It was an indication of his isolation and solitary nature that Lewis eagerly anticipated Arthur's return letters. Lewis confessed that on Tuesday evenings and Wednesday mornings he hung on for Arthur's mail "just like a schoolgirl".[2]

One feature of Lewis's correspondence with Arthur at that time was his sharing of sexual fantasies. They commonly referred to sexual experience as "IT" or "THAT". On one occasion he had called on the Master of University College, who lived in a house full of books in the college grounds. Unexpectedly, he had been invited in for a meal. The lunch was pleasant, with the Master's wife and niece present. In reporting the visit to Arthur, he mentioned fantasizing about the attractive niece; her figure was just what he liked. The fantasy went on to a desire to spank her.

While this was hardly fifty shades of Lewis, the adolescent fantasies he and Arthur shared at this time quite often moved in the direction of sadomasochism. This tendency seems to be more at his instigation than Arthur's, and was probably a legacy of coming to terms with the brutal canings he had seen inflicted as a terrified young boy at Wynyard School. It has to be seen in the context of the traditional moral views of the rest of his life (for example, his exploration of the justice of human suffering in *The*

Problem of Pain), and that it was purely fantasy. We would not know of this tendency but for Lewis's letters to Arthur Greeves – in fact Arthur attempted unsuccessfully to erase any references to these and other sexual fantasies in the letters from his friend.

Lewis's later repulsion at any sadistic attitude to the affliction of pain, with its lack of regard for another's suffering, is expressed no more vividly than in Aravis's remorseful recognition of her indifference to the lashes received by her maid in the Narnian tale *The Horse and His Boy*. It might well also account for the very lengthy exposé of the cruelty at Wynyard School in *Surprised by Joy*.

Such fantasies were only a small part of the letters, however. They were full of a diversity of matters, including what Arthur and he were currently reading. In a typical letter he mentioned reading *Orlando Furioso*, a sixteenth-century text, in the original Italian (slowly, but enjoyably), how he would love Oxford to be lifted up and placed by the sea between mountains in "beautiful Donegal", reading a book on psychic research, which was kindling his old fascination with the occult, seeing the Poet Laureate, Robert Bridges, in an Oxford street, and how much he was enjoying the company of Cherry Robbins, a second cousin of his who was a volunteer at a military hospital in Oxford.[3]

It was in this quiet period that Lewis had got to know her. Cherry was the daughter of his mother's cousin, Katie. Though Cherry was not, in Lewis's view, "pretty", he clearly was attracted to her. Most of all, he noted, she was a "lover of books", a high accolade. In fact, to Lewis's increasing delight, she shared many of the "pet tastes" he owned with Arthur, such as Wagner's Ring, and Arthur Rackham's illustrations. Cherry and Lewis were able to continue seeing each other during the coming months. Later he wrote of her playing the piano (his favourite instrument at that time) when visiting his college, and of her being plain in a pleasant way.

Reading Lewis's letters of the time one wonders where the relationship might have led, had he been free to pursue it after his war service. Cherry is a rare example at this time of a woman friend. He, like many of his peers at that time, believed that true friendship was unusual between a man and a woman, as they were unlikely to share a view of the world or to meet mind to mind. Later events of his life were to educate his attitudes and to deepen his understanding and range of friendships with women.

Lewis's in many ways idyllic stay at University College ended when he eventually was able to join a cadet battalion based in another college early in June 1917, as No. 738 Cadet C.S. Lewis, "E" company.

At the end of April 1917, Lewis had enlisted in the University Officers' Training Corp, awaiting a posting. His preparatory military duties before joining a battalion included morning parade from 7:00 to 7:45 a.m., and an afternoon one from 2:00 to 4:00 p.m., with occasional evening lectures on map reading and similar topics. The medical records state Lewis's height as 5 feet 10¾ inches (almost 180 cm) and his weight as 13 stone (182 pounds, or about 82 kilos). At this height and weight, he was clearly already well built.

He noted a typical morning in the weeks of his "Phoney War" before proper officer training. He awoke at 7 a.m., then read until 8:30 (William Morris and also *Le Chanson de Roland*), before taking first a hot then a cold bath (as was the habit in college). He had an invitation with the other freshmen to "brekker" (breakfast) with a senior student, Theobald Butler. Butler was a fellow Irishman, a Sinn Feiner. Fresh on his bookshelves, Lewis noticed, was a volume of poems by Joseph Plunckett, executed after the Easter rising the previous year in Dublin. Lewis liked Butler a great deal, and the conversation turned to Ireland, W.B. Yeats, and then books. After breakfast they decided to bicycle to the river to bathe, Lewis being lent a bike. After a quarter of an hour cycling through quiet Oxford streets they arrived at Parson's Pleasure, an area of riverbank customarily reserved for men, eliminating the need for swimming clothes. Here two branches of the River Cherwell come together, forming in the tract between them the islet of Mesopotamia – a local name, after the biblical lands between the Tigris and Euphrates.

The battalion Lewis joined for officer training was encamped at Keble College. He was able therefore to remain in Oxford for another four precious months. This meant he could keep in contact with his friends at University College, and with Cherry Robbins. It also allowed a momentous encounter. The alphabet dictated that his room-mate was fellow Irishman Edward "Paddy" Moore, a trivial-seeming fact that was to dictate much of the shape of his future life. As an "L", Lewis was placed in a tiny, carpetless room with the "M", Moore. The two beds in the stark room were in sharp contrast to his comfortable rooms at University College. Paddy was the son of Mrs Janie King Moore, who had escaped an unhappy marriage and Ireland ten years before to live in Bristol with Paddy and his younger sister. Her husband, a civil engineer unaffectionately known as "the Beast", paid her a regular allowance.

With Paddy's commission, Mrs Moore and her daughter, Maureen, had moved temporarily to Oxford to be near him. She and Lewis first met in June that year, along with others of Paddy's friends. Immediately attracted to the Moore family, Lewis increasingly was to be found in their company. Maureen, who was eleven at the time, remembered: "Before my brother went out to the trenches in France he asked C.S. Lewis… 'If I don't come back, would you look after my mother and my little sister?'"[4] Lewis increasingly became emotionally attached to Paddy's mother, a feeling heightened by Albert Lewis's inattention to his son at this time. It was soon to turn to infatuation. Mrs Moore and Maureen were staying in temporary rooms in Wellington Square, not far from Keble College.

The life of an army cadet was not a natural habitat for Lewis, and he found some consolation, as the weeks of training went on, in meeting up with Cherry Robbins, and also in visiting Mrs Moore and Maureen with Paddy and others of their set of trainee officers. For Janie Moore, Lewis stood out. She later wrote to Albert:

Your boy of course, being Paddy's room mate, we knew much better than the others, and he was quite the most popular boy of the party; he is very charming and most likeable and won golden opinions from everyone he met here.[5]

Lewis was very happy at this stage to write to his father about meeting Janie Moore, telling him in June 1917 that he had met her "once or twice". He urged "Papy" to visit Oxford for a week. They could, he said, both stay at University College – he was allowed to invite a guest, as a scholar of that college. Albert, reluctant as ever to travel, didn't follow up his son's invitation. Soon, however, Lewis was able to visit Albert in Belfast, when granted a brief leave in August. He was careful to make the journey in uniform as young men thought shying conscription were frowned upon. By this time Lewis was seeing much more of Paddy's mother, as the two billet mates visited her together. This was soon to lead to a conflict of interest on Lewis's part between seeing his father and seeing Mrs Moore.

As the time for active service loomed larger, training became more intense. In September, as part of their officer training, Lewis, Paddy, and the other cadets went to the Wytham Hill area near Oxford to bivouac, and to try out model trenches, made more like the real thing by recent heavy rain. The experience of sleeping out proved to be more pleasant than Lewis expected, as there was an abundance of bracken to make a soft bed, and the rain kept off. Soon after this, Lewis was given a temporary commission as a second lieutenant in the 3rd Battalion, Somerset Light Infantry. Within two months he was to be at the front lines in northern France.

He began a month's leave, upsetting Albert by using three weeks of this to stay with Paddy and the Moores at their permanent home in 56 Ravenswood Road, Redland, Bristol. He claimed to Albert that he was unwell with a sore throat, and had to remain to rest, but the real reason was that he preferred Mrs Moore's company to his father's.

During this period, Paddy was posted to France with the Rifle Brigade, disappointed that he was not to serve with Lewis in the

Somerset regiment. Towards the end of his leave, in mid-October, Lewis finally turned up in Belfast, leaving him only a few days with his father. He was able to confide in Arthur Greeves, who lived close nearby, about his friendship with and growing love for Paddy's mother.

After leaving Belfast, Jack joined his new regiment at Crownhill, near Plymouth, south Devon. Here he became friendly with Laurence Johnson, who had been commissioned just a few months before him, and like him had been elected to an Oxford college (in his case, Queen's College). His new friend had markedly similar interests to those Lewis shared with his Ulster soulmate, Arthur Greeves, and was very soon to die in France from the same shelling that badly wounded Lewis.[6] Johnson seems to have encouraged him to pursue philosophy.[7] He told the Christian Arthur to take it up, to save him from the stagnation of being totally satisfied with a "traditional religious system". Certainly, Lewis told Arthur in a letter that philosophy, particularly metaphysics, was his "great find" at the moment.[8] He was reading the Irish philosopher Bishop Berkeley (1685–1753). In fact, it was the beginning of his long-standing interest in Berkeley's form of idealism, because of the philosopher's spiritual emphasis when it came to understanding our perception of natural things.

Though Berkeley thought from a Christian worldview, Lewis may have been attracted to his denial of the self-sufficient existence of material things. Lewis's materialism was becoming much more complex and diluted than it had been, in his quest for the spiritual and the beautiful. As the war progressed, his view of nature and the material world became much darker, and his response to beauty and the spirit more separate from his current intellectual beliefs.

In the space of a few months, Lewis had found two people, Cherry Robbins and now Laurence Johnson, who had affinities with him and also, he believed, with Arthur. It is notable that, although Lewis had had exclusive male companionship forced upon him in his schooldays, and now in college life at Oxford, he seems at this stage to have had no reservations about including at least some women in his close friendships – that is, friendships that related to his inner life or soul.

Just under a month after the visit to his father, Lewis suddenly was ordered to go to the front, being allowed only a 48-hour leave. Unable to visit his father in Ireland within that time, Lewis decided to spend it with Mrs Moore and Maureen in Bristol, which was, conveniently, on the way back from Plymouth to his departure point for France, sending a desperate telegram to his father to rush to Bristol to see him. "HAVE ARRIVED BRISTOL ON 48 HOURS LEAVE. REPORT SOUTHAMPTON SATURDAY. CAN YOU COME BRISTOL. IF SO MEET AT STATION.... JACKS." Confused, Albert Lewis simply wired back: "DON'T UNDERSTAND TELEGRAM. PLEASE WRITE." Thus father and son did not meet again before Lewis was invalided out of France the following spring.

Lewis reported to Southampton harbour at 4 p.m. on 17 November 1917, and crossed to France, to a base camp at Monchy-Le-Preux, a place that later inspired one of his war poems, "French Nocturne".[9] By his nineteenth birthday, 29 November, Lewis found himself at the front line and introduced to life in the trenches. His brother was elsewhere in France and in a safer location with his deployment in military supplies.

Infantry men usually alternated between the front lines and base camps behind the war front, depending on the ferocity of fighting at a particular time. The front lines were a network of trenches that stretched along a course shaped by the need to repel the enemy advance from anywhere along the borders of Belgium and Germany. The zone of trenches was relatively static. Sometimes the sacrifice of hundreds of thousands of men moved the front line a few miles.

In mid-December 1917, Lewis was billeted in the French town of Arras. Though it bore the scars of three and a half years of war, it would be devastated even more the following March, when the enemy pushed forward in their last major offensive. Lewis and his colleagues were transported there from the trenches in buses.[10]

Before Christmas, Lewis was back up in the cold trenches for a few days, some distance from the main battle lines, his battalion attached to an unnamed company for further training in bombing.

By New Year's Eve, Lewis was still experiencing a relatively normal day in the trenches. As usual, many shells sang over his head, to descend on the British gun batteries far behind. This was a "quiet" section of the line, where the dugouts were relatively comfortable and very deep. On one occasion, however, a shell fell close by the latrines as he was using them. Thinking back over an eventful year, Lewis wrote to Arthur that his hope was that he had gained the new (meaning Janie Moore) without losing the old (that is, Arthur).[11] In an earlier letter from the front lines, Lewis thanked him for writing to Mrs Moore (which is what he called her to Arthur), adding that "she appreciated it very much and you may perhaps understand how nice & homely it is for me to know that the two people who matter most to me in the world are in touch".[12]

The new year, 1918, at first continued as usual. Lewis's battalion was still stationed in the reserve lines, and some of the men were helping to rebuild damaged trenches. Albert, using his limited influence as a well-known Belfast solicitor, had been trying to get Lewis moved to what he thought would be a safer position with the gunners. His son informed him that he had decided to stay with his present company. The same letter played down the discomforts of life in the trenches and its horrors. Troops usually gave an edited version of their experiences to family back home.[13]

Trench life could not have been as idyllic as the letter to Albert suggested, because by the end of January or beginning of February, Lewis was hospitalized for three weeks at Le Tréport, miles away from the front line, with trench fever or, more technically, PUO (pyrexia, unknown origin). In some cases this disease could be deadly; it forced J.R.R. Tolkien to be invalided out of the theatre of war near the end of the Battle of the Somme in 1916. Le Tréport, Lewis soon discovered, was a small fishing village about eighteen miles up the coast from Dieppe. This reminded him sharply of the holiday he and Warnie spent with their mother close by in the year before she died, over ten years before.

It was not until the end of February that Lewis rejoined his battalion at Fampoux, a village to the west of Arras. He was now in the direct line of the final German large-scale attack of the war on the Western Front. Almost immediately he began a four-day tour of the battle front, during which he had as many hours sleep. It may have been these days that he remembered in *Surprised by Joy*, where he said that exhaustion and the constant rain were the soldiers' main foes. He recalled falling asleep while marching and then waking to find himself still on the march. The icy waters in the trenches could be above knee height.[14]

When Lewis returned to comparative safely outside the fighting area, he spent the whole night digging, in anticipation of the German advance southwards. All hell broke loose a little over two weeks later, on 21 March 1918. In the early hours of that morning German General Erich Ludendorff launched an offensive designed to drive the allied forces from the Western Front – the French from the Aisne and the British from the Somme – and to open the door to the capture of Paris. The initial bombardment lasted five hours, using more than 6,000 heavy German guns, supported by another 3,000 mortars. Two million poison-gas shells would descend on British lines over the next two weeks.[15]

A few days into the battle, elsewhere along the front, at Pargny, Paddy Moore was fighting with his 2nd Battalion of the Rifle Brigade, resisting the great German offensive. He was last seen alive the morning of Sunday 24 March.[16] Mrs Moore later was told that he died instantly from a bullet to the head as he was receiving emergency treatment for a wound. Meanwhile Lewis's battalion was being moved around the battle front near Arras.

Between 12 and 15 April, still in the area north of Arras, quite near the Belgian border, Lewis was caught up in the Battle of Hazebrouck. The action he saw took place around the village of Riez du Vinage. During the battle, he took sixty retreating German prisoners.

He was wounded on Monday 15 April by "friendly fire" at Mont Bernenchon, a slightly elevated hamlet just south-west of Riez du Vinage. At least one British shell burst close by him, killing nearby Sergeant Harry Ayres and fatally wounding Laurence Johnson, who were standing beside Lewis. Shards of the shell ripped into Lewis's body in three places, including his chest. Ayres was thirty-two years old and Johnson, who died later, merely twenty. Lewis then started to crawl back over the cold mud towards help and was picked up by a stretcher-bearer. A couple of days later Albert in Belfast received a telegram from the War Office: "2ND. LT. C.S. LEWIS SOMERSET LIGHT INFANTRY WOUNDED APRIL FIFTEENTH."[17]

K.J. Gilchrist may be right in thinking that stanzas in Lewis's long narrative poem, *Dymer* (1926), may draw on this experience.

> … Beside a lane
> In grass he lay. Now first he was aware
> That, all one side, his body glowed with pain:
> And the next moment and the next again
> Was neither less nor more. Without a pause
> It clung like a great beast with fastened claws;
>
> That for a time he could not frame a thought…[18]

Pieces of shrapnel remained in Lewis' chest for much of his life.

Everard Wyrall, in his official *History of the Somerset Light Infantry*, gives an account of the battle that took place between 14 and 16 April, in which Lewis was seriously wounded and friends killed:

> The 13th was a quiet day. Apparently the German advance was, for the time being, at a standstill, his infantry having got well ahead of his artillery so that the latter had to be brought up. His forward guns were only moderately active, but during the evening Mt Bernenchon was shelled and a group of buildings set on fire. Daylight patrols ascertained that the enemy was holding Riez du Vinage, a small wooded village

north of the [canal] and north-east of Mt Bernenchon….
As the leading Somerset men approached the eastern exits of
Riez [on 14 April], the enemy launched a counter-attack from
east of the village and the northern end of the Bois de Pacaut.
This counter-attack was at once engaged with Lewis-gun and
rifle fire and about 50 per cent of the Germans were shot
down. Of the remainder about half ran away and the other
half ran towards the Somerset men with their hands in the air
crying out "Kamerad?" and were made prisoners….[19]

Warnie, stationed at Behucourt, eventually heard from Albert
that his brother was wounded and hospitalized at Etaples (south
of Boulogne, on the French coast). He borrowed a motorcycle
and navigated the fifty miles west to the coastal hospital. Racked
by anxiety, he was able to force himself to concentrate on
nursing his engine over rough stretches of road and coaxing it to
maximum thrust over straight sections. His fear turned to joy and
thankfulness when he found Jack sitting up in bed. Though serious,
Warnie found, the wounds were not life-threatening, as Albert had
interpreted in his panic.

  From the Liverpool Merchants' Mobile Hospital at Etaples, a
few days later, Lewis was able to write his father that he had been
hit in the back of the left hand, on the left leg a little above the
knee, and in the left side under the armpit. The army medical
records recorded:

The Board find he was struck by shell fragments which
caused 3 wounds. 1st, left chest post-axillary region, this
was followed by haemoptysis and epistaxis and complicated
with a fracture of the left 4th rib. 2nd wound: left wrist quite
superficial. 3rd wound: left leg just above the popliteal space.
Present condition: wounds have healed and good entry of air
into the lung, but the left upper lobe behind is dull. Foreign
body still present in chest, removal not contemplated – there
is no danger to nerve or bone in other wounds.[20]

In the mobile hospital in Etaples, Lewis worked at understanding his horrific experience in the light of his atheistic beliefs. As his poetry written at that time reveals, he sought to retain a place for beauty and the spirit in his materialist worldview.[21] He thought about the "lusts of the flesh" that so often buffeted him. He had found himself becoming almost monastic about them. This is because, he reasoned, desires of the flesh, such as hunger or sex, increased the mastery of matter over the human spirit. On the battlefield he had seen spirit constantly evading matter: dodging bullets and artillery shells. He saw the equation starkly now as Matter equals Satan. Beauty, on the other hand, equals Spirit. Beauty was the only non-material thing that he could find. What everything boiled down to was, in effect, Beauty versus Satan. The material world was a prison house from which humans alone on the earth were capable of escape, through the hopes of the human spirit. There was, however, no God to aid us. Lewis's was a materialist's mysticism, owing much to his reading of the influential thinker, Arthur Schopenhauer.[22]

Lewis was transported later in May to the Endsleigh Palace Hospital, in central London. He was pleased to find this a comfortable place, where he even had a separate room. He was also happily aware of the fact that he could easily order from the many bookshops nearby. By the next month he was able to attend a Drury Lane theatre one evening to hear Wagner's *The Valkyrie,* conducted by Sir Thomas Beecham. One Sunday he took the train to Bookham, to visit the Kirkpatricks.

As the days drew on, Lewis missed his family. He wrote many pleas to Albert to visit him. "Come and see me. I am homesick, that is the long and short of it."[23] Warnie commented years later, after his brother's death:

> One would have thought that it would have been impossible
> to resist such an appeal as this. But my father was a very
> peculiar man in some respects; in none more than in an
> almost pathological hatred of taking any step which involved

a break in the dull routine of his daily existence. Lewis remained unvisited, and was deeply hurt at a neglect which he considered inexcusable. Feeling himself to have been rebuffed by his father, he turned to Mrs Moore for the affection which was apparently denied him at home.[24]

Unlike Albert, Janie Moore was a frequent visitor to London. She transferred to Lewis the attention she had paid to Paddy when he was alive, even eventually to the extent of moving to be near Lewis as he was moved from camp to camp by the army when he was pronounced fit for duty.

Lewis arranged to convalesce in Bristol, to be near Mrs Moore and Maureen, and was moved there near the end of June. His recovery was slower than anticipated – he remained in Bristol until mid-October. While in Bristol, Lewis was able to report some good news to Arthur Greeves. He had sent a slim manuscript of poetry to a publisher. After what seemed to the aspiring poet a considerable time, William Heinemann had accepted it for publication. Lewis told Arthur that it would be called *Spirits in Prison*, and that it was woven around his belief that nature is a prison house and satanic. The spiritual – and God, if he exists – oppose "the cosmic arrangement". The collection was eventually published under the revised title of *Spirits in Bondage* in March 1919, when Lewis was twenty. Some of the book was war poetry, but in fact most of the poems were written before he went to the front, and are quite remarkable for one so young.

The war ended on 11 November 1918. Two days before Christmas, Warnie arrived home in Little Lea from the Belfast ferry, on leave. He believed that he would not see his brother, who was still at a military camp. But late on 27 December he recorded in his diary:

A red letter day. We were sitting in the study about eleven o'clock this morning when we saw a cab coming up the avenue. It was Jacks! He has been demobilized thank God.

Needless to say there were great doings. He is looking pretty fit. We had lunch and then all three went for a walk. It was as if the evil dream of four years had passed away and we were still in the year 1915. In the evening there was bubbly for dinner in honour of the event. The first time I have ever had champagne at home. Had the usual long conversation with Jacks after going to bed.[25]

5

Student Days: Oxford, and Mrs Janie Moore

From January 1919 until June 1923, Jack Lewis resumed his studies at University College, Oxford. Within weeks of starting his first term of study, he was reporting back in letters to Arthur Greeves, and to his father, Albert. To Arthur in his weekly letter on 26 January 1919, he announced his good luck that he was able to attend, twice a week, lectures by Gilbert Murray on Euripides' *Bacchae*. As he had read the play before, it made the lectures more meaningful. The following day, writing to Albert, he expressed his thankfulness over returning to Oxford, which was greatly different from the shadow he had known before, during wartime. The college was still reduced in number – only twenty-eight students – but they were able to dine in the hall, and the dust sheets were gone from the Junior Common Room. What was to become a familiar pattern of lectures, games, tutorials, and debates had started.

A few days after those letters, Lewis joined a literary and debating society of the college called the Martlets. Membership was by invitation only and limited to twelve. He was to have a long-standing involvement with the club, and it gave a sounding board for his incipient ideas. The Martlets also provided a literary focus, which chimed with Lewis's deep-rooted interest. His studies showed his outstanding ability and scholarship in a wide range of subjects – philosophy, ancient classical languages, literature, and history, as well as older forms of the English language. Literature, however, was at his heart. It was closely related to Lewis's imaginative side, which was as powerful, if not more so, than his formidable intellect.

Literary and other debating societies were common among Oxford undergraduates, as they still are. The Martlets stood out, however, in that its minutes were archived in the university's distinguished Bodleian Library. The members met in each other's college rooms in rotation. The club was an immediate source of friends.

Lewis was to read a number of papers to the Martlets, not only through his undergraduate years, but throughout much of his subsequent academic career. His first was given in March of his first year, and was on a writer he much admired, William Morris. The minutes for that meeting tell us: "The general sense of the Society was that rather too high a position had been claimed for William Morris." Lewis had claimed, noted the minutes: "As a teller of tales he [Morris] yielded to none except Homer. In his prose works he had endeavoured, with some success, to recall the melody and charm of Malory." Other papers he gave as an undergraduate to the Martlets include one on narrative poetry, and another on the poet Edmund Spenser (who greatly influenced Lewis's future writing).

Shortly after Lewis started his studies in 1919, Janie Moore and her young daughter, Maureen, once more found accommodation in Oxford to be near him. Eventually, they permanently left their Bristol house. They were to live in a succession of rented flats and houses for the next ten years and more, most of this time with Lewis as part of the household, and much of this time enjoying financial support from his small scholarship and supplementary payments to him from Albert.

One immediate reminder of the war for Lewis was the pieces of shrapnel left in his body, which stopped him swimming as energetically as before.

Like a number of those who would become friends in Oxford, he never, however, indulged in the fashionable literary spirit of disillusionment after the First World War. There was not a fundamental conflict between his beliefs and the horrors of his wartime experience. This seems the opposite of what is argued in K.J. Gilchrist's thorough study, *A Morning After War: C.S. Lewis & WWI*. Gilchrist argued that Lewis suppressed the reality of his wartime experience, because otherwise this would have devastated the romantic yearnings that held his life together. In his later poem *Dymer*, however, Gilchrist argues, he was able to face the end of romantic ideals. Gilchrist is completely right, however, in concluding:

> The things Lewis met in France and the fragments – metal or metaphorical – that he carried within him from that place gave him a knowledge of grief, of loss, of the atrocities that humankind is capable of producing, of relationships awry and relationships lost, of the wanderings of youth – knowledge that after his conversion [in 1931] continued to inform his views of life, the cosmos, and his faith beyond a point where many people can follow.[1]

The strongest memento of war, however, was not Lewis's memories and scars, but the loss of his friend, Paddy Moore. This was not because he was a close friend. Paddy was not of the first-order of friendship, unlike Arthur Greeves. It was not also that Paddy had been particularly close to his mother before he left for war; there were tensions and frictions (probably quite normal between an eighteen-year-old and his mother). The fact was that Lewis had a promise to keep. Even at that time, Lewis was morally serious, a trait he had throughout his life, despite his failings. He was intent on fulfilling his promise to look after Janie Moore, even though this would inevitably complicate his life. Not least of the complications was that Mrs Moore was still married to the Beast, Courtenay Moore, who lived back in Dublin, and was receiving an allowance from him. Word of Lewis's living with her could jeopardize this lifeline, and could potentially affect Albert Lewis's provisions for his son, which covered the modest living needs of a single student. It could even jeopardize his studies at Oxford, according to A.N. Wilson,[2] as sharing a house with someone else's wife was likely to be scandalous.[3]

Lewis had no choice over where to live in his first year of study. He was required to stay in the college. After the first year, students could find digs in the town if they wished. It was not until after the end of his first year, therefore, that he was able to move in with Mrs Moore, effectively his adoptive mother, and Maureen. It is not clear when he set himself free from college accommodation, and settled in with his adopted "family". By May 1920, however, about the time Mrs Moore moved permanently to Oxford with her daughter, he was staying with them in rooms in a superior detached house in a picturesque part of Old Headington, at Courtfield Cottage, 131 Osler Road. This was the home of a Mrs Marshall, a "strange lady", according to Lewis, and her daughter.

Lewis expressed to Arthur his relief in not having to drag himself back to college each evening, even though the rent was expensive.[4] One of Lewis's delights was to walk into college from Headington via Cuckoo Lane, an attractive and often narrow walk that is roughly parallel to the Headington Road, and eventually took him past Mesopotamia.

Even though Lewis was resident in the college in that first year at least, he nevertheless closely tied his life into that of the Moores, spending as much of the vacations as possible living with them, while continuing to deceive Albert. Mornings in term he would work in the college library or attend lectures. Then he frequently took lunch and had afternoons with Mrs Moore, returning for dinner in the college hall, after which evenings were employed working in his spacious rooms.

What are we to make of Mrs Moore? Much ink has been spilled by biographers of C.S. Lewis over whether or not he was sexually intimate with her, even though there is not enough evidence to say either way. This is an issue that is unavoidable, because of the number of years he shared a house with her, and how strange their relationship seemed to some of those who knew them both (such as Warnie). What is clear is that in his late teens Lewis was in love with an attractive older woman who showed affection and care towards him. Even when she was in her late fifties, his brother Warnie referred in his diary to Janie Moore's "good looks".[5]

Lewis refers in *Surprised by Joy* to this period of his return to Oxford after military service, and to a "huge and complex episode" that he is obliged to leave out of his account of his life. He concedes, however: "All I can or need say is that my earlier hostility to the emotions was very fully and variously avenged."[6] Even if he had felt free to recount the story, he adds, he doubted that it had much relevance to the subject of *Surprised by Joy*: how he passed from unbelief to Christianity.

He talked and wrote of his love for Janie Moore openly with Arthur, confident that his friend would keep his secret.[7]

At first, too, he had spoken openly to his father about his links with Mrs Moore. Indeed, she corresponded directly with Albert. A.N. Wilson claims, "While nothing will ever be proved on either side, the burden of proof is on those who believe that Lewis and Mrs Moore were *not* lovers – probably from the summer of 1918 onwards."[8] But this is to oversimplify the matter by not considering the full context of the affection Lewis and Janie Moore felt towards each other.

In 1918, Mrs Moore lost her only son in a violent death. She had been informed that he had died of a bullet through the head while being tended for his shot leg on the battlefield.[9] Understandably, she was devastated by his death, and grieved deeply. Her daughter revealed, many years later, that her mother rarely went out after Paddy was killed. One rare excursion was to visit his grave in Pargny, France. Janie Moore, Maureen remembered, no longer had the heart for the things she used to do, becoming "more and more obsessed with household things and the hands and the gardens".[10] Emotionally and realistically, these are not the circumstances for a love affair, with someone replacing her son, even had Janie Moore been free of her marriage to the Beast.

Paddy Moore's death was not made official until September 1918. Upon this news Albert wrote to Mrs Moore expressing his sympathy. She replied on 1 October, saying how she had lived her life for her son, and now how very difficult it was to go on. She told Albert of Paddy's request to his son to look after her if he did not return from France. She remarked of Jack Lewis: "He possesses for a boy of his age such a wonderful power of understanding and sympathy."[11] As some mothers might, Mrs Moore continued to think of Lewis as a "boy", and years later she would shout for him and Warnie with the call, "Baw-boys!"

His son's mysterious "entanglement" with Mrs Moore greatly troubled Albert. He once confided in a letter to Warnie:

> I confess I do not know what to do or say about Jack's affair. It worries and depresses me greatly. All I know about the lady is that she is old enough to be his mother — that she is separated from her husband and that she is in poor circumstances. I also know that Jacks has frequently drawn cheques in her favour running up to £10 — for what I don't know. If Jacks were not an impetuous, kind-hearted creature who could be cajoled by any woman who had been through the mill, I should not be so uneasy.[12]

Albert's anxieties about Lewis's relationship with Mrs Moore were to lead to a major falling out between father and son early on in his undergraduate studies. The summer of 1919 they had a serious quarrel to do with finances, and over Albert's habit of snooping into his son's mail. Albert described the initial spat in his diary afterwards.

> Sitting in the study after dinner I began to talk to Jacks about money matters and the cost of maintaining himself at the University. I asked him if he had any money to his credit, and

he said about £15. I happened to go up to the little end room and lying on his table was a piece of paper. I took it up and it proved to be a letter from Cox and Co stating that his a/c was overdrawn £12 odd. I came down and told him what I had seen. He then admitted that he had told me a lie. As a reason, he said that he had tried to give me his confidence, but I had never given him mine etc., etc. He referred to incidents of his childhood where I had treated them [he and his brother] badly. In further conversation he said he had no respect for me – nor confidence in me.[13]

After this, Lewis got in the habit of having his post to Belfast sent to Arthur's house, Bernagh, across the street. He continued dutifully to write to Albert regularly, despite the tensions in their relationship.

Albert was pleased to hear some very good news from his son in April, the following year. He had got a First Class mark in Classical Honour Moderations (Mods), the preliminary part of his studies. This was a gruelling examination in Latin and Greek. The final stage in the Honour School would be Greats. This was a combined course in history and philosophy, mainly of the classical period of Greece and Rome, but supplemented by study of modern philosophy, that is, from Descartes onwards. After the exhilarating announcement of Lewis's First, however, there followed the bad news. He was, Lewis continued, fulfilling a promise by taking a holiday in Somerset "with a man who has been asking me for some time to go and 'walk' with him". This would keep him from visiting Little Lea during the somewhat short Easter vacation. The truth was that Lewis was actually on holiday in Washford in Somerset with Mrs Moore and Maureen.[14]

From sometime early in 1920 onwards, therefore, it seems Lewis lived with the Moores, while pretending to his father (who supported him through this period) that he was still resident in the college. He had by then fully adopted Mrs Moore as his mother, while having deeper feelings for her.

Although Janie Moore would have been aware of his infatuation, her own feelings for him are likely to have remained motherly – Jack Lewis became the replacement for her only son. Her attitude to him was deeply affectionate, but practical rather than sentimental. She expected obedience to her iron rule over the household, and he was forced, like any real son in that situation, either to rebel against the regime or to come up with strategies for living in a way that ensured he remained intact in himself.

Because he had adopted Mrs Moore, he took on a disposition of basic contentment that became second nature, even when irritated by the frequent storms of their domestic life. Indeed, his adopted family life taught him about ordinary human living at a time when he could easily have become a scholarly recluse, or part of a narrow circle, as biographer A.N. Wilson points out.

It is likely that Lewis's immersion in ordinary rather than an exclusive scholarly life deeply influenced the course of his writing. As part of this deluge of the familiar, Mrs Moore became known by her nickname, Minto, probably after a fondness for a popular mint confectionary, Nuttall's Mintoes. Lewis's life with Janie Moore (and with Maureen for many years) partly helps to account for many of the books that have made him popular. In the early Oxford days after the war, his ambitions were to be a great poet and a scholar. He didn't at this time seem to be the future author of any science-fiction stories, *The Screwtape Letters*, or *The Chronicles of Narnia*. Though somewhat tongue-in-cheek, A.N. Wilson points to the heart of what Lewis learned in the school of Mrs Moore:

> He is the great chronicler of the minor domestic irritation, of the annoying little trait bulking up to (literally) hellish proportions. Domestic life with his father had been the training school for this distinctively Lewisian vision. Minto not only provided him with stories of *Screwtape*-style domestic situations. She also had a rich enjoyment of the comedy of human character, which was one of the things she shared with Lewis. [15]

Lewis coped with his adopted mother's limitations with forbearance. His diary recording his ordinary life, which he began keeping for several years from 1922, provide instances of friction, and his response. One such is recorded on Sunday 16 May 1926, some years after he moved in with Mrs Moore (whom he frequently referred to as "D" for no obvious reason) and her daughter. Maureen (then aged nineteen) had generously offered to wash up the dishes after supper (usually Lewis's task). "Like a fool (or a knave)," Lewis recorded,

> I acquiesced and she began, not according to D's fundamental principles. D rushed into the scullery and took the implements out of her hands and a violent altercation followed, Maureen claiming to be judged by results, and D saying that if every servant had to learn her ways she didn't see why her daughter shouldn't etc. etc.

The evening deteriorated after that, and Lewis at one point exacerbated matters by speaking up for Maureen. He generously concluded that Mrs Moore was suffering the effects of a headache ("She is still very poorly").

A glimpse of Lewis's demanding double life as an undergraduate and as fellow householder with Mrs Moore and Maureen was granted to Arthur in a letter after the household returned to more settled accommodation in 28 Warneford Road, in a suburb off the Cowley Road. Lewis wrote:

> It has been all the usual thing. I walk and ride out into the country, sometimes with the family, sometimes alone. I work: I wash up and water the peas and beans in our little garden: I try to write: I meet my friends and go to lectures. In other words I combine the life of an Oxford undergraduate with that of a country householder: a feat which I imagine seldom performed. Such energies as I have left for general reading go almost entirely on poetry – and little enough of that. [16]

Minto was deeply hospitable, inviting many into her Irish household. For the few years Lewis kept a diary, many people featured in its pages that were full of his domestic life. In all, it totals about 250,000 words, which Walter Hooper, in editing the diary for publication, abridged by a third, at the request of the Lewis Estate and publishers.

The very choice of events and contents recorded between 1922 and 1927 often appears to have in mind Janie Moore, to whom Lewis read many of the entries as they were written. As a result, as his friend Owen Barfield discovered, there was no record of the "Great War" of ideas between himself and Lewis (see below). The diaries vividly rendered the daily domestic life that Lewis shared, as well as weather, walks, writing, books, and uncertainties over employment. There is often a discernable undercurrent of constant anxiety, very much related to a lack of money, which did not dissipate until Lewis was finally employed by Oxford University in 1925, after a year of temporary tutoring in philosophy.

The early part of the diaries capture the final terms of his undergraduate years. Lewis's remarkable powers of concentration helped him to adapt to a family habitat. Maureen at one time had to practise music around five hours a day, sometimes in the same room the student was working in, but he remained focused upon his books, shutting out everything else.

Arthur Greeves also walked through the pages of Lewis's diary at times, as he did throughout Lewis's correspondence. In 1920 he was contemplating becoming an Oxford student, but also weighing up the counter claims of studying at the prestigious Slade School of Fine Art in London. In his letters, Lewis provided much counsel on preparing for Oxford entrance, and commented upon tutoring that Arthur was having back home in Belfast. At one point he mentioned the idea of Arthur having the medieval scholar Helen Waddell as a tutor. She was well known to Lewis and his friends in Strandtown and Belmont, and was also a friend of Jane McNeill. Lewis and Arthur often discussed Jane, a mutual friend, in their correspondence. Waddell became particularly famous for her study of the tragic love between Abelard and Heloise in her novel, *Peter Abelard*.

In the end, Arthur decided upon the Slade, playing to his strengths as a painter, beginning his studies there in 1921, and graduating with a certificate two years later. Some time afterwards he did further study of art in Paris.

During his undergraduate years at University College, much of Lewis's thought and attention was taken up by Mrs Moore and issues of finance and accommodation. Somehow he was able to succeed brilliantly in each stage of his studies, despite their demands and range. These took in the rigours of ancient Greek and Roman language, literature, thought and history, as well as the demanding English School, providing the foundations for an academic career.

Lewis's hope was to gain a fellowship to an Oxford college, which would mean both tutoring and lecturing in one of the disciplines he was to study, whether philosophy, English language and literature, or Classics. He therefore set upon a course in which he was thoroughly grounded in the Classics and philosophy before reading English. He eventually received the triple First Class BA degree mentioned earlier: a First in Classical Honour Moderations (Greek and Latin literature) in 1920, a First in Greats (philosophy and ancient history) in 1922, and a First in English in 1923. In Oxford fashion, this in time became an MA.

In the summer of 1921, the resolutely stay-at-home Albert Lewis was persuaded by relatives to pursue a holiday in England. Albert subsequently arrived in Oxford to visit his son, accompanied by his brother-in-law and sister-in-law, Augustus and Annie Hamilton. Together the four set off to tour around southern England for a week in Uncle Gussie's pale-grey four-seater Wolseley convertible. In a letter, Lewis told an anecdote about Albert that was typical of his father. Half an hour south of Oxford, cruising at a little over thirty miles an hour, Albert in the back seat suddenly asked, "Are we in Cornwall yet?" When the party eventually did reach north Cornwall, Lewis was pleased to find the landscape uncannily like the County Antrim coastline of his childhood memories.

The following spring of 1922, not long before Lewis achieved another First Class distinction after sitting the Greats examination, he wrote to his father about his ideas for the future, acutely aware that Albert was his main benefactor. He passed on the news that a tutor of his had suggested that it would be better to hang on in Oxford after Greats than to take employment in a hurry. The college, the tutor revealed, would be likely to continue his scholarship for another year. Another tutor had suggested he take a course in English literature; if he were to get a First in that, he would be in a very strong position indeed.

6

The Aspiring Poet and Scholar in Hard Times: The Inspiration of Owen Barfield

The generosity of University College in extending his scholarship for another year allowed Lewis to study in the English School. His wide reading, astonishingly retentive memory, and formidable past reading in English literature allowed him to complete these studies in a short period, during the academic year 1922–1923. With this third course, he had achieved a triple First Class in his undergraduate studies, opening the way for his longed-for academic career. Albert gamely continued to supplement the modest scholarship, while unsure about whether he was in fact helping to support Mrs Moore as well.

Not only did Lewis's four years of studies between 1919 and 1923 thoroughly ground him in a number of disciplines, but they also led him into close friendships, some of which were lifelong. One of these was with Nevill Coghill, a student at another Oxford college, Exeter, who would eventually become a member of the Inklings when it formed about a decade later. He had studied history, and was now in the English School.

Lewis met Coghill, who was a few months younger than him, through an English discussion class run by Professor George Gordon, newly arrived from Leeds University. Lewis penned a sketch of Coghill in his diary, after first meeting him: "He seems an enthusiastic sensible man, without nonsense, and a gentleman..."[1] Though attracted by his seemingly effortless courtesy, Lewis was disturbed to discover that this "most intelligent and best-informed" member of the discussion class was a Christian, whose belief in the supernatural basis of reality sharply contrasted with his own materialism.

Literary critic John Carey points out that Coghill had grown up in the

> old-world atmosphere of the south of Ireland, where sailing, fishing, hunting, shooting, and the painting of pictures provided gentlemanly pleasures... A tall, handsome figure with rather leonine features, he was known in Oxford for the charm and vivacity of his conversation and the fineness of his taste.[2]

As well as his future involvement in the Inklings, especially in its early years, Coghill would become famous for popularizing the fourteenth-century poetry of Geoffrey Chaucer with his highly readable modern translation in rhyming couplets of *The Canterbury Tales*. He also became well known for his Oxford theatrical productions, which included introducing the talents of Richard Burton and other students. Later he co-directed, with Burton, a film adaptation of Christopher Marlowe's *Doctor Faustus* (1967) in which Burton also acted, along with Elizabeth Taylor. All this was on top of a distinguished academic career at Oxford.

Both C.S. Lewis and Nevill Coghill read outstanding papers to Gordon's discussion class, the latter student on one occasion covering the subject of "realism" in a wide range of literature, including Shakespeare's *King Lear*.

In another meeting of the class, Lewis's contribution was on a poet who was to prove one of the most important influences upon his future writing, the sixteenth-century author of *The Faerie Queene,* Edmund Spenser. Both Coghill and Lewis were delighted by each other's papers to the discussion class. On the occasion of Lewis's paper on Spenser, Coghill's task was to record the minutes. He did so in accomplished verse stanzas, in the style of Spenser, with allusions to Chaucer thrown in. After a brief prologue, which spoke of scholars of "Oxenford" being gathered "in a goodlye companye," he recorded:

> Anon turned Lewis to a bluë boke [book]
> He swalwed thrice; hys dewy fingers shooke
> And he bigan with right a myrie cheere
> His tale anoon; and spake in this mannere.[3]

Coghill then proceeded to give the gist of the paper (or "tale") in the same verse form. One stanza reports Lewis stating about the poet Spenser:

> So leave him, more than lovely, less than great;
> He was a poet; he was nothing more:
> Nay – but a poet's poet; and there sate
> Milton and Keats within his forest door.
> Young dreamy boys delight in Spenser's lore
> And eat his satisfying faery food
> And Wordsworth on his native mountain shore
> Caught echoes from that dim enchanted wood;
> Then enter ye who dare, ye who have understood.[4]

In the second term of Lewis's year in the English School, on a Sunday in February 1923, Coghill and Lewis took the first of many long walks together, fervently talking about literature and life as they skirted the Hinksey hills to the south of Oxford. Over forty years later, Coghill remembered these intellectually intoxicating times:

We used to foregather in our rooms, or go off for country walks together in endless but excited talk about what we had been reading the week before – for [F. P.] Wilson [a tutor they both shared] kept us pretty well in step with each other – and what we thought about it. So we would stride over Hinksey and Cumnor – we walked almost as fast as we talked – disputing and quoting, as we looked for the dark dingles and the tree-topped hills of Matthew Arnold. This kind of walk must be among the commonest, perhaps among the best, of undergraduate experience. Lewis, with the gusto of a Chesterton or a Belloc, would suddenly roar out a passage of poetry that he had newly discovered and memorized, particularly if it were in Old English, a language novel and enchanting to us both for its heroic attitudes and crashing rhythms… his big voice boomed it out with all the pleasure of tasting a noble wine… although at that time he was something of a professed atheist, the mystically supernatural things in ancient epic and saga always attracted him.…[5]

Coghill also remembered tempestuous differences and emphatic agreements in their newfound friendship, with

none more thunderous or agreeing than over [John Milton's] *Samson Agonistes*, which neither of us had read before and which we reached, both together, in the same week; we found we had chosen the same passages as our favourites, and for the same reasons – the epic scale of their emotions and their over-mastering rhythmical patterns.… Yet when I tried to share with him my discovery of Restoration comedy he would have none of it.[6]

Lewis's rapture over Milton's poetry and coolness to drama of the Restoration period was characteristic. He had strong ambitions to be a major poet, and throughout his life, drama was not a real interest. With Shakespeare, his taste centred upon the poetry of the plays. Lewis's ambition at the time, in fact, could be summed up in a line of Coghill's minutes of his paper on Edmund Spenser for Gordon's discussion class:

He was a poet; he was nothing more…

Other important friendships were forged at this time. Lewis, in fact, had a great talent for friendship. In *Surprised by Joy* he writes of some of those made at this period as an undergraduate, and friendship is a theme that he often turned to in his future writings. Sometimes his very writings would be shaped by his friendships. Typically, he saw the making of friends to be character-building or, in older terms, to be a "school of virtue". He, in fact, took a classical view of friendship, which in later years, after his conversion, was gradually adapted into a Christian perspective. Properly lived out, he gradually discovered, friendship could open one's eyes to previously unseen aspects of reality, whether this be the world of nature, realms of the imagination, or the hard-won reaches of human thought.

Lewis came to believe that friendship could restore health in how we viewed things, and could even change our very perceptions of reality. He was aware of the dangers in friendships, too, as changes in perception can lead to the bad as well as good. He revealed the good impact of friendship particularly well in comments he made about two friends – a fellow undergraduate, Alfred Kenneth Hamilton Jenkin, and his Ulster soulmate, Arthur Greeves.

In *Surprised by Joy* he records:

The first lifelong friend I made at Oxford was A. K. Hamilton Jenkin, since known for his books on Cornwall. He continued (what Arthur had begun) my education as a seeing, listening, smelling, receptive creature. Arthur had his preference for the Homely. But Jenkin seemed able to enjoy everything; even ugliness.

Lewis explained that he got from Jenkin the idea of complete total surrender to whatever was being offered at a particular time. If they were in a drab town, the thing to do would be to hunt for "those very places where its squalor rose to grimness and almost grandeur". When a day was dreary, then of course they would search out the "most dismal and dripping wood". If the weather was breezy, the idea would be to head for the most exposed ridge.

Rather like the way Lewis saw the texts of literature, he became aware that a friend provides another vantage point from which to view the world. For Lewis, his different friends opened up reality in varying ways. Another fellow undergraduate, Owen Barfield, for instance, was very different from Arthur Greeves, who had revealed to Lewis that he was not alone in the world. Though Barfield shared with Lewis a view of what was important, and asked strikingly similar questions, the conclusions he came to usually differed radically from those of his friend. During the 1920s, the two were to wage what Lewis later called a "Great War", a long dispute over the kind of knowledge that imagination can give us. As Lewis put it, it was as if Barfield spoke his language but mispronounced the words.

It is no exaggeration to say that his friendship with Barfield was one of the most important in his life; as important at least, in its different way, as that with Arthur, and with a few others whom Lewis met later. In a talk in the USA almost a year after Lewis's death, Barfield remembered their friendship:

> Now, whatever he was, and, as you know, he was a great
> many things, C.S. Lewis was for me, first and foremost, the
> absolutely unforgettable friend, the friend with whom I was in
> close touch for over forty years, the friend you might come to
> regard hardly as another human being, but almost as a part of
> the furniture of my existence.[7]

Lewis tried to explain the difference between "Arthur and Barfield" (as he called them) in *Surprised by Joy*. In a way, he said, they were representative of every person's "First" and "Second" friend. Arthur is the First Friend. He is the one "who first reveals to you that you are not alone in the world by turning out (beyond hope) to share all your secret delights"; you merge "like raindrops on a window". Barfield is the Second Friend. Rather than being your *alter ego*, he is the "anti-self", the one "who disagrees with you about everything". Obviously your interests are shared, but he approaches all these from "a different angle". "Out of this perpetual dog-fight," Lewis concluded, "a community of mind and a deep affection emerge."[8]

Owen Barfield happened to be born within weeks of Lewis in 1898, but in north London rather than east Belfast. He was a child of agnostic parents: Arthur, a London solicitor, and Lizzie, a suffragette. They had been brought up as non-conformists but abandoned any church participation. They retained a respect for Christianity, and for the man Jesus Christ, but lived in an entirely secular way. Barfield remembered it as a happy home, alive with music, books, and visiting aunts, uncles, and cousins. Lizzie Barfield, a skilful pianist, taught her husband to play, and he would join her in duets. Arthur Barfield excelled in reading aloud, and his particular delight in Dickens's novels was infectious.

Barfield was born in Muswell Hill, and lived there until he was six or seven. He had two sisters and a brother. Lizzie Barfield taught him to read and provided his early education. Just before he was eight, he went to preparatory school in nearby Highgate. Then he attended upper school in Highgate until he was seventeen. At school he was keen on gymnastics, which anticipated his later involvement in dance.

In the spring of 1917, with the First World War in its third year, he was called up to the army; he was then eighteen. He served with the Royal Engineers, and joined the Signal Service. In the Wireless Department, Barfield studied the theory of electricity. He had already learned Morse code from his elder brother.

While he was still training, the armistice was signed, so he had no combat experience at all, though he was sent to Belgium. There he had very little to do, as pigeons were still used for communications. He had already won a scholarship to Oxford. It was while he served in the army that his fervent interest in English literature began, so much so that he decided to try to switch his intended studies at Oxford from Classics to English literature. At this time, he began writing a little.

Demobilization from the army was a slow process, and Barfield did not get up to Oxford until October 1919, the start of the first term of the new academic year. He studied at Wadham College, obtaining permission to read English, and developing his own writing. One undergraduate friend of Barfield's, Leo Baker, shared his interest in poetry, and introduced him at a tea in the college to Lewis, whom he had recently befriended. Lewis at this time was still studying Classics. Baker was one of several who would become abiding friends of his; in fact, he was one of Lewis's first close friends at Oxford, and was one of the very few introduced to his secret "hideout" in Headington. "Mrs. Moore" Baker remembered as an "an Irish lady with an ebullient temperament. I was often invited up there, for meals even, and greatly enjoyed her exceptional rice puddings, of which she was justly proud."[9] Baker was not deterred by his friend's secrecy or by his fervent materialism. "For me," he recalled,

> fundamental atheism was a new experience. One day over the tea cups in my room, Lewis cried out in an angry crescendo, "You take too many things for granted. You can't start with God. *I don't accept God!*" I was surprised into silence.[10]

Thanks to Leo Baker, Barfield and Lewis soon found themselves walking together, or asking each other to lunch, but did not really see a lot of each other until after graduation, when the first skirmishes of their always friendly Great War started, and later in the decade intensified. Barfield recalled:

> The Lewis I first met late in 1920 or early 1921 was an extremely well-educated but hard-up undergraduate, twenty-

one years of age, with a ruling ambition to become a great poet. At that time, if you thought of Lewis, you automatically thought of poetry.[11]

He remembered that Lewis was rather slight of build then, unlike in later years, probably because of the financially lean years he was going through, as before those years he was of thicker build. Barfield was mightily impressed that Lewis had already published a collection of his poetry (*Spirits in Bondage*), and he liked many of them. He soon found out that unlike him, Lewis preferred longer, narrative poems, and was soon reading sections from such a long poem, *Dymer*, which took Lewis a number of years to complete, not helped by the complexities of his home life with Mrs Moore and Maureen, and the pressures of his studies and then his search for employment.

While an undergraduate, Barfield experienced what has aptly been described as an "intellectual epiphany"[12] while studying the Romantic poets. That moment of illumination seems to have set the course for his entire life. He became fascinated not only with what happens in the mind of a reader of poetry, but with the mystery of human consciousness itself, in play when we recognize faces, see flowers in a meadow, or observe a rainbow.

As with J.R.R. Tolkien, whom he met some years after graduation through Lewis, Barfield's main intellectual stimulus came from language. He recalled long after:

> What impressed me particularly was the power with which not so much whole poems as particular combinations of words worked on my mind. It seemed like there was some magic in it; and a magic which not only gave me pleasure but also reacted on and expanded the meanings of the individual words concerned.[13]

Language, he believed, had the power to transform human consciousness and to embody historic changes in our way of seeing reality. Barfield's ideas about how poetry and reading brought about changes in how we see the world were to have an enormous impact upon Lewis, and later Tolkien.

One of Barfield's schoolboy friends at Highgate School, Cecil Harwood, was an undergraduate in Oxford at the same time as him, though at Christ Church College. The two had remained fast friends, and Lewis was drawn into their wider circle, becoming a lifelong friend of Harwood. A couple of everyday incidents from the undergraduate years illustrate their friendship.

One fine day in May 1922, before Lewis started the English course, he left Mrs Moore around midday (Maureen was in school during the day) and took the bus from Headington into Oxford, where he met Barfield outside the Old Oak public house. They strolled together to the delightful gardens of Barfield's college, Wadham, and sat under the trees. They argued stubbornly about the dreams of Romantic literature. The love dream, insisted Lewis, made people incapable of real love, while the hero dream made them cowards. To Lewis's surprise, when the subject turned to his poem in progress, *Dymer,* Barfield's verdict was warmly favourable. He said that it was "by streets" the best thing Lewis has done, and asked, could he keep it up? Barfield added that their mutual friend Cecil Harwood had "danced with joy" over it.

About a month later, on Friday 30 June, Lewis bicycled into central Oxford down Headington Hill, for a planned meeting with his tutor in college, who turned out to be absent. Returning up Headington Hill, and then riding through Barton into the countryside, he pressed on through wind and rain to Bee Cottage, Beckley, where he was to stay for the weekend, and where he was warmly welcomed by his friends Owen Barfield and Cecil Harwood. The two had taken digs together there.

Later, the three of them got into a literary conversation about fancy and imagination. After supper they ventured out for a walk, through woods that were darkening with the approaching twilight. Pierrot, their black and white cat, followed them like a dog. Barfield, who was already a skilled and vigorous dancer, unself-consciously danced around Pierrot in a field, watched by the amused Harwood and Lewis, and by three horses nearby. Did the dancer perhaps have Edward Lear's limerick in mind?

There was an Old Man on the Border,
Who lived in the utmost disorder;
He danced with the cat,
And made tea in his hat,
Which vexed all the folks on the Border.

On the way back to Bee Cottage in the dark, they composed a nonsense poem, each taking on a line in turn.

The weeks and terms rolled on, and Lewis's final exams in the English School were in sight. With them only three months away, he was plunged some of the worst weeks in his life – and this was someone who had endured his mother's death, a small boarding school led by a man going insane, and the trenches of the First World War.

Lewis had become fond of one of Janie Moore's brothers, Dr John Askins, who was familiarly known as "the Doc". He had trained in medicine at Trinity College, Dublin, served in the Royal Army Medical Corp, and was wounded in 1917. His wartime experiences appear to have deeply affected his health, and in peacetime he became absorbed in the practice of psychoanalysis and the occult.

The Doc had brought his family to live in Iffley, to be near Oxford and his sister. During what was intended to be a brief visit, Askins suddenly suffered what Lewis described as "war neurasthenia", in which he endured nightmarish mental torment. Mrs Moore insisted that he must stay with them, which meant accommodating his wife, Mary, as well. Many a night, the student took his turn sitting with him. In *Surprised by Joy* Lewis remembered:

It had been my chance to spend fourteen days, and most of the fourteen nights as well, in close contact with a man who was going mad... And this man, as I well knew, had not kept the beaten track. He had flirted with Theosophy, Yoga, Spiritualism, Psychoanalysis, what not?[14]

The Doc suffered fits, and contortions, and would scream uncontrollably. Lewis and others, including Mrs Moore, frequently had to forcibly restrain him until his drugs took over. All this time, Lewis's university studies were being neglected and, dog-tired, he tried to continue to give tutorials in Latin to a family friend, Mary Wiblin, whom they had nicknamed Smudge. This was in exchange for her giving violin lessons to Maureen. In the end, Askins was admitted to hospital at Richmond, where death soon released him from his terrors.

Another severe drain on Lewis's time after the period of caring for the Doc ended up bringing a measure of stability into his life. Since he had become part of Mrs Moore's household, they had frequently moved house, from one rented place to another. In May, when his studies leading to his final exams in June were at their most intense, a fresh move took them to Hillsboro, 14 Western Road, in Headington (later renamed Holyoake Road).

For weeks prior to the move, it had been necessary for Lewis to spend many hours painting the prospective house. Then, when the move took place, so much had been left undone by a slipshod decorator called Mr Tolley that Lewis – along with Mrs Moore and Maureen and their French lodger – was forced to camp for a fortnight before the place was ready for the furniture to be delivered. Settling in took a considerable time. Lewis notes in his diary as late as 5 July that he and Mrs Moore, were hanging photos over her son Paddy's desk. But Hillsboro turned out to be a home for seven years, before Lewis, Mrs Moore and Maureen moved into a permanent house of their own in the vicinity. This was The Kilns, which proved to be Lewis's home for the rest of his life.

Despite these setbacks, and his constant anxiety over making ends meet, Lewis astonishingly achieved his goal. When the results appeared on Monday 16 July 1923, they revealed that Lewis and Nevill Coghill had obtained "First Class Honours in the Honour

School of English Language and Literature". But he would have to wait two years for a permanent position in an Oxford college, and the financial security that it entailed. Owen Barfield and Cecil Harwood had received their degrees two years before, in 1921, and were now postgraduate students. Barfield was awarded a First in English Literature, and Harwood a First in History.

Warnie Lewis commented some years later, in *The Lewis Papers*:

> When we reflect on the circumstances of Clive's life during the time he was reading this school – the shortness of the period at his disposal, his ill health, a constant anxiety inseparable from supporting a family out of an undergraduate allowance, his fears for the future, the unceasing domestic drudgery, the hideous episode of Dr John Askins' final illness, and the move to Hillsboro – we are astounded at the extent of an achievement which must rank as easily the most brilliant of his academic career.[15]

With the momentous award achieved, Lewis could not afford to relax. He spent that summer correcting Higher School Certificate examination papers to earn money, and for the next academic year did what he could to bring income to the household. One September day, worried about the future, Lewis took a walk suffering from depression and ill health. He made his way through Mesopotamia, between the branches of the River Cherwell, and then on to Marston. Here he had a glass of beer and a packet of cigarettes, an extravagance he had not been able to indulge in for a while.

Ten days later, he arrived in Ireland to see his father. He stayed for nearly three weeks and left heartened by Albert's continued generosity. The day after his farewell to his son, Albert noted in his diary:

> I repeated my promise to provide for him at Oxford if I possibly could, for a maximum of three years from this

summer. I again pointed out to him the difficulty of getting anything to do at 28 if he had ultimately to leave Oxford.

Lewis had some breathing space in his quest for academic employment there.

Earlier that year, in April, Owen Barfield had married Maud Douie. Like him, she danced, and he had met her at the English Folk Dance Society. She was looking for a male dancer for a concert party around Cornish villages, partly for protection against the crudities of some of the local men. She was thirteen years older than her new husband. Maud came into a little money, and for the next few years Barfield would be a freelance writer, doing various odd jobs to supplement his income. With his marriage, there was no lessening of his deep friendship with Lewis. What had alarmed Lewis even more than the possibility of marriage making his friend inaccessible was noticing that Barfield had completely abandoned his materialism, so that, for him, "the night sky is no longer horrible".

Owen Barfield had come under the spell of a charismatic mystic thinker called Rudolf Steiner, as had his friend Cecil Harwood. The movement around Steiner was called Anthroposophy, and this name was to be dominant in conversations and exchanges between Lewis and Barfield for the rest of Lewis's life, but most intensely in the remaining years of the twenties. It was the basis of the Great War between them, which eventually led to an amiable truce. Barfield was intent on demolishing Lewis's materialism, and Lewis on undermining Barfield's new supernaturalism. The two locked into battle, using the resources of their brilliant minds to defeat each other. For each, the motive was to save his dear friend from error. The battle was so important that the future of each lay in its outcome.

Maud, Barfield's new wife, was an Anglican, and antipathetic to her husband's espousal of Steiner and Anthroposophy. She only very gradually modified her resistance, and he in turn became an Anglican nearly thirty years later. For him, Steiner's insights were a way of knowledge, rather than a religion, which provided the true key to understanding Christianity, including the biblical texts on which it rested. Christianity for him meant the "working of the Logos [the Word, or Christ] in human destiny and human life". Like Rudolf Steiner, he became convinced that the incarnation, life, and death of Christ were at the centre of the "evolution of consciousness". Also like Steiner, he believed in reincarnation (which may have been the sticking point for Maud). He had encountered the writings of Steiner, and Anthroposophy, as early as 1922.

Steiner's teaching melded well with Barfield's love of literature, particularly the Romantic Movement, and the thought and poetry of Samuel Taylor Coleridge in particular. The influences upon his thinking took in the Romantic poets and writers, including the German poet and philosopher Novalis, as well as Steiner's theosophic mysticism. Barfield also appreciated George MacDonald, whose adult fairy tale, *Phantastes,* had so enraptured Lewis, as we have seen.

Barfield and Maud lived for a time near Oxford in the Buckinghamshire village of Long Crendon, making it easy for him and Lewis to see each other. The two friends also carried on an extensive correspondence (through which much of their battle was fought in its more intense period).

Keen to continue his literary exploration of poetry, Barfield had begun a post-graduate B.Litt in 1921, which eventually became his book *Poetic Diction* (1928).[16] He recalled that the university was unable to find him a supervisor versed in the area he wished to pursue. In the end, they decided to let him get on with the B.Litt without one! In 1925, he brought out an accomplished children's book, *The Silver Trumpet*, published by Faber and Gwyer, which later was a success in the household of J.R.R. Tolkien. Lewis read it in manuscript form and, soon after starting, he enthused in his diary (October 20):

I began to read Barfield's faery tale "The Silver Trumpet" in which with prodigality he squirts out the most suggestive

ideas, the loveliest pictures, and the raciest new coined
words in wonderful succession. Nothing in its kind can be
imagined better.

In 1926, Barfield's study *History in English Words* appeared. It was
clear from the variety and innovation of his publications in the
twenties that he could have had a brilliant career as a writer and
academic. Instead he eventually decided to work as a lawyer in his
father's legal firm in the City of London, where he remained until
retirement age. After this long hiatus, surprisingly, his literary
career took off.

While Barfield was pursuing his B.Litt and writing *The Silver
Trumpet,* Lewis amid his tribulations was plodding along with
Dymer, determined to make his mark as a poet. Warnie Lewis
perceptibly commented, after his brother's death:

> The remarkable thing about his literary career is that it never
> occurred to him until a relatively late date that his great
> achievement would be in prose. *Spirits in Bondage* appeared
> in 1919, a collection of poems, some of them written in his
> Bookham days: *Dymer*, a narrative poem, would be published
> in 1926, the fruit of much pain and effort during a peculiarly
> difficult period. During all these early years, he thought of
> himself (though with no great confidence) as essentially a
> poet. A certain feeling of alienation from the poetic currents
> of his time led him to publish pseudonymously: those first
> two books were by "Clive Hamilton" (his own first name, and
> his mother's maiden surname), and the many poems that he
> published in later years were signed "Nat Whilk" (Anglo-Saxon
> for "I know not who") or, more simply, "N. W."[17]

Dymer gives a vivid insight into Lewis's thinking and imagination
in the long period before he returned to Christian belief. In the
period he was living, though, the twenties, the "new psychology"
created a distrust of the romanticism that had so marked the

pre-First World War scene. The distrust was reinforced by bitter memories of the war. Though Lewis never succumbed to fashionable disillusionment, he was, he confessed, affected by this distrust, which forced him to rethink the whole basis of Romanticism and literary fantasy, a process that eventually led to his move from atheism, via a Stoic idealism, and then pantheism, to belief in theism (admitting to a personal God, instead of a distant Absolute Spirit unmoved by human experience), and finally to his conversion to Christianity in 1931.

Dymer is a poem pitched against all totalitarian regimes, and has some similarities with themes in Spirits in Bondage. It was based on a story that came to Lewis in his youth. In the story, a man had intercourse with a mysterious bride, the fruit of which was a monster. When the monster murdered his father, it turned into a god. The monster's father was Dymer, the hero of the poem. In the story, Dymer escapes from a perfect but inhuman city into the soothing countryside. Various adventures overtake him. In contrast to Dymer's high ideals, a revolutionary group rebel against the Perfect City in anarchy, claiming to be doing it in Dymer's name. Fresh in Lewis's mind when he wrote were the bloody events of the Russian Revolution and of his native Ulster. He regarded popular political causes as "daemonic".

In Dymer, Lewis attacks Christianity bitterly, regarding it as a tempting illusion that must be overcome and destroyed in one's life. Christianity is lumped together with all forms of supernaturalism, including spiritism.

Old Theomagia, Demonology,
Cabbala, Chemic Magic, Book of the Dead,
Damning Hermetic rolls that none may see
Save the already damned – such grubs are bred
From minds that lose the Spirit and seek instead
For spirits in the dust of dead men's error,
Buying the joys of dream with dreamland terror.[18]

By the time Lewis finished writing *Dymer*, he had rejected out-and-out materialism in favour of idealism, acknowledging an Absolute Spirit as prime reality, rather than the material world as source of all that is real, hence the reference to losing "the Spirit" by seeking instead "spirits in the dust of dead men's errors".

Lewis's long discussions with Owen Barfield were in part the cause of the changes in his thinking that led him out of a bleak materialism and, some years later, atheism. The other friend who was part of his change in direction was J.R.R. Tolkien, who moved from teaching in Leeds University to Oxford in 1925.

7

The Young Don:
Meeting J.R.R. Tolkien

In the academic year following his gaining his First Class degree in the English School (1923–1924), Lewis could not make do simply with his father's allowance. He was forced into a combination of some tutoring and intermittent work such as Higher School Certificate exam marking. He wrote some of the *Dymer* poem, which at this time was nearly finished. A short poem was published in a literary magazine. During that year he had tenaciously sought academic posts in any of Oxford's colleges, even contemplating teaching subjects other than English literature. His various First Class honours awards meant that in principle he could turn his hand to a variety of subjects. In reality, posts were few and far between. In his diary, he noted how Mrs Moore felt "keenly (what is always on my mind) how the creative years are slipping past me without a chance to get to my real work".[1]

In January 1924, Lewis tried for a fellowship in philosophy at St John's College. In support of his application, he submitted an essay on "The Promethean Fallacy in Ethics". He was unsuccessful, but his friend Nevill Coghill obtained an English fellowship at the college at which he had been an undergraduate,

Exeter. Lewis also contemplated a research fellowship at All Souls College, and registered for a D.Phil degree.

The next month, Lewis dined at High Table in University College, his old college, as guest of the distinguished philosopher E.F. Carritt, his former tutor. Carritt told him of a fellowship in philosophy that was to be awarded at Trinity College, worth £500 a year, and advised him to apply for it. They then took themselves to a meeting of the Philosophical Society. As Lewis walked home to Headington late that night, he looked at the written details of the Trinity fellowship in the light of street lamps as he passed them. He found himself in a strange state of excitement, even though there was only a very slender chance of obtaining the fellowship. It would mean, he realized, the end of the poverty of the last years for his adopted family. In the end, his application came to nothing, like his registration for a D.Phil.

Three months later, however, Sir Michael Sadler, Master of University College, offered him a temporary post for the coming academic year, to take on E.F. Carritt's work as philosophy tutor while he was absent, teaching in America. Lewis accepted, once again having cause to be grateful to University College. It meant a lot of preparation in the months before he started, and a disappointment; the pay would only be £200, as he was not asked to take on all of Carritt's duties. Those he was given, however, included lecturing as well as tutoring undergraduates, which was good experience to include in future applications.

So it was that from October 1924 until May 1925, Lewis served as philosophy tutor at University College during E.F. Carritt's absence. He heard that there was a vacancy at Magdalen College coming up and decided to apply, though he felt that the chances of being successful were small. It turned out that the advice he had been given to study in the English School after Classics was invaluable. It gave him an edge, and the years of intensive study were rewarded.

On 20 May 1925 C.S. Lewis was elected to a fellowship in Magdalen College, Oxford, as Tutor in English language and literature for an initial five-year period. He lost no time in informing his father. Albert's reaction to Lewis's appointment was recorded by Warnie in *The Lewis Papers* (taken from his father's diary entry for that day). Albert was waiting to be called for dinner. Mary Cullen, the stalwart housekeeper (or the Witch of Endor, as she was affectionately called by Albert and his sons), came into his study to let him know that the post office was on the phone. Albert went to take the call, and was informed that there was a telegram for him. "Read it," he said. The message was brief: "Elected Fellow Magdalen. Jack." Albert thanked the anonymous voice and then climbed the stairs to his son's room. There he burst into tears. With joy filling his heart, he knelt down by the bed and thanked God. His entry simply concludes, "My prayers have been heard and answered." On 22 May *The Times* announced: "The President and Fellows of Magdalen College have elected to an official Fellowship in the College as Tutor in English Language and Literature, for five years as from next June 25, Mr Clive Staples Lewis, MA (University College)."

Lewis joined the Oxford University English School (with his appointment to Magdalen College) the same year that J.R.R. Tolkien took up his post as Rawlinson and Bosworth Professor of Anglo-Saxon in it, but they were not to meet until the following spring. Tolkien was a fellow of Pembroke College. It was the practice to affiliate a professor with a particular college.

Magdalen – the college of St Mary Magdalen – was founded in 1458, and its name is still pronounced as it was by its founder, William Waynflete: Maud-elen. The landmark tower of Magdalen was completed in 1503. During the Reformation, the medieval features of the chapel were stripped away, but the interior was restored in the nineteenth century.

The college lies on the banks of the River Cherwell, crossed by Magdalen Bridge. The pattern of Lewis's life would change in some ways in arriving at Magdalen, and its routines would remain in place for the thirty years he would be a don there. One change was that, in termtime, he would sleep in his college rooms during the week, but continue to spend most afternoons in Headington. His term-time days, and often others as well, approached the ideal of the pattern of the Bookham days a decade or so before.

Before the term started, Lewis spent more than a fortnight in September 1925 with his father, at Little Lea. Relations were much improved, and Lewis was relieved that he no longer had to rely on his father for his living. After Lewis left Belfast on 1 October from Donegall Quay, Albert noted in his diary: "Jacks returned. A fortnight and a few days with me. Very pleasant, not a cloud. Went to the Boat with him. The first time I did not pay his passage money. I offered, but he did not want it."

Early in October, Lewis moved into his college rooms at Magdalen. These were in New Building, Staircase 3, Room 3. He was delighted with the accommodation, though some furnishing was needed. He was pleased by the views from his windows at both the front and rear of the building. His big sitting room looked north. Remarkably, as the college is near the bustling Oxford High Street, from the windows of this sitting room the scene was rural – there was no clue from the view that he was in a small city. He looked down upon close-cropped lawns, which took his eyes to a distant woodland. There the trees burned an autumn red. Over the grass, a herd of deer grazed. To his right he could glimpse the beginning of what would become a favourite walk, a path through the college grounds beside the River Cherwell, known as Addison's Walk. To the front of the building, Lewis's smaller sitting room and bedroom provided a view southwards, across to the main buildings of the college, with Magdalen tower standing tall beyond it.

As well as tutoring students (an early and recalcitrant pupil was John Betjeman, later Poet Laureate), an important part of Lewis's duties was to give lectures. Over the years he would become one of Oxford's most popular lecturers, and some of his lecture series were eventually published, and are still in print today.

One series, which he was to give several times, was created to introduce students to the medieval world, both its thinking and the splendour of its imagination. He showed how a mental and imaginative model of the world was then created that was inspiring and a challenge to many of our basic assumptions about reality. When contrasted with our modern image of the world, that old model stimulates many questions. An important one is the influence of our own familiar model upon our minds and behaviour.

In helping his modern students to step inside this distant world, Lewis took away barriers to their reading of its texts. He was not giving the lectures for

> those who prefer not to go beyond the impression, however
> accidental, which an old work makes on a mind that brings
> to it a purely modern sensibility and modern conceptions;
> just as there are travellers who carry their resolute Englishry
> with them all over the Continent, mix only with other English
> tourists, enjoy all they see for its "quaintness", and have no
> wish to realise what those ways of life, those churches, those
> vineyards, mean to the natives.[2]

The book, *The Discarded Image: An Introduction to Medieval and Renaissance Literature*, is one of Lewis's finest literary studies, marked by clarity and readability. It was not published until after his death, in 1964.

Lewis's very first lecture of a series of eight in the Oxford English School was given on 23 January 1926, after frantic preparations. The series was entitled "Some Eighteenth-Century Precursors of the Romantic Movement". He had planned to lecture on selected poetry of that period, but discovered just in time that a distinguished colleague intended to cover the poets "from Thomson to Cowper", which completely overlapped his series. He therefore was forced to turn to the relevant prose writings of the pre-Romantics, which were much less familiar to him. Modestly he underestimated the size of his audience, and had to lead them to a larger room. This meant a crowd of gowned students surging across Oxford High Street, holding up the traffic.

The young don was still locked into his atheism, though now believing that the origin of all things was in an impersonal Absolute Spirit, not in matter. He had a shock a few months later that greatly disturbed him, and was a significant moment in his journey to eventual belief in God and then Christianity.

Many of his colleagues at that time at Magdalen made an impression on Lewis. One was the philosopher T.D. Weldon. On Monday 26 April, Lewis and Weldon – who had dropped by – were sitting by the fire in his larger sitting room in college. Over whisky, they got on to the subject of the historicity of the New Testament Gospels. Both agreed that there was much in them that could not be discounted. To Lewis's astonishment, Weldon – this hardest-edged of all the atheists that he knew – suggested that the evidence for the historicity of the Gospels was surprisingly good. The atheist then made a reference to the anthropologist Sir James Frazer's *The Golden Bough,* on worldwide magic and religion, which was vogue reading at the time. "Rum thing," Lewis remembered Weldon remarking. "All that stuff of Frazer's about the Dying God. Rum thing. It almost looks as if it had really happened once."[3]

During that evening, Lewis and Weldon could easily have been discussing the impending General Strike, which gripped Britain the following month. Instead, the focus had become the surprising subject of the New Testament Gospels. This was one of a number of unexpected turns Lewis's thinking was reluctantly to make in the next several years. Many of his ideas at this time were to be transformed, or at least taken in new directions, or even restored from neglect, by J.R.R. Tolkien.

On Tuesday 11 May 1926, Britain's first nationwide General Strike had been underway less than a week. It had been brought to a head by the breakdown of negotiations between coal miners and their employers over a large pay cut and longer working hours. Oxford undergraduates, stockbrokers, solicitors, and white-collar workers throughout the country rallied to beat the strike by staffing abandoned trains and buses. Some signed up as special constables, expecting a breakdown in civil order. It looked as if a class war might divide the nation. The Chancellor of the Exchequer, Winston Churchill, emotively labelled the strikers "the enemy".

Lewis made his way from Hillsboro into Oxford. His destination was Merton College, a short distance from Magdalen. Here a four o'clock "English tea" was planned, a meeting of the Oxford English School that was likely to be discussing important issues that even a General Strike could not postpone. The school was a relatively new institution, and different approaches to the subject – particularly the views of its professors – could strongly influence its future direction. In 1926, the school had only three chairs, one of which had been occupied the year before by Professor Tolkien, whom Lewis was interested in meeting.

When Lewis entered the meeting room, he would have taken in the various people already assembled, some of whom he had already met. They included the Reverend Ronald Fletcher (chaplain and tutor in English language and literature at St Edmund Hall), George Gordon (Merton Professor of English Literature), Margaret Lee (a tutor in English), and Professor Tolkien. The latter was a slight man, rather smart in dress, shorter than Lewis and not very much older. He spoke quickly, and Lewis had to listen carefully to catch all he said. He was, in Lewis's words, jotted in his diary that night, "a smooth, pale, fluent little chap".

The meeting seemed cocooned from the outside world. Lewis noted later that there was hardly any talk of the strike. Tolkien finally managed to get the discussion around to the English School syllabus, but wasn't allowed to say very much. Lewis was interested in hearing more about his approach.

Talking to Tolkien afterwards, Lewis discovered that the professor felt that he couldn't read Spenser (one of Lewis's favourite authors) "because of the forms". He considered "language is the real thing in the school". Not only that, Tolkien expressed his opinion that "all literature is written for the amusement of *men* between thirty and forty". Lewis recorded that according to Tolkien, "We [in the English School] ought to vote ourselves out of existence if we are honest – still the sound-changes and the gobbets are great fun for the dons." (Gobbets are short extracts from old texts for translation in exams.) Lewis summed up his new acquaintance: "No harm in him: only needs a smack or so."

One seemingly throwaway observation Lewis made in his diary about the man who would soon be his close friend uncannily got to the heart of Tolkien's make-up: "Technical hobbies are more in his line."[4] This referred to what Tolkien called his "secret vice" or hobby of inventing languages. Lewis was shortly to discover that there was a whole lot more to Tolkien's private hobby when he and Tolkien started to meet regularly and to share with each other their writings. Lewis would become one of the few to be introduced to stories from the world of Middle-earth that Tolkien was inventing, integral to which were the languages that he was creating.

Lewis would soon find out also that Tolkien wished to bring the teaching of English language and literature together in the English School. In this aim, he was drawing upon an older view of learning that had its roots in the earlier ages that he and Lewis loved.

By the end of 1929, a little over three years after their first meeting, Lewis would be supporting Tolkien's proposed changes to the Oxford English School, changes that would eventually integrate language and literature more, and conclude the literature syllabus with the Romantics at around 1830. This was the point, as they saw it, after which the modern reader was familiar with the predominant worldview of literary authors and thus, in their opinion, did not need the kind of support teachers in the English School were best suited to give. This was help in obscure texts, shifts in the meaning of words, and in tasting the imaginative worlds of previous ages, especially the imaginative glory of the Middle Ages.

Lewis's lectures ranged from those that provided a context to the texts that students had to study to others that focused closely on the actual texts. He was trying to help his students as much as he could, drawing upon both his own wide reading and his analytical thinking. Many lectures, in fact, combined both context and textual study. His range of subject can be seen in a couple of series that he taught. In the autumn (or Michaelmas) term of 1926, Lewis gave a twice-weekly course of lectures on the subject "Some English Thinkers of the Renaissance (Elyot, Ascham, Hooker, Bacon)". He began a rather different series a year later, on "*The Romance of the Rose* and its Successors", material that would eventually appear in his *The Allegory of Love* (1936), a book that was written over a long period.

Lewis once explained to his father his approach to giving lectures (he was referring to a lecture series on philosophy, but his approach was the same for literary topics). He was, he said, plodding on with his preparation for fourteen lectures. He was not writing them out in full, only in note form. Though the introduction of this extemporary element was dangerous for a beginner, lectures that were read simply sent his students to sleep. He had decided to take the plunge from the very beginning of his academic teaching career. He would force himself to talk rather than recite.

Lewis's lecture notes tended to be made up of complex headings, but with his frequent quotations from texts written out in full. In fact, he was gifted with an extraordinary, almost photographic memory, so in theory he did not need to write out quotations. Probably, doing so was an aide-memoire for the whole lecture. He seems to have held entire books in his mind by remembering the positions of sections or of entire chapters, and knew even the placing of particular sentences on a page. Alistair Fowler, one of his later students and a friend, called it "memory of the substance, aimed at grasp of contents through their structure", leading to a superlative "literary competence".[5]

Lewis's ability as a philosopher is easily overlooked because of his subsequent fame as a literary figure. He had, of course, taught philosophy for a complete academic year in an Oxford college. His ongoing Great War with Owen Barfield was often carried on at a high philosophical level (teaching Barfield much in the process), and his philosophical interests were well known to others. Indeed, he continued teaching some philosophy after taking up his lecturing in English.

On 12 May 1926 (the day after meeting Tolkien for the first time) he conducted a philosophy class, as usual, at Lady Margaret Hall with several female students. (Contrary to some accusations of misogyny, Lewis seemed to treat male and female students as equals.) In his diary, later, he recorded with approval their continued interest in the thought of Bishop Berkeley, who saw all existence as dependent on God's perception (*esse is percipi*), and things in the world as existing through derivative human perception.

To the group of women students, he also explained a distinction made by the contemporary philosopher Samuel Alexander that had been a very important discovery for him. It was so important that it shaped his thinking for the rest of his life. This was a distinction between "contemplation" and "enjoyment" (both terms being used technically by Alexander, it should be said). When you see a chair you *enjoy* the act of seeing, and *contemplate* the chair. If you focus on the act or experience of seeing a chair, however, your inner state becomes the object of contemplation instead of the chair itself. It is an either/or situation.

Lewis pointed out to the women that there is a fundamental difference between looking *at* and looking *with* one's perceptions and sensations (rather like how you can either look *at* or look *with* a pair of spectacles). It was a matter of where you placed your awareness; whether you were focused on your own moods, experiences and other inner states, or you were attending to something or someone other than (and outside of) yourself. In one attitude, you were fixed upon your inner state; in the other, you were focused upon an object.

This either/or distinction was becoming more and more important to Lewis. It had already undermined his materialism, and would eventually help him to leave his atheism and convert to belief in a personal God. This would prepare the way for his later conversion to Christianity. Lewis was particularly pleased that one student, Joan Colbourne, understood the crucial difference between enjoyment and contemplation. Joan responded to another student's comment that she wished to "know" the self: "It is as if, not content with seeing with your eyes, you wanted to take them out and look at them – and then they wouldn't be eyes."[6]

According to the eminent literary critic William Empson, Lewis was "the best read man of his generation, one who read everything and remembered everything he read". His completely bookish nature suited him to his task of lecturing and tutoring in the English School. What emerged from this background of reading was a wealth of thought, imagination, and writing that enriched all he taught, thought, and wrote. He gradually became a humble man who, rather than seeking constantly to be original and celebrated, took pleasure in building upon the work of others, especially if they were writers or thinkers from distant ages. Yet he was as quick to acknowledge his debts to contemporaries such as Samuel Alexander, or Owen Barfield.

From childhood onwards, Lewis read voraciously and eclectically. Later in his career, he typically defended the value of "lowbrow" reading, such as Rider Haggard and John Buchan, in the face of literary elitism. This bookishness and eclecticism was an important characteristic throughout his life, reflected in his diaries, conversation, and letters, and in the books he wrote.

Lewis's appetite for almost permanent reading made him a natural library-dweller from his undergraduate studies onwards. Oxford's Bodleian Library held a central place in his life, work, and also his affection, as he explained on one occasion in a letter to his father. He wrote of spending his mornings in the Bodleian and remarked that had he been able to smoke and relax in an upholstered chair, this would be one of the world's paradises.

The literary critic Helen Gardner noticed his reading habits in the Bodleian Library in later years with admiration:

One sometimes feels that the word "unreadable" had no meaning for him. To sit opposite him in Duke Humphrey

[Library] when he was moving steadily through some huge double-columned folio in his reading for his Oxford history was to have an object lesson in what concentration meant. He seemed to create a wall of stillness around him.[7]

Lewis saw the world with the help of texts, as part of the correct way to perceive reality. This is why, while experiencing the horrors of trench warfare, he reflected: "This is War. This is what Homer wrote about." Homer wrote about the first-hand experience of battle in several places. Perhaps Lewis was thinking of the lines:

And from there we sailed on,
Glad to escape our death
Yet sick at heart for the comrades we had lost.[8]

Lewis's new friendship with Tolkien became an important part of his social life. When they first met, Lewis's interest had been piqued when Tolkien mentioned to him his linguistic and writing hobbies. They were clearly the fire that burned within Tolkien. Soon Lewis was attracted by the Professor of Anglo-Saxon's invitation for him to come along to the Coalbiters, an informal reading club that Tolkien had just started. Its purpose was to explore the original Icelandic literature such as the *Poetic Edda*, which was full of tales of Norse gods and heroes, and a great dragon, Fafner, which had enchanted Lewis as a child.[9]

The readings took him back to his discoveries when young, where the sudden thrill of "northernness" struck him as a palpable sensation. Tolkien, he already knew, shared such a love of a vast, northern world, with cold, pale skies, dragons, and vulnerable gods, one of whom was Balder the Beautiful. The name of Tolkien's reading club referred to those who huddled so close to the fire that they appeared to "bite the coal". The small band of members included his old friend Nevill Coghill, of Exeter College.

In one of his frequent letters to Arthur Greeves, Lewis wrote that a number of his very old dreams were materializing because of the Coalbiters, which included reading *Sir Gawain and the Green Knight* in the original Middle English, and learning Old Icelandic. As a result of the sessions, Lewis and Tolkien were soon meeting regularly and talking far into the night.

In another letter to Arthur, in December 1929, Lewis recorded that after one meeting, Tolkien came back with him to his college rooms and "sat discoursing of the gods and giants of Asgard for three hours". These conversations were to prove vital both for the two men's writings, and for Lewis's eventual conversion to the Christian faith in 1931. As Lewis the Ulsterman remarked in *Surprised by Joy*:

> Friendship with... J.R.R. Tolkien... marked the breakdown of two old prejudices. At my first coming into the world I had been (implicitly) warned never to trust a Papist, and at my first coming into the English Faculty (explicitly) never to trust a philologist. Tolkien was both.[10]

Tolkien and Lewis's evolving friendship would turn out to have great significance for both men. Tolkien found in Lewis an appreciative listener for his developing stories and poems of Middle-earth. He acknowledged that without Lewis's encouragement over many years, *The Lord of the Rings* would have never appeared in print. Lewis equally had cause to appreciate Tolkien, whose views on myth, story, and imagination helped him eventually to completely change his views about the foundation of reality. When they met, Lewis's atheism meant that he saw nature "as the whole show".[11] They eventually came to see mind to mind on both imagination and the truth of Christianity, despite important differences, such as their Protestant and Roman Catholic divide. Their shared vision would strengthen the foundation of their remarkable friendship. It is clear that from the beginning, Lewis recognized Tolkien's remarkable literary and linguistic gifts. On Tolkien's side, too, there was much for which to be grateful. He wrote in 1929: "Friendship with Lewis compensates for much."

Tolkien recalled their conversations at this formative period:

> C.S. Lewis was one of the only three persons who have so far read all or a considerable part of my "mythology" of the First and Second Ages, which had already been in the main lines constructed before we met. He had the peculiarity that he liked to be read to. All that he knew of my "matter" was what his capacious but not infallible memory retained from my reading to him as sole audience.[12]

He also remembered: "In the early days of our association Jack used to come to my house and I read aloud to him *The Silmarillion* so far as it had then gone, including a very long poem: Beren and Luthien."[13]

When their friendship had deepened, Tolkien decided he could give the "Lay of Leithian" – the poetic version of one of his central stories from his developing mythology – to Lewis to read. This was the tale of Beren and Lúthien. His friend read it during one winter evening. His response was enthusiastic and swift – he wrote to Tolkien the very next day. "I can quite honestly say," he told him, "that it is ages since I have had an evening of such delight... The two things that came out clearly are the sense of reality in the background and the mythical value..."[14]

Soon afterwards, Lewis, perhaps aware of his friend's sensitivity over exposing his private world, offered comment on the unfinished poem in the form of a pretend academic commentary. His comments ran to fourteen pages. The commentary was as from several spoof literary critics, representing various critical schools. The fictional boffins were Schick, Schuffer, Pumpernickel, Bentley, and Peabody. Lewis had already discovered that Tolkien's usual response to any critical analysis of his work, however friendly, was either to ignore it, or to go back to the beginning and start a total rewriting. Lewis felt that the poem had considerable merit, but would benefit from some changes, although not a radical rewrite.

Tolkien's regular habit became to call in at Lewis's college around mid-morning on Mondays (a day when his friend had no students). The two usually crossed the High Street and went to the Eastgate Hotel or to a nearby public house for a drink. Sometimes they remained in Lewis's college rooms. Less often, they met at Tolkien's home in Northmoor Road, or after meetings of the Coalbiters. Lewis wrote to Warnie about these increasingly regular weekly meetings with Tolkien. Meeting his friend, he said, was one of the most pleasant spots in the week. They might talk about university English School politics (they were concerned about implementing changes to the undergraduate syllabus), or comment on each other's poems. They easily wandered into theology or "the state of the nation". They might verbally spar with repartee and pun.

By the Christmas of 1926, Lewis had been teaching at Magdalen College for well over a year. That Christmas vacation was the last time that he, his father, and his brother spent all together. Warnie would soon be embarking for China, in another overseas assignment with the British Army.

Relations between Albert Lewis and his two sons had improved. For the sons, he was always the "P. B." or "the Pudaita-bird", a nickname based on his occasional lapse in pronouncing potato. Albert's Irish brogue was a constant source of amusement to his sons. In *Surprised by Joy*, Lewis portrayed his father as having little talent for happiness, withdrawing into the safe monotony of routine. Biographer A.N. Wilson, however, believes the picture Lewis painted of his father as a "comic character" is one-sided. Albert Lewis was in fact a complex person, scarred by the loss of his wife.

The richest heritage his father gave to Lewis was, literally, a houseful of old books. Lewis was able to share many things with Albert, including what he was reading. Albert, in fact, also had an interest in writing in common with his son, and a power of rhetoric, including recounting "wheezes" (pithy observations, often of humorous events). When Lewis held forth in debate, as he often did, a spectral Albert Lewis in action in a Belfast courtroom declaimed behind him.

On 2 May 1928, Albert retired with an annual pension from his position as Belfast Corporation County Solicitor. Just over a year into his retirement, on 25 July 1929, he had his first X-rays to investigate a recurring complaint. The illness was serious enough for Lewis, on 13 August, to hasten to Belfast. Albert's condition seemed to stabilize, but on 25 September he died, quickly succumbing just after Lewis had returned to Oxford to care for some urgent matters.

Two days later Warnie received a telegram in Shanghai – "Sorry report father died painless twenty fifth September. Jack." It was shocking news, as letters to Shanghai from Lewis telling Warnie of his father's illness, and how his condition was developing, had not yet reached him. With his older brother away, it was left to Lewis to arrange the funeral and settle the estate.

8

The Most Reluctant Convert

The death of Albert perhaps had some bearing on what was going on in Lewis's mind during the busy course of ordinary life, and as he settled into those early years as an Oxford don. Both his parents were now gone, and his brother was overseas. There had been that long, painful period of emotional estrangement from Albert, even though Lewis had always continued to visit and write. His friendship with Tolkien was deepening, but Lewis had soon discovered he was a Christian, seeing the world in a very different way from that of an atheist. Owen Barfield continued to hammer away at his basic beliefs, and their Great War had, if anything, intensified through their need to carry on their debate by correspondence. Barfield's stays in London eventually became permanent.

As we saw, Lewis had already come to the conclusion that the whole universe was, in the last resort, not fundamentally material but mental. He rejected, in other words, a simple materialism in favour of a current form of idealism called Absolute Idealism, which spoke of an Absolute Spirit. This move was influenced by Owen Barfield, and also Cecil Harwood. Lewis's letters record many of the numerous arguments and discussions they had. In contrast to Barfield, he and other friends could talk really zealously about the Absolute Idea, the real Spirit behind the appearances of the material world, without there being any danger of its doing anything to them. As he put it in *Surprised by Joy*: "It [the Spirit] would never come 'here', never (to be blunt) make a nuisance of Itself.... There was nothing to fear; better still, nothing to obey."[1]

Lewis's temporary post, teaching philosophy at University College in 1924–1925, forced him to be more specific about his idea of the Absolute. Doubtless, what was to shape into the later Logical Positivism of A.J. Ayer and others was beginning to be felt as a challenge in philosophical circles at this time also. This asserted that all metaphysical statements (those that spoke of freedom, causes, God, and similar intangibles) are without meaning. Significantly, one of the basic concerns of Lewis and Barfield in their frequent discussions was the meaning of poetic language, at a time when these new philosophers were beginning to assert that only "scientific" statements were meaningful.

Lewis began more and more to be dissatisfied with his Idealism. Even on the moral level, when he tried to live by his idea of the Absolute, which he sincerely struggled to do, he was shocked at the tangle of badness he found inside himself. In his usual pithy way, he concluded: "Idealism can be talked, and even felt; it cannot be lived."[2] Very reluctantly, and very slowly, he started to accept the possibility that the impersonal spiritual "It" was really a personal being. There came a point where he felt that he had made a vastly significant move, which he spoke of as a conversion. He had opened himself up and was terrified about what he would find. Lewis wrote: "Amiable agnostics will talk cheerfully about 'man's search for God'. To me, as I was then, they might as well have talked about the 'mouse's search for the cat'."[3]

Lewis's hesitant conversion was at that time to theism, not to Christianity. His pilgrimage was not yet over. He didn't yet grasp the Trinity and the importance of salvation from a state of sin that blighted human life. He was only beginning to see what he had let himself into by admitting God's existence and abandoning his atheism. On one occasion, he wrote to Owen Barfield with some consternation:

Terrible things are happening to me. The "Spirit" or "Real
I" is showing an alarming tendency to become much more
personal and is taking the offensive, and behaving just like
God. You'd better come on Monday at the latest or I may have
entered a monastery.[4]

Lewis turns the event of this momentous change from atheism to
belief in some kind of God into the story of the "most dejected and
reluctant convert in all England" in his memoir. While the story is
undoubtedly a true account, it is difficult to pin down some details.
By then, Lewis had ceased diary-keeping (abruptly in February
1927) as part of a firm decision to reject continual self-absorption,
which correlates well with such an eventual acceptance of a divine
self behind the existence of the universe and a surrender to that self.

Apart from *Surprised by Joy*, written long afterwards, and a
rejected earlier version, we have to build up an account of his
abandonment of atheism from his letters. These give a picture of
gradual but real change, but do not date precisely that dramatic
experience of conversion as featured in *Surprised by Joy* (though
two letters, one probably and one certainly written in 1930, seem
to point directly to it).[5]

As it is, as well as Lewis's own date of spring 1929, the earlier
year 1927 has some plausibility, as has the following year,
1930. Dating is not helped by a letter Lewis wrote in 1939 to
the scholarly Sister Penelope CSMV, based at the Anglican
Community of St Mary the Virgin at Wantage, near Oxford (who
later became a lifelong friend). In the letter, Lewis appears to
give his later conversion to Christianity as around 1927 instead
of the well-documented 1931![6] The two letters of 1930 perhaps
give a pointer to that year being the time of Lewis's conversion to
belief in God, rather than 1929 or 1927, though it is clear from his
letters that this was a slow process.[7]

There are two parts to Lewis's account of his conversion from
atheism to belief in God. One is a bus journey up Headington Hill
on his way to his home at Hillsboro, in Western Road. This took

place before "God closed in" on him. The other is when he kneels and prays in his college rooms at Magdalen. The two events happen in a sequence – the bus journey before the kneeling in prayer – and are both part of the conversion experience of accepting God's existence. Lewis doesn't say how much time lay between the events, except that the final surrender is after a period in term-time of nightly struggle. He remembers the term as that of the Trinity (summer) one of 1929.

On the journey up to Headington and home, he started to struggle with a momentous decision, which evoked the whole question of human freedom. Unprovoked by any particular event on the bus journey, Lewis suddenly felt presented with a fact about himself. It was an interruption without words and perhaps, he remembered, even without images. He could describe the encounter in a variety of images that he supplied to try to capture the experience, however. It was like he had been shutting something out, holding something at bay. It was as if he were wearing uncomfortable clothing, rather like a cumbersome suit of armour or rigid lobster-skin, or a high-collared uniform (perhaps similar to what he had to wear when he was sent off to boarding school). It was as if suddenly there was a door before him that he could push open, or leave shut. He decided in an instant that he would go through the door, that he would shed his skin of harsh clothes. Yet at the same moment, he felt compelled to do so. As he decided, he knew he was freer than ever before, yet the choice was demanded by his deepest nature. Here the imagery changed again. Lewis felt that he was a man made of snow, beginning to melt, with drips becoming trickles down his back.

Perhaps this remarkable image of the melting man made of snow foreshadows the time when spring comes to Narnia after the interminable period in which the land had been cursed by winter and never Christmas. Possibly, too, the image of uncomfortable clothes or a hard, armoured skin may have later transformed into the dragon-skin that Eustace was desperate to shed in the Narnian story *The Voyage of the "Dawn Treader"*. The portrayal of Eustace prior to his dragoning owed much to Lewis's perception of himself as an arrogant adolescent.

At some point after this experience on the Oxford bus, Lewis knelt and prayed to his unknown God, who as yet appeared barely personal. He described himself then as the 'most ... reluctant convert'.[8]

Because of the epiphany on the Oxford bus, and the culmination of many other conversations (such as with Barfield and Tolkien), and books that he had encountered, Lewis eventually became a theist and bowed the knee. He acknowledged some kind of personal God behind the show of reality: "In the Trinity Term of 1929 I gave in, and admitted that God was God, and knelt and prayed..." The movement of Lewis's thinking at this time would be vividly captured some years later, when he wrote:

> I never had the experience of looking for God. It was the other way round; He was the hunter (or so it seemed to me) and I was the deer. He stalked me like a redskin, took unerring aim, and fired. And I am very thankful that that is how the first (conscious) meeting occurred. It forearms one against subsequent fears that the whole thing was only wish fulfilment. Something one didn't wish for can hardly be that.[9]

Lewis had no clear script for his first faltering steps as a "reluctant convert" to belief in God. Now that he had gone through the door, he was as determined to find his way as he had been in his quest to find self-identity and moral foundation as an atheist. He chose to do a number of things in response to his new theism. He decided to start churchgoing, even though there was no Christian element, so far as he could see, in his newfound belief in God. He had to start somewhere on his new journey, and beginning here made sense to him, steeped as he was in the Christian tradition in literature. This religious step allowed him, as he put it in January 1930, to be "on the main road with all humanity". Lewis attended Magdalen College chapel during term weekdays, and his parish church of Holy Trinity on Sundays. He also resolved to start reading the New Testament. His characteristic thoroughness, combined with his extensive classical knowledge, meant that he read in the original Greek. A further decision was to set time aside in order to continue disciplined meditation.

Meditation was deliberately different from the self-absorption of his atheist period, where he had realized eventually that constant self-analysis was unhelpful and, in fact, poisonous. This self-absorption had allowed him to be ravished by a climate of a "new psychology", which had alienated him from the insights of his imaginative life. Barfield had perhaps been partly right in suspecting that in a way, his friend was deeply in love with the imagination, but had overprotected it as having nothing to do with truth, to his deep loss.[10]

The "new psychology" was perhaps the strongest current swirling through Oxford at that time, stemming most of all from the theories of Sigmund Freud (later satirized by Lewis as Sigismund Enlightenment in his *The Pilgrim's Regress*). His preface to the 1950 edition of *Dymer*, Lewis's narrative poem first published in 1926, explained the context of its writing. Lewis said:

> In those days the new psychology was just beginning to make itself felt in the circles I most frequented at Oxford. This joined forces with the fact that we felt ourselves (as young men always do) to be escaping from the illusions of adolescence, and as a result we were much exercised about the problem of fantasy or wishful thinking.[11]

Fantasy had increasingly been seen as unreal and escapist. Barfield had constantly fought against this view, pointing out to Lewis again and again how imagination, poetic insight, and metaphor in all language undergirded and gave meaning to even the most abstract kinds of word-based thinking.

In Lewis's letters, particularly to Arthur Greeves, there are recurring references to his "meditation". In one letter he said that he meant by meditation "mind-emptying".[12] In his letters in general, also, there is a discernable change of mood. Lewis's official biographers, Roger Lancelyn Green and Walter Hooper, remark:

> One of the most striking changes in Lewis's letters is a sense of personal well-being and happiness. More than ever he delighted in his afternoon walks, conversations and books. As the frail securities of his recent atheism crumbled, they made way for a deep and genuine humility. He even admitted to *liking* the Christianity in the works of John Bunyan and George MacDonald and felt as though his youth had been given back to him.[13]

Lewis describes his conversion to believing in a yet unknown God in words that approach the mystical:

> In the region of awe... in the deepest solitude there is a road right out of the self, a commerce with something which, by refusing to identify itself with any object of the senses, or anything whereof we might have biological or social need, or anything imagined, or any state of our own minds, proclaims itself sheerly objective.... the naked Other, imageless (though our imagination salutes it with a hundred images).[14]

At this stage, it is clear Lewis still only believed in God, but without acceptance of Christian belief.

Coinciding with the changes spreading through Lewis's thinking and deepest attitudes was a great change in the circumstances of the household Lewis shared with Mrs Moore and Maureen. They had lived for seven settled years in Hillsboro, Western Road, Headington. Warnie had been invited by them to share Hillsboro after he retired from the army, a generous act that touched him deeply. Now, all things considered, Lewis and his adopted mother felt that it was time to move and to buy rather than lease a home. They started to search the neighbourhood for a suitable property.

In October 1930, Mrs Moore and Lewis, with some welcome help from Warnie, purchased The Kilns, just outside the city boundaries near Headington, with the title being taken solely in the name of Janie King Moore. The sale of Little Lea, in Belfast, helped to make this possible. The Kilns was more spacious than Hillsboro, and had a rural setting, while still being close to Headington, and to transport into Oxford. The Lewis brothers held rights of life tenancy. Warnie, on one of his many visits from his army base, noted his first impressions of the prospective house in his diary.

> J[ack] and I went out and saw the place... the eight-acre garden is such stuff as dreams are made of.... The house... stands at the entrance to its own grounds at the northern foot of Shotover [hill] at the end of a narrow lane... to the left of the house are the two brick kilns from which it takes its name – in front, a lawn and hard tennis court – then a large bathing pool, beautifully wooded, and with a delightful circular brick seat overlooking it: after that a steep wilderness broken with ravines and nooks of all kinds runs up to a little cliff topped by a thistly meadow, and then the property ends in a thick belt of fir trees, almost a wood: the view from the cliff over the dim blue distance is simply glorious.[15]

A happy touch was that the pond in the grounds had, according to Warnie, links with a poet whom Lewis liked. It was known locally as Shelley's Pool. Tradition had it that the poet "used to meditate there". If so, it was a place where both an atheist poet and a newly theistic (but less successful) one did their meditations, though well over 100 years apart.

After the war, Warnie Lewis had served first in Sierra Leone and then later in Shanghai, and was at this time, after a three-year absence from home, stationed at Bulford, near Amesbury, within easy reach of Oxford by motorcycle. It was in May 1930 that his brother and Mrs Moore had warmly invited him to share their home, an invitation which, after some careful thought, he gratefully accepted. Following another posting to China in 1931–32, during which the Japanese forces attacked the city at which he was stationed, Shanghai, Warnie, now promoted to major, applied for early retirement. He left the British army in 1932 at the age of 37 with a pension and moved into The Kilns at the very end of that year. He had by then served over eighteen years.

In his rather pleasant military base in Bulford, in May 1930 Warnie had set out in his mind the plusses and minuses of accepting the invitation, given his reasonably happy state then in his present army posting. His ruminations, recorded in his diary, throw interesting light on the situation at Hillsboro.

> I considered very seriously the pros and cons of Hillsboro life as a permanency... against it in general there is a loss of liberty which in the particular manifests itself in the impossibility or at any rate extreme difficulty of doing any reading: but this could I think be adequately met, given full membership of the household, by doing the bulk of my reading in College and for the rest, turning my bedroom into a bed sitting room, and reading at night: and in any case in mess life,[16] one's reading, even in one's room, may be considerably interfered with by the mess bore. Secondly there is the substitution of a scheme of life under which one's day is woven into the general stuff of a communal day in contradiction to the army scheme of a day which consists of periods of rigidly defined duty alternating with periods of absolute liberty... at Hillsboro I should have to explain when I was going and when I was coming back, and if I did not come back by the bus I had named there would be uneasiness: further, I should almost certainly be given a shopping commission to do... To this point... the answer seems to be that just as the discomforts of my "lone wolf" existence are inseparable from its luxuries, so one cannot expect to have the good of domesticity without the bad. Finally there is the consideration of the assets of Hillsboro

life to which the army can show not only no corresponding assets but actual debits – a closer intimacy with J[ack] and a correspondingly fuller intellectual life: a healthy life too, by the cutting out of those hours spent in social and ceremonial drinking, and if a poorer life financially (which is by no means certain) at any rate one which such income as I have will be spent to much better advantage....[17]

It needs to be noted that at this time and the earlier years since he had met and got to know Janie Moore, he often wrote affectionately and appreciatively of her. It was in later years that his comments about her became increasingly miserable and bitter, years that correspond with her declining years. In 1930, the year of her move to The Kilns, Mrs Moore was fifty-eight, already quite elderly by the expectations of the period. Also of note is Warnie's reference to "social and ceremonial drinking", which hinted at an awareness of an unhealthy lifestyle. By this time he was already struggling with a thirst for that which would in later years turn him into an alcoholic. When describing drinks in his diary, he had long had a tendency to dwell lovingly over their details.

When Warnie moved into The Kilns he soon felt at home, despite any misgivings about Mrs Moore. She and Lewis had had two rooms added onto the building in preparation for his coming, for a study and a bedroom. As the years drew on, he increasingly perceived Minto as unsuited for his brother, mainly due to the narrow range of her interests, as he saw it.

Maureen Moore remembered that her mother made The Kilns "a very Irish household", centred on herself. Soon after its establishment, there were "hands" (housemaids and similar) about the place, as well as dogs and cats (which frequently came into Lewis's letters). Maureen described The Kilns as very much a "country place", which is why her mother had liked it. A later visitor, Leonard Blake, who was courting and later married Maureen, recalled how Lewis and Warnie would carry on conversation "at fortissimo strength".

There were frequent references to Mrs Moore's "marmalading" in Lewis's diary period and in letters, an event that would dominate household life. Lewis was often drawn into domestic chores, on top of his cheerful willingness to wash dishes, prepare vegetables, and do other such tasks. In later years, he told David Wesley Soper, who was researching his writings, that "he had to write by snatches, between walking the dog and peeling the potatoes". It was such impositions that particularly irked Warnie, on behalf of his brother, who in fact rarely complained about them.

During life at The Kilns, Maureen remembered being drawn into the pattern of Lewis's day after a car was acquired. Throughout each Oxford eight-week term, Lewis slept in college and would have tutorials there from 9 a.m. until 1 p.m., and then from 5 to 7 p.m. Maureen would drive down to pick up Lewis at 1:10 p.m. to return to The Kilns for lunch. Then he would take the dog out for a walk. Maureen would later return him to Magdalen about 4:30 p.m. His "social life", she recalled, was at the college. In fact, she socialized more with Warnie than with Lewis, once they all lived together at The Kilns.[18] The pattern was complicated when Lewis installed Warnie in one of his college rooms during mornings; Warnie could use the room for his writing and editing, and would have easy access to the town, including the research facilities of the Bodleian Library.

When Warnie moved in with his brother's ménage, he continued an enormous task (which he had started during visits on leave from the army) of arranging the Lewis family papers (letters, diaries, photographs and various documents), typing and arranging the material in what ended up being eleven large typewritten volumes of 3,563 pages. Warnie added numerous explanatory notes. Albert Lewis had accumulated these papers and, after his death, the brothers had brought them to Oxford. The edited collection was entitled *The Lewis Papers: Memoirs of the Lewis Family:1850–1930*. The volumes were completed in 1935.[19]

Since the wartime years, throughout all of which Warnie had served in France, he had developed a fervent interest in French social history of the seventeenth century. Now that he had the leisure, Warnie turned his hand to writing on this period, following his efforts on *The Lewis Papers*. He was to publish a number of books, including *The Splendid Century: Life in the France of Louis XIV* and *The Sunset of the Splendid Century: The Life and Times of Louis Auguste de Bourbon, Duc du Maine, 1670–1736*. The first of these he dedicated to his brother, and the second to their Belfast mutual friend, Jane McNeill.

Students turning up to Lewis's tutorials in New Building at Magdalen College got used to glimpses of a balding man approaching middle age. Warnie was always courteous to them and sometimes delivered cups of tea. One former student of Lewis's, John Lawlor, remembered: "Lewis's eleven o'clock tutorial pupil was the fortunate recipient of a cup of tea (a large one, of course). Then Warnie would retreat to the little inner study and resume the steady tap-tap on the ancient machine."[20]

Lewis's frequent meetings with Tolkien continued to be of great importance to both men. One of the many issues that Tolkien and Lewis discussed was that of the nature of language, the way a language changes over time, and the manner in which languages carried and were shaped by myth. These were all features of language that Tolkien was building into his slowly evolving world of Middle-earth. His invented languages, especially Elvish, grew and were shaped by its geography and history, and even, it seems, by the influence of its angelic powers in the stories that lay behind events, and not just human and Elvish doings.

In the process of painstakingly creating his fictional world, with its alternative history of what was roughly the ancient north-west of what is now Europe, Tolkien was actually learning more about the nature and growth of real language itself. This was in a way that he couldn't achieve in his academic studies in philology. He was, in essence, creating some kind of world model of language development and change. This is somewhat like the way meteorologists have used computer world-models to predict weather more knowledgably than was possible before. Tolkien's

On the entrance steps of Little Lea, Strandtown, Belfast, in 1905. On the front row (left to right): Warren ("Warnie") Lewis, Jack Lewis, Leonard Lewis (cousin), and Eileen Lewis (cousin). Back row: Agnes Young Lewis (aunt, and mother of Leonard and Eileen), maid (name unknown), maid (name unknown), Flora Hamilton Lewis (mother), Albert Lewis (father), cuddling the family dog, Nero.

C.S. Lewis with his father, Albert.

i

Below: The Lewis family attended St Mark's Church, Dundela, where the infant Jack Lewis was baptized.

Above: County Down, Northern Ireland, with the Mourne Mountains in the distance. This landscape helped to inspire Narnia, with the mountains of Archenland to the south.

Right: Dunluce Castle, County Antrim, which may have inspired Cair Paravel in Narnia.

Below: The view eastwards from Mussenden Temple, near Castlerock, County Londonderry, a resort where the young C.S. Lewis spent long summer holidays.

Above: Malvern College, on the flanks of the Malvern Hills, where Lewis experienced a period of formal schooling. Later, he returned to Malvern a number of times for holidays and breaks.

Left: Owen Barfield, one of Lewis's closest friends, 1920s.

Below: At a teashop at St Agnes Cove, Cornwall, on holiday in August 1927 with Mrs Janie Moore (far right) and her daughter Maureen. The family dog is Mr Papworth (aka, "Tykes").

Right: 28 Warneford Road was one of many rental properties that C.S. Lewis shared with his adopted mother Mrs Moore, and her daughter, Maureen. This one was off Oxford's Cowley Road, at that time quite rural.

Above: Courtfield Cottage in Old Headington was rented briefly by Mrs Moore at the time she moved permanently to Oxford with her daughter, joined at the cottage by C.S. Lewis.

Right: Leasing Hillsboro, 14 Western Road, in Headington (now renamed Holyoake Road) gave Lewis, Mrs Moore, and Maureen several years of stability after constant house moves.

Left: Buying The Kilns in Risinghurst near Headington gave a permanent home to Mrs Moore, daughter Maureen, and C.S. Lewis, where they were soon joined by Warnie Lewis.

iv

Right: The large grounds of The Kilns, at the northern foot of Shotover Hill, included a flooded quarry pit ideal for swimming and punting. In Narnia-like woodland, Lewis and his brother made paths.

Below: Poet and critic Charles Williams was an inspiring friend who influenced much of Lewis's later output.

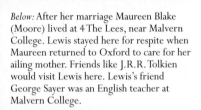

Below: After her marriage Maureen Blake (Moore) lived at 4 The Lees, near Malvern College. Lewis stayed here for respite when Maureen returned to Oxford to care for her ailing mother. Friends like J.R.R. Tolkien would visit Lewis here. Lewis's friend George Sayer was an English teacher at Malvern College.

Left: When taking a break in Malvern with friends like J.R.R. Tolkien, Hugo Dyson, and his brother Warnie, The Unicorn was a favoured pub.

Below: C.S. Lewis was fellow and tutor in English at Magdalen College, Oxford for almost 30 years, before moving to Magdalene College, Cambridge at the end of 1954 to become Professor of Medieval and Renaissance literature there.

Above: Magdalen College, Oxford from Addison's Walk, one of Lewis's favourite places. Here, one night in 1931, the wind stirred the trees as he, Tolkien, and Hugo Dyson had a conversation that was to change Lewis's life.

Below: The grounds of Magdalen College, Oxford, which gave C.S. Lewis great pleasure. They include a deer park.

Above: The Eagle and Child in St Giles, the pub most associated with C.S. Lewis and the Inklings in Oxford.

Right: Holy Trinity Church, Headington Quarry, Oxford, the local church C.S. Lewis attended after abandoning atheism. The photograph is taken from near Lewis's grave.

Above: Poet and novelist Joy Davidman, wife of C.S. Lewis.

Left: C.S. Lewis's simple grave in the churchyard of Holy Trinity Church, where he is buried with his brother, Warnie. The Shakespearean inscription reads, "Men must endure their going hence."

employment of imagination in gaining real knowledge had a strong appeal to Lewis.

Tolkien had read Owen Barfield's *Poetic Diction* soon after it was published back in 1928; Lewis, who had read it years before in manuscript form, may have lent him a copy. In an undated letter to Barfield, possibly written in 1929, Lewis observed:

> You might like to know that when Tolkien dined with me the other night he said *à-propos* of something quite different that your conception of the ancient semantic unity had modified his whole outlook and that he was almost just going to say something in a lecture when your conception stopped him in time. "It is one of those things," he said, "that when you've once seen it there are all sorts of things you can never say again."[21]

Barfield's ideas helped Tolkien to focus his own thoughts about how mythology and story are part of language. Expunging them from a language would be to kill it. Not only did Barfield help Tolkien to focus the insights he had developed, but so did Lewis. His atheism and then continuing questions after "reluctantly" believing in God led Tolkien to defend his own Christian belief in terms that might persuade Lewis. He in fact called in Lewis's own imagination as a witness to the truth of Christian belief. It took Tolkien some time to persuade Lewis that his imaginative response to poetry, myth, and story was on the side of Tolkien's argument, rather than supporting his resistance to it. Then, finally, one night in the autumn of 1931, a long time after converting to theism, Lewis's defences were breached.

The evening of 19 September was a still one, with an occasional gust of wind that stirred the leaves of the trees, which were growing brittle as their colour changed. Lewis had met with Tolkien, and a mutual friend, H.V.D. Dyson, at Magdalen College. He had already recently been introduced to Dyson, who was lecturing in English at Reading University but often had occasion to visit Oxford. Lewis liked his quick wit and exuberance. The talk had moved to serious matters that they all wished to pursue, with no thought of the passing hours. They decided to go outside and to cross the little bridge onto Addison's Walk, a favourite stroll of Lewis's.

In his exploration of belief in God, and attempts to come to terms with the fact that he faced Someone tangible and utterly concrete rather than an abstraction, Lewis had got held up over the Christian belief in Christ as a sacrifice for the whole world, and indeed for an individual. He couldn't grasp, he confessed, how the life and death of someone 2,000 years ago could help or save us today, except perhaps as an example. But the New Testament, he saw clearly, spoke of Christ's death as far more than an example.

A few days after that momentous night conversation, Lewis explained to his friend Arthur how he had become aware of a failure of imagination on his part:

> Now what Dyson and Tolkien showed me was this: that if I met the idea of sacrifice in a Pagan story I didn't mind it at all: again, that if I met the idea of a god sacrificing himself to himself... I liked it very much and was mysteriously moved by it: again, that the idea of the dying and reviving God (Balder, Adonis, Bacchus) similarly moved me provided I met it anywhere *except* in the Gospels. The reason was that in Pagan stories I was prepared to feel the myth as profound and suggestive of meanings beyond my grasp even tho' I could not say in cold prose "what it meant".
>
> Now the story of Christ is simply a true myth: a myth working on us in the same way as the others, but with this tremendous difference that *it really happened*: and one must be content to accept it in the same way, remembering that it is God's myth where the others are men's myths: i.e. the Pagan stories of God expressing Himself through the minds of poets, using such images as He found there, while Christianity is God expressing Himself through what we call "real things".[22]

Whereas the human imagination might work through fiction and poetry, and with God's help can glimpse what is real and true, Lewis saw that God is able to work directly through actual events in human lives and history. He much later wrote a powerful essay on the harmony of story and fact in the Gospels, spelling out this idea, remembering that life-changing conversation with Tolkien and Dyson:

> This is the marriage of heaven and earth, perfect Myth and Perfect Fact: claiming not only our love and obedience, but also our wonder and delight, addressed to the savage, the child, and the poet in each one of us no less than to the moralist, the scholar, and the philosopher.[23]

He realized that the claims and stories of Christ demand an imaginative as much as an intellectual response.[24] In a letter, Lewis said, "Dyson and Tolkien were the immediate human causes of my conversion."[25]

For the first time in his life, both sides of Lewis − the philosophical and the imaginative person − were to become fully engaged. Just over a week later, he rode in Warnie's sidecar of his Daudel motorbike, while Mrs Moore and an Irish friend were driven in the slower family car by Maureen, together with their pet dog. They were on a day trip to the recently opened Whipsnade Zoo, about forty miles east of Oxford. Lewis recalled: "When we set out I did not believe that Jesus Christ was the Son of God, and when we reached the zoo I did." Another door had been offered to him, and he chose to go through it. Up to now, his dream had been to be a great poet. From then his apprenticeship was for becoming "an apostle to the skeptics" (as a perceptive American commentator called him), and a master of prose.

But there was a whole other dimension to his movement from atheism, via idealism and pantheism, and then belief in God, to Christian belief, which went right back to the biscuit tin lid that Warnie had made into a toy garden when Lewis was an infant.

This was the quest for Joy (Lewis's special term), which turned into a search for something other than Joy itself, which evoked its sweet longing. Nothing else could satisfy that longing. This was to become a major theme in many of his writings, from his earliest prose fiction, *The Pilgrim's Regress* to *The Chronicles of Narnia*, and including theological writings (such as in the chapter on heaven in *The Problem of Pain*). His experience with Joy was particularly explored in his autobiography of his life up to his conversion to Christianity in 1931, *Surprised by Joy*, and in *The Pilgrim's Regress*.

Shortly after his conversion from atheism to theism, Lewis had begun writing a forerunner to *Surprised by Joy*. His aim was to account for the importance of his experience of Joy in his early life, which was associated with an inconsolable longing or sweet desire. This book was never finished, and is made up of seventy-two handwritten pages and a few loose sheets. It was not, he pointed out, an intellectual defence of theism as such. Rather, it told the story of a persistent experience that led him to belief in God:

> In this book I propose to describe the process by which I came back, like so many of my generation, from materialism to a belief in God… I arrived where I am, not by reflection alone, but by reflection on a particular recurrent experience. I am an empirical Theist. I have arrived at God by induction.[26]

The manuscript is of great interest, as it is written in the transition between believing in an unknown God to accepting Christian belief and a God of definite character – a God who, by the knowing of him, could fulfil all human desire to experience tangibly the good and the beautiful.

This unfinished autobiography indicates Lewis's depth of meditation after accepting theism. The conflict between his intellectual and his imaginative life began to be over. In the same spirit, Lewis wrote to Arthur Greeves of his satisfaction in completing daily readings from George MacDonald's *Diary of an Old Soul* (1880) very early in 1930. He saw this as another of the beauties of coming, I won't say, to religion but to an attempt at religion – one finds oneself on the main road with all humanity, and can compare notes with an endless succession of previous travellers. It is emphatically coming home....[27]

As he recounted his early life, in *Surprised by Joy,* Lewis reported his sensations of Joy, some of which were responses to natural beauty, while others were evoked by literature and art. He hoped that other people would recognize similar experiences of their own as they read his account. His early tastes of beauty taught him longing, and early on made him, for good or ill, he said, a votary of the Blue Flower. This was a symbol of *sehnsucht* or inconsolable longing – his "Joy" – in German Romantic literature and Scandinavian poetry.

With his conversion to Christianity, Lewis rejected the grand impersonality of systems generated by materialism, and even by idealism. He grew to prefer the individuality of places and people, seasons and times, moods and tones of feeling. God himself, he eventually concluded, was the most tangible and articulate of existences. Christ's incarnation had a seductive logic to it. The Gospel accounts were (as he learned through Tolkien) the highest point of human storytelling and myth-making, with an astounding dimension of historical veracity. Everything was true in the actual, primary world, without losing the quality of myth that engendered Joy.

The Gospel narratives thus demanded both an imaginative and a reasoned response. In his own story, his two sides – the philosophical and the imaginative – had married.

A God who is fully personal, Lewis discovered, was much more interesting than any abstract "Spirit" or "Mind" behind the universe. The deity, who could truly be called "Father", was involved in the tiniest details of the world, including the very stuff of history; he was not an unchanging, abstract entity (even though his character is unchanging), as Lewis was to argue elegantly in his book *Miracles*. He wrote, in *Surprised by Joy*: "Every step I had taken, from the Absolute to 'Spirit' and from 'Spirit' to 'God', had been a step towards the more concrete, the more imminent, the more compulsive."[28]

9

The Company of Friends

The Inklings were a group of literary friends that coalesced around Lewis, and existed for around thirty years. It was in many ways unlike coteries of Oxford dons with whom the immensely clubbable Lewis had mixed in his early years as a fellow and tutor in English at Magdalen College.

Oxford coteries frequented by Lewis before (and after) the Inklings was formed often belonged to the English School of the university. As was the fashion of the time, the attendees were known to each other by their surnames, or by nicknames that they had acquired.

The Inklings did not have such a narrow academic focus, although in much of the group's existence they did have, in Lewis's summing up, a "tendency to write" and were Christians. Some were Oxford dons, but from several of the university schools, and the rest belonged to other professions. One was a retired soldier (Warnie Lewis), another a family solicitor based in London (Owen Barfield), and later members included a GP (Dr "Humphrey" Havard) and a book editor (Charles Williams). Though these at first were known by surname or nickname (Tolkien was called "Tollers" at times), in later years first names started to slip into use.

The Inklings group was informal. It resists a rigid division into those who were central and those who were more peripheral. As it was consciously a writers' group, the publications of various Inklings is a useful yardstick. But this only takes us so far, as it was also very much a conversation group, which liked at times to meet in pubs as well as in the more literary venue of the members' college rooms, or (mostly) Lewis's rooms in Magdalen. These rooms, not the pubs, were the places to read out writing in progress, for instant and high calibre criticism.

One of the Inklings who clearly was central to the group (he is one of the few Lewis lists or mentions as a member) was H.V.D. "Hugo" Dyson, who wrote little in either prose or poetry, but was a brilliant conversationalist with an incisive wit. Of the more committed writers, Charles Williams's books were nearly all published before he joined the Inklings and breathed its atmosphere. His writings, however, were to have an enormous impact on Lewis's own books.

What picture we can gain of the group has to be built up from Inklings' letters, diaries, and also memoirs and interviews from later in life. After his brother's death, Warnie wrote sadly in a memoir about him: "Had I known that I was to have outlived Jack I would have played Boswell[1] on those Thursday evenings, but as it is, I am afraid that my diary contains only the scantiest material for reconstructing an Inklings."[2]

The first of the Inklings were Lewis's friends before the club started, which was sometime early in the thirties, most likely 1933 (though some think it was a little earlier or later). These friends were J.R.R. Tolkien, Owen Barfield, Nevill Coghill, H.V.D. Dyson, and also the Reverend Adam Fox. To this we need to add Warnie. On abandoning his atheism, Lewis humorously described himself as a fox driven out of the Hegelian Wood (a reference to the nineteenth-century philosopher Hegel who stood for much of what Lewis left behind when he started believing in God rather than an Absolute Spirit). He went on to describe the pack of hounds hunting him down, just a field behind at most, which, he said, included Barfield, Tolkien, and Dyson.

Of the "hounds", Tolkien and Dyson were the most immediate human causes of Lewis's surrender to belief in Christianity. Barfield also had a part to play in the pursuit, in having the pitched battle with Lewis over most of the years of the 1920s, with the aim of revealing the inadequacies of his friend's beliefs. Warnie had returned to Christian faith while still with the army, just months before his brother rode in his sidecar to Whipsnade Zoo and assented to Christian belief during the otherwise uneventful journey.

The Inklings originated not just from Lewis's circle of friends, but specifically from Christian friends.

In his diary,[3] Warnie Lewis gives us a tantalizing glimpse of the pre-Inklings circle of friends around his brother. In the early summer of 1933, he and his brother were invited by Tolkien and H.V.D. Dyson to dine at Exeter College. The party of nine dined in the Common Room, as was the custom during the vacation. Several other friends of Lewis were present, some of whom Warnie met for the first time. The party included "a little unobtrusive clergyman", unnamed by Warnie but who may have been Adam Fox, who was to join the Inklings in its early years. Warnie noted that Tolkien and Dyson "were in most exuberant form". The menu, Warnie felt, suited the hot evening. It included cold soup and lobster salad, accompanied by sweet draught cider. Warnie liked the man sitting opposite to him at the meal, whom he learned was Nevill Coghill, and described as "big, pleasant, good looking in a sort of musical comedy way, except for a vicious mouth. What I could overhear of his talk sounded good."

After the meal the party broke up, and Lewis, Warnie, Tolkien, Dyson, and the unnamed clergyman walked to Magdalen College and into the moonlit deer grove below Lewis's rooms. Tolkien saluted a deer that they had disturbed with, "Hail fallow well met!" Not to be outdone in verbal buffoonery, Lewis came out with a Spoonerism that was considered a good one, "Locke's Rape of the Pope".[4] With his Ulster Protestant background, Lewis probably said it with some relish. Warnie, of course, did not have the benefit of hindsight in composing his diary entry later that night but, all in all, the evening augured the atmosphere of future Inklings meetings.

Whoever the clergyman was in Warnie's account, he is not recorded as impeding the flow of verbal banter that evening. If indeed he was Adam Fox, this would correlate with his acquaintance with Lewis. He was the eldest member of the Inklings, being about fifteen years older than Lewis and nine more than Tolkien. After a period of school teaching, he had become a fellow and Dean of Divinity at Magdalen in 1929. Fox and Lewis had become friends after frequently meeting at morning prayers and breakfast in term-time.

Lewis's pilgrimage from theism to Christian belief might have heightened his interest in the theologian, who shared with Lewis a deep interest in the Greek philosopher Plato. Fox wrote verse, but only a few things were published. These included a narrative poem a few years later, *Old King Coel: A Rhymed Tale in Four Books*, which came out in 1937, the year before he was appointed Professor of Poetry, with the encouragement of his fellow Inklings and some engineering on their part. Fox went on to write books popularizing Plato, and other books trying to do the same for New Testament Greek.

Through his brother, Warnie had already met Dyson earlier in the year, in February. Dyson was on one of his frequent visits to Oxford from Reading University, where at that time he was lecturer and tutor in English. Warnie had brilliantly recorded his impression of Dyson that night in his diary, writing that he was "a man who gives the impression of being made of quicksilver: he pours himself into a room on a cataract of words and gestures, and you are caught up in the stream – but after the first plunge, it is exhilarating…"[5]

On this or another occasion, Dyson may have mentioned to the retired army major that he had fought in the war with the Queen's Own Royal West Kent Regiment, in which he had been severely wounded in battle and had had an "out of body" experience. In a letter to Warnie two years before, while he was posted in China,

Lewis had mentioned visiting Dyson and his attractive wife, Margaret, in Reading, and how Dyson was scarred by his wartime experience – "a burly man, both in mind and body, with the stamp of war on him".[6]

Another early member of the Inklings – how early we do not know – was originally a friend of Tolkien's rather than Lewis's. This was Charles L. Wrenn. He had read English at Queen's College and, after more than ten years teaching in a variety of colleges and universities, returned to Oxford in 1930 as a lecturer in the English School, where he helped Tolkien in the teaching of Anglo-Saxon. He and his family became friendly with the Tolkiens; this pleased Tolkien's wife, Edith, who felt isolated in Oxford after the warm community she had experienced while Tolkien was teaching at Leeds University. The Wrenn family and Tolkiens even took holidays together.

J.R.R. Tolkien very informatively described the origin of the Inklings in a letter to an American scholar who was researching Lewis's thought and writings. He told William L. White that he and Lewis had been invited to belong to an undergraduate club at University College, Lewis's old college (presumably to give it a bit of gravitas and help it to make its mark). Members read work in progress for on-the-spot criticism, and minutes were taken. The instigator of the club was Edward Tangye Lean (brother of the notable filmmaker David Lean), who went on to have a career in journalism and writing, after having two novels published while still an undergraduate. The club was named the Inklings, presumably a double pun on the spilled ink of composition and having a glimmer of an idea or of a distant reality.

The club failed to outlive Lean's graduation in the summer of 1933. As Tolkien put it:

The Club soon died but C.S.L. and I at least survived. Its name was then transferred (by C.S.L.) to the undetermined and unelected circle of friends who gathered about C.S.L., and met in his rooms in Magdalen. Although our habit was to

read aloud compositions of various kinds (and lengths!) this
association and its habit would in fact have come into being
at this time, whether the original short-lived club had ever
existed or not. [7]

The reason Tolkien gave for the inevitably of an Inklings-type
group beginning was Lewis's irrepressible zest for hearing pieces
read aloud, and his enjoyment of the give and take of spontaneous,
instant criticism. He and Lewis, in fact, often met up before the
Inklings were in existence and read work in progress to each other.
Even when the club was meeting regularly, Lewis and he would
meet up together to talk of the things that concerned them, maybe
to enjoy a beer, and to share their writings, a habit that was to
continue for many years. In a sense, what the Inklings was about
was more than the original Thursday evening meetings in Lewis's
rooms, and later additional Tuesday morning meetings in a pub,
often the Eagle and Child in St Giles.

At the heart of the Inklings was what happened when two or
three of them met up, whether casually or habitually, outside
of the Thursday or Tuesday meetings. They were a little like the
church; in existence where two or three gathered. Of course,
casual or more habitual meetings of just Lewis and Tolkien, for
example, might have been less documented in letters and diaries
than the more noticeable Thursday and Tuesday institutions. With
Warnie on the scene after his retirement in 1932, he was often
present when Lewis met up with Tolkien. He tried to take it
stoically when his brother occasionally wanted to be alone with
Tolkien for an afternoon, or on other occasions.

Lewis's views of friendship are set out in his book *The Four Loves*.
He argues it doesn't have to arise out of any biological need, such
as sexual desire.

> Friendship arises out of mere Companionship when two or
> more of the companions discover that they have in common
> some insight or interest or even taste which the others do

not share and which, till that moment, each believed to be his own unique treasure (or burden). The typical expression of opening Friendship would be something like, "What? You too? I thought I was the only one."[8]

Lewis wrote these words near the end of his life. He had by then widened his views about friendship between men and women, partly because of his experience of friendship with and marriage to Joy Davidman in the 1950s, and his friendships with Dorothy L. Sayers and the poets Ruth Pitter and Kathleen Raine, to mention a few. Also, changing social conditions meant that men and women were more likely to work together as equals, and to have interests in common.

Meeting and being changed by Joy Davidman was one of the great ironies of Lewis's life. However, he still retained something of an "objective" view, typical of the period of his upbringing, which saw friends as sharing a common outlook, in which interest in the everyday life and history of a particular friend was of secondary importance, indeed inappropriate.

In this view, he was shaped by his classical background, with its hierarchy of form over matter (form being seen as masculine, and matter as feminine), which was spiritualized in medieval times into one of grace over nature. This was why, to him, bodily differentiation, as in gender or ancestry, was of lesser relevance to friendship than spiritual nature, characterized by the leadership of the mind and subservience of the body. For this reason, he believed that friendship more easily happened between man and man, free of the distractions of gender; erotic love, he argued, had a very different character from friendship love. As Lewis put it, lovers are usually imagined face to face; friends are best imagined side by side, their eyes ahead on their interests in common.

For this reason, Lewis would have known little, in this sense, of his great friend Tolkien and his background and upbringing. In another sense, he knew Tolkien more intimately than almost anyone, because of being granted access to the inner world of his rich imagination. Indeed, it may have not been until Lewis was gathering information for his anonymous obituary of his friend for *The Times* very many years later that he got to know him more in the usual sense. In fact, his description of his friend's life in that obituary is one of the best brief biographies in existence, the other being Tom Shippey's entry on Tolkien in the *Dictionary of National Biography*. It is ironic that Lewis wrote *The Times* obituary that appeared a day after Tolkien's death on 3 September 1973, which was nearly ten years after his own death.

The published article evidently retained most of Lewis's wording, with only slight updates by an editor (such as recording Her Majesty the Queen's award to Tolkien of a CBE the year before his death). Though Lewis would have learned a few things about his friend's life over the years, much was probably discovered later on, such as Tolkien's birth in South Africa, childhood near and in Birmingham, loss of his father as an infant, and then of his mother – he was not much older than Lewis had been when his mother died. Lewis would have known from almost the beginning of their friendship that Tolkien had served in the First World War. This would be almost taken for granted at that time. Some friends' service was obvious; Dyson, for instance, limped from a severe war wound.

This period was a happy time for Lewis. His brother had joined him in his life with Mrs Moore and Maureen at The Kilns. He appreciated his circle of friends in Oxford and, with the beginning of the Inklings, could satisfy his love of hearing things read out; he also could enjoy giving and taking criticism in a group of his peers, rather than having to be in a teacher-student relationship. The latter he tried to soften in his daily work at Oxford by the conviction that teacher and pupil were fellows together in learning. This kept him an inspirational teacher who, from the same principle, was also very demanding of his students.

As well as the daily demands of tutoring and lecturing during termtime, Lewis was coming towards the end of his literary study of courtly love in the Middle Ages, *The Allegory of Love,* which was eventually published in 1936, and remains in print over seventy-five years later. He had begun work on the book in 1928. In a letter he wrote as *The Allegory of Love* neared completion, he suggested that the secret to understanding the Middle Ages, including its concern with allegory and courtly love, was to get to know thoroughly Dante's *The Divine Comedy*, *The Romance of the Rose*, the Classics and the Bible (including the apocryphal books of the New Testament). The Middle Ages, in fact, are at the centre of both Lewis's scholarship and his storytelling.

When Lewis pitched the idea of the book to Oxford University Press after completing it in 1935, he summed it up as follows:

> The book as a whole has two themes: 1. The birth of allegory and its growth from what it is in Prudentius [a fourth-century Christian poet] to what it is in Spenser [author of *The Faerie Queen*]. 2. The birth of the romantic conception of love and the long struggle between its earlier form (the romance of adultery) and its later form (the romance of marriage).[9]

In this book, and other literary studies, Lewis helped to give new life to a historical study of literature. While Lewis's conclusions in this, his first major academic work, are by no means always accepted today, as historical scholarship *The Allegory of Love* is still widely admired.

While working on the later stages of the book, Lewis was wrestling with his imaginative writing. His conversion first to theism and then to Christianity helped him to step outside of his ambition to become a major poet. He did, however, write two long poems of some merit in this transitional period – one of which, *The Queen of Drum*, was about the escape of a queen from a dictator into Fairy Land.

He would continue to write and publish short, lyrical verses for the rest of his life. His energies, however, were thoroughly switched to imaginative prose fiction – fiction with a strong symbolic element that was a vehicle for exploring his new view of the world. It was a huge and momentous transition, an expression of those changes in his life, first in accepting God and then what he later called "mere Christianity" (a term he was to borrow from the Puritan writer and preacher Richard Baxter). *The Queen of Drum* and another, *The Nameless Isle*, were his last narrative poems, as far as we know. After this, his storytelling was in the aforementioned prose fiction – sometimes deeply poetic prose. In what he wrote, his voice became clearer, his imagination more free, and his art more powerful.

The first outpouring of prose fiction was *The Pilgrim's Regress*, which flowed fluently but not always with success, during a short holiday in Belfast in August 1932. Little Lea was now of course sold, and Lewis stayed over the road from it in Bernagh, the home of Arthur Greeves. He had been anxious to meet up with Arthur while on holiday in Ireland. He stayed as his friend's guest from 15 to 29 August, and drafted the whole book in that fortnight, which is almost beyond belief. Not only did he write it in that brief period, but he also read it in instalments to Arthur as it was being composed.[10]

His attempts to recount the story of his conversion from atheism, and the place that the experience of Joy had in it, had hitherto eluded him. Now that he had passed the further stage of conversion to Christianity, his creativity was suddenly focused and released by telling, in *The Pilgrim's Regress,* the story of a modern pilgrim somewhat in the style of John Bunyan's seventeenth-century *A Pilgrim's Progress*. It is fitting that the childhood of John in the story (the name may be a tribute to Bunyan) is set in Puritania, which has some resonance with the north of Ireland of Lewis's own childhood. The dialogue of John's parents, his Uncle George, and the Steward has an Ulster lilt. The *Pilgrim's Regress* carries a dedication to Arthur Greeves.

Despite the unevenness of the book, and sometimes the obscurity of its references to thinkers and intellectual trends, the narrative has a strong pulling power, taking the reader with John through his quest for a mysterious island he had glimpsed as a boy, and which filled him with the acute longing Lewis called Joy. In a new edition, ten years after its first publication in 1933, Lewis added running headers to explain his allegory. Twenty years later, with the new edition still in print, he found it necessary to write to one of his readers apologizing for the story's obscurity.

> I don't wonder that you got fogged in *The Pilgrim's Regress*. It was my first religious book and I didn't then know how to make things easy. I was not even trying to very much, because in those days I never dreamed I would become a "popular" author...[11]

Even in its first edition, however, Lewis did provide his readers with a helpful *Mappa Mundi* (world map) in which the human soul is divided into north and south, the north representing arid intellectualism and the south emotional excess. A straight road passes between them. Needless to say, John's wanderings strayed a long way off the straight and narrow. Like the young Lewis, he tended towards intellectual rather than sensual follies. The quest helped John to avoid the various snares and dangers he encountered and to reach the Island that he had so long desired. The story gave a vivid picture of Lewis's intellectual climate in the 1920s and early thirties, some features of which are inherited in our own day.

On his journey, John encounters a rich variety of characters. They include Mr Enlightenment from the city of Claptrap, Mr Vertue, who becomes John's companion, and Medea Halfways, from the city of Thrill. At one point, John is imprisoned by the Spirit of the Age, and rescued by the tall, blue-clad figure of Reason. She teaches him many things and directs him back to the main road.

John's way is a *regress* rather than a *progress* because he in fact was going away from rather than towards the beautiful island that he sought. That island was Lewis's equivalent to the Celestial City of Bunyan. When John the modern pilgrim gained the knowledge of how to achieve his Island, through Mother Kirk, he had to retrace his steps.

It is best to enjoy the book as a story and not be too concerned with the meaning of every allusion. Reading it as a quest for Joy, in Lewis's special sense, and in parallel with *Surprised by Joy*, clarifies its main meanings.

When corresponding later with Arthur after his August visit, Lewis asked him if he minded the book being dedicated to him. Lewis added: "It is yours by every right – written in your house, read to you as it was written, and celebrating (at least in the most important parts) an experience which I have more in common with you than anyone else."[12]

Lewis, as always, devoted a great deal of time to his letter-writing to Arthur, other friends such as Owen Barfield in London, and numerous other people. Meanwhile, in his loquacious diary, his brother Warnie recorded many of his days. These letters and diary entries from the brothers give us often vivid glimpses into the ordinary life of family and friends Lewis enjoyed, outside of his academic teaching and work on his books and scholarly papers.

Walking tours during vacations played an important part in Lewis's relaxation. Sometimes they were with Owen Barfield, Cecil Harwood, and mutual friends such as Walter "Wof" Field, a teacher at a Rudolf Steiner school. By this time, Warnie and his brother had established the habit of a walking tour of their own. Between Tuesday 3 and Friday 6 January 1933 they embarked on the second leg of their ascent of the Wye Valley on the borderland of Wales and England, which they had started two years before. On that occasion, they set out from Chepstow and soon passed the ruins of Tintern Abbey. On their second trip, they picked up their trail about fifty miles upriver.

In later years, Lewis's walking holidays with friends were only seriously interrupted by Mrs Moore's illnesses during her decline, and then his change of lifestyle after marrying Joy Davidman Gresham.

Back at home in The Kilns, the daily routine of Lewis and his brother overlapped during termtime. In his diary Warnie outlined a typical day, when he would share space in Lewis's college rooms in Magdalen College during the week. Warnie would work during the morning (mainly, in the first years, compiling *The Lewis Papers*), go home to The Kilns with Lewis for lunch, and then in the afternoon participate in what Lewis typically dubbed "public works". They would work in the wooded area of the extensive grounds of The Kilns. They were slowly were building an ambitious footpath made of rubble and sand through the "wilderness and wood which ran up the hill to Shotover".

At that time, Warnie later observed, "Mrs King's [Mrs Moore's][13] autocracy had not yet degenerated into… tyranny." On Sunday evenings, Warnie played orchestral and other musical recordings on his gramophone to the assembled family, Minto, Maureen, and Lewis. Warnie loved to have gadgets and mechanical items such as a motorbike or a portable typewriter. Later, in 1936, he was to buy a small, two-berth cabin cruiser, called *The Bosphorus*, which he kept on the River Thames. He would frequent the network of rivers and canals accessible from Oxford.

In his diary, that spring of 1933, Warnie recorded a holiday that illuminates Lewis's creative processes. Warnie, Lewis, Maureen, and Mrs Moore holidayed for two April weeks at Flint Hall, Hambleden in Buckinghamshire. Flint Hall was (and still is) a farmhouse in the Chiltern Hills, surrounded by rolling fields and woodland. The family was accompanied by their dog, Tykes, also known as Mr Papworth, who often appeared in Lewis's letters. There was no real holiday element in having him with them, as Warnie had already tired of what he called the "compulsory daily walk" of the dogs Tykes and Troddles.[14]

While at Flint Hall, Lewis, with Warnie's help, corrected the long galley proofs of *The Pilgrim's Regress*.[15] The book came out the following month. On Good Friday, they attended an amateur performance of a Passion play in a rural church in the village of Frieth, in the Hambleden valley. On Easter Sunday, Lewis had an idea for a book (probably while in church), which he outlined to Warnie, who subsequently recorded in his diary: "A religious work, based on the opinion of some of the [Church] Fathers, that while punishment for the damned is eternal, it is intermittent: he proposes to do sort of an infernal day excursion to Paradise."[16] It was not until over a decade later that the idea was realized as *The Great Divorce*, about a bus trip from hell to the outskirts of the heavenly country.

Just three years before, Warnie had described Mrs Moore as "being of the most uncompromising school of churchwomen" after a conversation about nonconformity with Lewis.[17] She had begun to react strongly, however, to his conversion and the brothers' churchgoing. She ridiculed Holy Communion. "Back from the blood feast," Minto would comment upon their return from church.[18]

Maureen, however, accompanied the brothers on Sunday mornings without her mother. Elsewhere, Warnie noted in his diary:

[Mrs Moore] nags J[ack] about having become a believer, in much the same way that P [Pudaita-bird, his father] used to nag me in his latter years about my boyish fondness for dress, and with apparently just the same inability to grasp the fact that the development of the mind does not necessarily stop with that of the body.[19]

The autumn of 1933 proved a turning point in Maureen's life, as she began teaching in a public school in Monmouth. At beginning and end of term and other times, her head teacher would give her a lift in her car, as her route took her past Oxford. On 5 November, Guy Fawkes's Day, Maureen was due to return to Monmouth, and was picked up in the early evening. At her departure, Mrs Moore was at her most characteristic. Though her mother had not left the house that day, she confidently warned Maureen and the head teacher of the greasiness of the highways, and the perils of the thick fog they would surely encounter. Her parting shot was, "And if I don't hear from you by eleven o'clock tonight, I'll know there has been an accident."[20]

Evidently the mismatched family had had a fireworks party the evening before (perhaps because of Maureen's planned early departure the following evening). Warnie noted that Mr Papworth had been "much alarmed and disgusted" by the fireworks. He added in his diary that on Guy Fawkes's Day:

> In the afternoon J.[ack] and I and the dogs did the Railway walk under conditions which were sheer delight. Everything was still, and a faint blue haze, the merest suggestion of a fog, softened all the colours to a compatible shabbiness – the sort of day when the country seems more intimate, more in undress, than at any other time. J.[ack] pointed out to me that one of the best bits of that whole walk is the clump of trees on the [railway] embankment seen from the south side of the level crossing.[21]

Warnie's picture of the walk reveals his ability to capture the atmosphere of a natural scene – in this case, an autumnal one.

Later that year, Lewis had visits to The Kilns at different times by two of his closest friends, Tolkien and Barfield. Both had got to know Mrs Moore. With both of them, Lewis had slowly relinquished his secrecy over his unusual household. Tolkien came to tea on Thursday 23 November, then, less than two weeks later, Owen Barfield, down from London, came to stay. With Warnie occupying the two rooms especially built on for him, there was some room in the house for a guest.

One morning, Warnie had breakfast with Barfield as usual at 7:45 a.m. (Lewis was sleeping at college, it being termtime). The guest borrowed ten shillings from him and pocketed the banknote. Warnie was amused when, some minutes later, Barfield said, "I find I've no change: could you lend me a shilling?" The two then drove into town, where they were joined by Lewis at half past ten.

Warnie was secretly miffed when he discovered that his brother had arranged to go for a walk with Tolkien that afternoon. It seemed to Warnie, at that point, that he saw less and less of his brother every day. The fact was that Warnie was becoming more and more dependent upon the company of the younger brother he adored. Even his writing of books on French social history and compilation of *The Lewis Papers,* combined with his use of the Bodleian Library for reading and research, helped him to feel closer to his brother.

10

Storytelling and Reflections: Through the Changing Thirties with Tolkien

C.S. Lewis's friendship with J.R.R. Tolkien was particularly strong throughout the thirties. As we saw, Tolkien had played an important part in Lewis's coming to a belief in Christianity, some time after abandoning atheism. This newfound faith was greatly to shape Lewis's writings, both fiction and academic writing, in this decade. Though Lewis had the intellectual haven of the Inklings from 1933 or thereabouts, he also spent a lot of time in Tolkien's company. The Thursday evening meetings of the Inklings focused upon writings; in the later Tuesday morning pub ones, the Inklings were simply a conversation group. It is not clear when the gatherings in pubs began, in addition to the core Thursday meetings. These were not institutionalized, so far as can be told, until the war years. With less time in those early years in meetings of the Inklings, therefore, Lewis spent more hours with Tolkien.

As the most productive of the group at that time, the two needed each other to talk over their poetry and fiction in particular. They also explored ideas and theology together as Lewis quickly developed in his new perspective on the world and, in a sense, started to catch up with the more seasoned Tolkien. They had enormous common ground from the start, as scholars of the Christian Middle Ages. They both were "modern medievalists" as they tried out and honed their attempts to bring an older perspective into "modern" fiction, or fiction at least that would appeal to contemporary readers.

Lewis also made medieval thought and imagination accessible through his introductory lectures at Oxford, which became the book *The Discarded Image*. Both, too, shared the disappointment of failing in their ambitions to become major poets and having to reassess the direction of their writing. It appeared that they were not being very productive in other writing, either. Lewis had been working on his *The Allegory of Love* since 1928, and, at the beginnings of the Inklings, hadn't even approached a publisher. Tolkien had published little – a few journal articles and poems – since his *A Middle-English Vocabulary* in 1922 (later also included in Kenneth Sisam's *Fourteenth Century Verse and Prose*) and an edition of *Sir Gawain and the Green Knight* (with E.V. Gordon) in 1925. He had written much to do with his then private hobby, tales, poems, and other material to do with the development of Middle-earth and all that it involved. By this time, Lewis was in his thirties and Tolkien in his forties.

Not long after Lewis wrote his *The Pilgrim's Regress* in a burst of creativity at the home of Arthur Greeves, in August 1932, Tolkien handed him an unfinished manuscript. It was the tale of a creature called a hobbit, a Mr Bilbo Baggins, who reluctantly took off with a band of dwarves at the instigation of a wizard called Gandalf. His task was to burgle the ill-gotten treasure of a dragon who had usurped the ancestral halls of the dwarves of the Lonely Mountain, far to the east of the Misty Mountains. Lewis was delighted by the story. Tolkien also enjoyed *The Pilgrim's Regress,* including Lewis's poem about a dragon in the story, which he discussed in an early draft of a lecture that he was preparing on Beowulf, an Old English poem.

Lewis wasted no time in writing to Arthur to share his discovery of Tolkien's story that had emerged from his private world.

Reading his fairy tale has been uncanny – it is so exactly like what we would both have longed to write (or read) in 1916: so that one feels he is not making it up but merely describing the same world into which all three of us have the entry.[1]

At some stage in the ensuing years, Tolkien read instalments from *The Hobbit* to the Inklings, and it was finally published in September 1937. Lewis wrote a laudatory review, and the book's admirers grew, even to include the poet W.H. Auden. From an initial print run of 1,500 copies, its worldwide sales would one day exceed 100 million.

Lewis's embrace of Christianity and the subsequent formation of the Inklings out of his Christian friends had significance far beyond his immediate circle or even his growing readership. This significance becomes apparent in hindsight. The 1930s included a small but important landmark in English literature. The decade featured what literary historian Harry Blamires (a former student of Lewis's) called a "minor renaissance" of Christianity in English literature. This was not an overly self-conscious, and certainly not a triumphalist, movement. Some of the Christian writers were part of small circles, such as the Inklings, or isolated from movements or groups recognized at the time, such as the by then vintage Bloomsbury Group.

This revival took place against a trend to modernize Christian teaching, by which was meant removing by reinterpretation miraculous elements such as the virgin birth of Christ, his physical resurrection from the dead, and his prophecy of the fall of Jerusalem in AD 70. Many writers, however, unhappy with the secular and materialism in whatever guise, turned back to orthodox Christian belief, as Lewis did. Others, such as Tolkien and Charles Williams, had never lost their childhood belief. The Inklings, small as they were as a club, and Lewis and Tolkien, in particular, were very much part of this significant trend towards Christian belief embodied in English literature in the thirties.

An early sign that something was happening in the literary scene occurred back in 1928. George Bell, then Dean of Canterbury Cathedral, decided to bring theatre back into the church, picking up a great tradition that was now barely visible. He founded the Canterbury Festival, which soon attracted a following. In 1935, T.S. Eliot's new verse drama, *Murder in the Cathedral*, was performed there. The next year saw the staging of *Thomas Cranmer of Canterbury* by Charles Williams.

With T.S. Eliot, other Christian writers were to have an impact in the 1930s, including Graham Greene, Evelyn Waugh, and Christopher Fry. Dorothy L. Sayers was writing her Lord Peter Wimsey crime novels, which she had begun in the twenties, and Charles Williams was bringing out literary criticism and supernatural thrillers such as *The Place of the Lion*, which Lewis, Tolkien, and others of the Inklings read in 1936. At Williams's suggestion, Dorothy L. Sayers was approached to write for the Canterbury Festival. Tolkien published *The Hobbit* in 1937 and, in 1940, W.H. Auden began composing his poem "New Year Letter" under the influence of Charles Williams's highly unusual history of the church, *Descent of the Dove*, which had been published the year before.

Lewis and Tolkien were not as alienated from contemporary culture as they thought, as they reflected upon their poetic failure. This point is summed up admirably by Harry Blamires:

> Lewis began writing just at the point when this minor Christian Renaissance in literature was taking off. His *Pilgrim's Regress* came out in 1933. And the 1930s were a remarkable decade in this respect.... So when the literary historian looks back at the English literary scene in the 1930s and 1940s he is going to see C. S. Lewis and Charles Williams, not as freakish throwbacks, but as initial contributors to what I have called a Christian literary renaissance, if a minor one.[2]

This current in the literary waters of the 1930s may have been a minor one, but the fruit of many of the writers listed by Blamires is in the mainstream. As our perspective benefits more and more from hindsight, Lewis's name does not appear out of place beside artist and poet David Jones, T.S. Eliot, and Graham Greene. Tolkien's too has mainstream importance, as Tom Shippey has argued powerfully in *J.R.R. Tolkien: Author of the Century* (2000). Even the Inklings club, which for many of its years had a small membership of, at times, half a dozen or less, can now be seen as an important literary presence.

When Lewis's family doctor, Robert "Humphrey" Havard, joined the circle sometime between 1935 and 1939, he saw it as a group of Lewis's friends who liked to read out work in progress and discuss ideas that often touched on theology and philosophy. He had no idea that some of them would become famous, and was quite astonished when Tolkien and Lewis began to be popular through their fiction.[3]

Havard had been invited after visiting Lewis when he was ill with influenza, and the conversation had turned to medieval philosophy. Perhaps this was because the term "influenza" (alluding to the influence of planetary bodies as explanation for the malady) comes straight from the view of the world commonly held in the Middle Ages. Though a GP, Havard's interests were wide: he had conducted advanced medical research, and did some writing in addition to journal articles.

Though it is not clear when Inklings members began to gather in pub meetings as well as the Thursday sessions, the Tuesday meetings in the back parlour of the Eagle and Child (also known as the Bird and Baby) eventually became such a local institution that they were referred to, along with Burton beer, in Edmund Crispin's 1947 Oxford-based crime novel, *Swan Song*. This is one of a series of stories featuring Gervase Fen, an Oxford Professor of English language and literature, and a private detective.

> "Oh, for a beakerful of the cold north," said Fen, gulping at his Burton. "Impossible murders, for the present, must wait their turn."

They were sitting before a blazing and hospitable fire in the small front parlour of the "Bird and Baby".... Adam, Elizabeth, Sir Richard Freeman, and Fen were now toasting themselves to a comfortable glow. Outside, it was still attempting to snow, but with only partial success....

"There goes C.S. Lewis," said Fen suddenly. "It must be Tuesday."[4]

Lewis read far more widely and eclectically than any of his Inkling friends. Tolkien, for instance, increasingly focused his attention upon the English West Midlands of the Middle Ages, both in his fiction and in his linguistic work, though he did enjoy reading science fiction and other contemporary stories that featured the "marvellous" (a term Lewis preferred to the "supernatural" in fiction). The fruit of Lewis's close, broad reading was many literary essays. There were also the major studies such as *English Literature in the Sixteenth Century, Excluding Drama* (1954), Lewis's contribution to the *Oxford History of English Literature*. Lewis began writing the latter when he completed his groundbreaking *The Allegory of Love*, in 1935, after seven years of work on it.

To write for the *Oxford History of English Literature* series was a daunting task, even for the most brilliant of scholars. Lewis, with feeling, was soon to call the project the "Oh-Hell" (OHEL) after the series name. He took on the exhaustive task at the suggestion of Professor F.P. Wilson, one of the editors. It could have been called "the graveyard of the scholars", because of the demands it put upon its authors.

Frank Wilson had been Lewis's tutor when he was an undergraduate at University College. Like many, Wilson had been wounded – in his case, severely – in the First World War. Like Tolkien and Hugo Dyson, he had fought in the Battle of the Somme. Nearly twenty years after inviting Lewis to contribute to the series, he would be involved in his election for a professorship at Cambridge University.

The critic David L. Russell pointed out that "most literary

criticism is dated within its generation, but Lewis' remains highly readable, provocative, and, perhaps more significantly, in print more than three decades after his death – a forceful testimonial to his powers as a scholar".[5]

Many now consider *The Allegory of Love* to be among the outstanding works of literary criticism of the twentieth century. "To medieval studies in this country Lewis's logical and philosophical cast of mind gave a wholly new dimension," acknowledged J.A.W. ("Jaw") Bennett, a later member of the Inklings and prominent medieval scholar. The Middle Ages in fact provide the master key and the context for both Lewis's thought and his fiction, just as they do for Tolkien's. Much of Lewis's scholarly work centred on the period, and he regarded writers of the sixteenth century, and the entire Renaissance, as part of the intellectual and imaginative world of medieval times, even with the great cultural changes that were taking place in those later times. His science fiction stories celebrate a medieval picture of the cosmos, as do his Narnian tales (as Michael Ward has ably demonstrated in his study, *Planet Narnia* (2008)).

Lewis sought, as did Tolkien, to rehabilitate insights from this vast period for the contemporary reader, for their nourishment and enjoyment. In terms that I borrow from their mutual friend, Owen Barfield, through reading Lewis, contemporary readers are able to experience a felt change in consciousness, as they are taken into an older world. As their imaginations are engaged, modern readers can partake of a change in perception while reading a Narnian chronicle or a science fiction story of Lewis's such as *Perelandra (Voyage to Venus)*. This allows them to see their familiar world in a restored or new way. In his *The Allegory of Love*, Lewis wrote of the lost world of the medieval mind:

> We shall understand our present, and perhaps even our future, the better if we can succeed, by an effort of the historical imagination, in reconstructing that long-lost state of mind

for which the allegorical love poem was a natural mode of expression...

In his preface to *The Allegory of Love*, Lewis makes reference to three significant friends, Tolkien, Dyson, and Barfield (to whom the book is dedicated, and to whom Lewis acknowledges the greatest debt, after his father):

> There seems to be hardly any one among my acquaintance from whom I have not learned. The greatest of these debts – that which I owe to my father for the inestimable benefit of a childhood passed mostly alone in a house full of books – is now beyond repayment; and among the rest I can only select.... Above all, the friend [Owen Barfield] to whom I have dedicated the book, has taught me not to patronize the past, and has trained me to see the present as itself a "period". I desire for myself no higher function than to be one of the instruments whereby his theory and practice in such matters may become more widely effective.

Lewis's friendship with Tolkien was particularly important to him during the changes and challenges of the 1930s, just as in the twenties his friendship with Owen Barfield was highly significant in shaping his thought, and his clarification of the role of imagination in poetry, myth, and human knowledge. During this period of the thirties he first met Charles Williams, whose friendship was to be enormously influential during the war years to come, an influence that was to continue long after Williams's premature and sudden death in 1945.

His friendship with Williams came about after Lewis discovered his novel *The Place of the Lion*, early in 1936. Lewis visited Nevill Coghill at Exeter College in February, and heard from him the basic plot. On the strength of what was, in effect, Coghill's vivid retelling of its story, Lewis had borrowed his copy of the "spiritual shocker". Reading it enraptured him, and he shared his reaction afterwards in a letter to Arthur Greeves on 26 February. First, though, he told Arthur about the peaceful demise of his beloved dog, Mr Papworth, after sympathizing with his friend's loss of a dog called Tommy. Mrs Moore, he added, had been struck by a grief over Mr Papworth almost as intense as for the loss of a human. Then he went on to write about what he considered to be Williams's "really great book". He felt that reading it had been very appropriate with the approach of Lent. It brought out, he said, the "abuse of intellect", which was a sin to which academics were especially prone, and Williams's point had struck home.

Lewis set out to Arthur the novel as a blend of Plato and the biblical book of Genesis, and which concerned the days of creation. It was based, he said, on Plato's theory of the other world, where archetypes or originals of all earthly qualities exist. In Williams's story, these primeval archetypes were pulling our world back into them. The processes of creation in fact reverse, and the world is in ultimate danger. The primordial butterfly, for instance, was pulling all butterflies on the earth back into it.

One of the story's protagonists, Anthony Durrant, has a fiancée who is writing a dissertation on Platonic ideas, little realizing the potent powers that they represent.

The story opens with two London friends, Anthony, and Quentin Sabot, awaiting a bus on the Hertfordshire Road. There, they notice a search party for an escaped lioness. As they get caught up in the search, they spot the animal in the grounds of a large house. The two men see another lion, representing the primeval power of all that is lion, which begins to transform dramatically:

Anthony and Quentin saw before them the form of a man lying on the ground, and standing over him the shape of a full-grown and tremendous lion, its head flung back, its mouth open, its body quivering. It ceased to roar, and gathered itself back into itself. It was a lion such as the young men had never seen in any zoo or menagerie; it was gigantic and seemed to their dazed senses to be growing larger every moment.... Awful and solitary it stood.... Then, majestically, it moved... and while they still stared it entered into the dark shadow of the trees and was hidden from sight.

There was something of Aslan, the creator-lion of Narnia, in that majestic lion, but Aslan was not to emerge from Lewis's imagination for a dozen years or so.

By a strange turn of events, soon after this, Charles Williams read through the proofs of Lewis's *The Allegory of Love*. This was not to correct them, but to give them a quick read in order to prepare some copy to help in the marketing and selling of Lewis's book. Williams had been on the staff of the London office of Oxford University Press for many years, and had handled many books that he greatly admired and enjoyed, but he was unusually excited. He resolved to take the uncommon step of writing to its author, to express his appreciation and admiration. Before he could, however, he received a remarkable letter, on 11 March 1936, from Lewis, which praised his own *The Place of the Lion*, and invited Williams to attend an Inklings meeting in Oxford:

A book sometimes crosses one's path which is... like the sound of one's native language in a strange country.... It is to me one of the major literary events of my life – comparable to my first discovery of George MacDonald, G. K. Chesterton, or Wm. Morris.... Coghill of Exeter put me on to the book: I have put on Tolkien (the Professor of Anglo Saxon and a papist) and my brother. So there are three dons and one soldier all buzzing with excited admiration. We have a sort of informal club called the Inklings: the qualifications (as they have informally evolved) are a tendency to write, and Christianity. Can you come down some day next term (preferably not Sat. or Sunday), spend the night as my guest in College, eat with us at a chop house, and talk with us till the small hours?[6]

By return of post, Charles Williams replied:

> If you had delayed writing another 24 hours our letters
> would have crossed. It has never before happened to me
> to be admiring an author of a book while he at the same
> time was admiring me. My admiration for the staff work of
> the Omnipotence rises every day.... I regard your book as
> practically the only one that I have ever come across, since
> Dante, that shows the slightest understanding of what this very
> peculiar identity of love and religion means... [7]

Williams did visit the Inklings, perhaps soon after – the exact date is not recorded. Later, in a tribute to Williams after his death, Lewis remembered a London meeting which involved "a certain immortal lunch" with Williams, which was followed by an "almost Platonic discussion" in the churchyard of St Paul's Cathedral, which lasted for about two hours. [8] Then, Williams had presented his new friend with a copy of his *He Came Down From Heaven*, which had just been published by William Heinemann. On the book's flyleaf, Williams wrote, "At Shirreffs, 2.10, 4th July 1938". Shirreffs was Williams's favourite restaurant, now long gone, located at the bottom of Ludgate Hill, under the railway bridge. It was close by the office of the Oxford University Press at Amen Corner in the City of London, where he worked.

The area where Lewis and Williams met on that occasion was not far from the home of a number of publishing houses. Among them was George Allen and Unwin, Tolkien's publisher in Museum Street (named after the British Museum nearby). On 18 February 1938, Tolkien had written to Stanley Unwin about a science fiction story by his friend Lewis. It had been, he said, read aloud to the Inklings ("our local club"), which went in for "reading things short and long aloud". He explained that they had found it exciting as a serial, and all of them rated it highly.

Lewis's story, which was eventually published as *Out of the Silent Planet* (1938), was just one of many stories that were honed by the forthright yet fair criticism from fellow Inklings members. It originated out of his friendship with Tolkien. In the spring of 1936, he and Tolkien had a conversation about the kinds of books they liked to read, and the dearth of such books in contemporary writing. This may have been during one of their frequent Monday morning meetings in Lewis's room in Magdalen College.

In the light of Williams's novels, Lewis was beginning to think that it was possible to write popular fiction that would include the marvellous and other qualities of the books they relished. In fact, he wondered at one stage whether Williams's off-beat novels had been inspired by the fiction of G.K. Chesterton, who was a superb communicator of Christian belief through his stories and imaginative prose. Suddenly he said to Tolkien, in words something to this effect: "You know, Tollers, that there's too little around of what we enjoy in stories. We'll have to write them ourselves. One of us should write a tale of time travel, and the other, of space travel." Tolkien had agreed. Then Lewis had suggested tossing for it, to see who should do space, and who time. The coin turned over and over quickly in the air and then Lewis caught it. The result was that he got space travel, and Tolkien time travel.

Tolkien's story, *The Lost Road*, was started, and continued, read in part to the Inklings, but never finished. It was put aside in favour of his "new Hobbit", which eventually came to be called *The Lord of the Rings*, in which the theme of time is central. Lewis's story of a space journey rattled along with great gusto, and had a much surer eye for what would appeal to a popular readership than his earlier fiction, *The Pilgrim's Regress*. As *Out of the Silent Planet* was being written, its instalments were eagerly anticipated by the Inklings, as Tolkien later revealed to his publisher. In later years, Lewis would meet up with science fiction writers including Arthur C. Clarke, Brian Aldiss, and Kingsley Amis, who approved of some of his stories.

The closeness of Lewis's friendship with Tolkien, in the thirties, is indicated by his main protagonist, Dr Elwin Ransom, who is partly modelled on his friend. A clue is that Elwin means "Elf-friend". In his story, Lewis captures the intuitions, motives, and thinking of a linguist very like Tolkien in Ransom, who is a Cambridge philologist. Ransom carried a physical war wound (Tolkien's was emotional scarring) and was a "sedentary scholar". One of his publications carried a title that could have come from Tolkien's pen – *Dialect and Semantics*. Ransom combined heroic and intellectual qualities, but tended to disparage himself. He wasn't a complete copy of Tolkien, however, being a little younger and lacking his dress sense – Tolkien was always dapper in appearance.

In the story, Ransom was kidnapped by a wicked Cambridge colleague, the scientist Professor Edward Weston, and his henchman Dick Devine, and transported to Malacandra (Mars) in a spacecraft, where he was able to escape his captors. He was terrified of meeting alien life forms, called sorns, in the wild. Then something happened that brought all his philological instincts to bear, and turned his perception of the planet on its head. He encountered an alien creature:

> The creature, which was still steaming and shaking itself on the bank and had obviously not seen him, opened its mouth and began to make noises. This in itself was not remarkable; but a lifetime of linguistic study assured Ransom almost at once that these were articulate noises. The creature was *talking*. It had language. If you are not yourself a philologist, I am afraid you must take on trust the prodigious emotional consequences of this realisation in Ransom's mind.... The love of knowledge is a kind of madness. In the fraction of a second which it took Ransom to decide that the creature was really talking, and while he still knew that he might be facing instant death, his imagination had leaped over every fear and hope and probability of his situation to follow the dazzling project of making a Malacandrian grammar. *An Introduction to the Malacandrian Language – The Lunar Verb – A Concise Martian-English Dictionary...* the titles flitted through his mind. And what might one not discover from the speech of a non-human

race? The very form of language itself, the principle behind all possible languages, might fall into his hands.

Ransom's idea, "What might one not discover from the speech of a non-human race?" is the kind that would naturally occur to Tolkien. Indeed, the creation of Elvish languages – non-human languages of a kind – were for him an explanation of the inexhaustible possibilities of language for enhancing our knowledge of reality, both natural and supernatural, seen and unseen.

Tolkien was aware of the intended resemblance between Ransom and himself, writing several years later to his son, Christopher: "As a philologist I may have some part in [Ransom], and recognize some of my opinions Lewisified in him." His daughter, Priscilla, seemed quite convinced of the likeness.[9]

A strong connection between Tolkien and Lewis was their antipathy to the modern. This did not mean that they were opposed to everything that had happened since the Industrial Revolution: dentists with syringes full of anaesthetic, petrol-driven buses, draught beer, and other such features of their century, but what they viewed as an underlying mentality or even atmosphere of modernism. They were not against science or scientists, but the cult (what Barfield called "idolatry") of science, found in modernism, and its tendency to control and dominate knowledge. This results in denying alternative (and usually older) approaches to knowledge through the arts, religion, and ordinary human wisdom. Tolkien and Lewis felt that this mentality was a malaise that, if adopted by a society, posed a serious threat to humanity itself. The fictional character of Elwin Ransom embodied what the friends viewed as the contrasting old, perennial values common to humanity – values later referred to by Lewis in his book *The Abolition of Man* as the Tao. Ransom's enemy on the planet Mars, his Cambridge colleague Weston, stood for all that sprang from the worship of the modern.

The positive values that were championed by Lewis and his friend were displayed fictionally in Ransom's perception of things, which was in fact pre-modern, and essentially drew on medieval and even pre-Christian insights about nature and humanity. Lewis, like Tolkien, loved the medieval picture of the cosmos, its imaginative model of reality, and it is this world-picture that was "smuggled" into the minds of modern readers as they enjoyed Lewis's story. In deep space, en route to Malacandra in a spacecraft, Ransom found himself unexpectedly feeling well, despite the ordeal of his kidnapping. He began to regain what Lewis regarded as a lost "consciousness", to use a term from Barfield:

> He lay for hours in contemplation of the skylight. The Earth's disk was nowhere to be seen, the stars, thick as daisies on an uncut lawn, reigned perpetually, with no cloud, no moon, no sunrise to dispute their sway. There were planets of unbelievable majesty, and constellations undreamed of: there were celestial sapphires, rubies, emeralds and pinpricks of burning gold; far out on the left of the picture hung a comet, tiny and remote: and between all and behind all, far more emphatic and palpable than it showed on Earth, the undimensioned, enigmatic blackness. The lights trembled: they seemed to grow brighter as he looked. Stretched naked on his bed, a second Danaë, he found it night by night more difficult to disbelieve in old astrology: almost he felt, wholly he imagined, "sweet influence" pouring or even stabbing into his surrendered body.

Ransom's positive values are contrasted with the negative values of his kidnapper, Professor Edward Weston. The eminent physicist has abducted Ransom in the mistaken belief that the mysterious rulers of Mars require a human sacrifice, an act he considers completely justifiable. He has a disdain for all values of common humanity. His guiding value is biological survival, the replication of enlightened men at any cost.

After escaping his captors, Ransom was at first terrified and confused by the red planet and its variety of terrain and inhabitants. The latter turned out to be civilized and amiable, however. Ransom underwent what Lewis elsewhere calls "undeception". He was undeceived about the notion that extraterrestrial life must be a threat to humans. Ironically, it was the reverse that was true. Human beings whose planet is in quarantine from the rest of the universe (deep heaven) were the threat both to themselves and to other races outside of earth. Sharing their quarantine were demonic powers (fallen angels) who sought to complete their enslavement of planet Earth.

As readers, we see through Ransom's eyes. Ransom's change of perception leads to the reader's own change of vision. In travelling to Malacandra, in fact, Ransom goes through a kind of new birth (there are a number of images of gestation and birth) that eventually results in his own new way of seeing the planet. Its wonder never leaves him. This transformation is connected with overcoming his deep-rooted fears, such as of the apparent emptiness of space, and of alien monsters.

Lewis rebelled against the tendency of science fiction at that time to portray extraterrestrial beings as evil, as the enemies of humanity. In his view, the medieval image of the universe was exactly the reverse, and this appealed to him. His portrayal of peaceful, spiritual, alien life forms had an impact on science fiction that has lasted to this day. It is likely, for instance, that Lewis's reversal influenced Arthur C. Clarke's famous story *2001*. Half humorously, Lewis lamented in a letter in 1939 to Sister Penelope:

> You will be both grieved and amused to hear that out of about 60 reviews [of *Out of the Silent Planet*], only 2 showed any knowledge that my idea of the fall of the Bent One was anything but a private invention of my own… any amount of theology can now be smuggled into people's minds under cover of romance without their knowing it.[10]

This sort of response was one of the factors in Lewis's decision to continue writing theology and ethics on a popular front, and then increasingly to focus on theological fiction.

In an early study of historic speculation about flying in space, *Voyages to the Moon* (1948), Marjorie Hope Nicolson paid a tribute to C.S. Lewis that was full of insight:

> *Out of the Silent Planet* is to me the most beautiful of all
> cosmic voyages and in some ways the most moving.... As
> C.S. Lewis, the Christian apologist, has added something
> to the long tradition, so C.S. Lewis, the scholar-poet, has
> achieved an effect in *Out of the Silent Planet* different from
> anything in the past. Earlier writers have created new worlds
> from legend, from mythology, from fairy tale. Mr Lewis has
> created myth itself, myth woven of desire and aspirations
> deep-seated in some, at least, of the human race.... As I
> journey with him into worlds at once familiar and strange, I
> experience, as did Ransom, "a sensation not of following an
> adventure but of enacting a myth".[11]

11

The Wartime Years and After: Enter Charles Williams

The Second World War soon turned out to be a crisis for Western civilization, perhaps the greatest since the fall of Rome in the fifth century. As Britain faced invasion by the Nazis, Churchill rallied the country to resist, and captured its mood:

> If we can stand up to [Hitler], all Europe may be freed and the life of the world may move forward into broad, sunlit uplands. But if we fail, then the whole world... including all we have known and cared for, will sink into the abyss of a new Dark Age made more sinister, and perhaps more protracted, by the lights of perverted science.

An Oxford philosophy don, John D. Mabbott, contrasted the earlier world war and the new one:

> In 1914 all the undergraduates, except a few invalids and foreigners, rushed to enlist, and by October Oxford was empty. The younger dons all joined up too.... In 1939 everything was completely different. The scientists were

directed to complete their courses. For the Arts men, some academic work could be combined with military training for a year or so. It was not expected that a vast civilian army would be needed. Nor did it seem likely that the 300,000 casualties of Passchendaele would be repeated and a whole generation practically wiped out. So the Colleges went on at half strength in tutors and pupils.[1]

One Sunday, less than a year into the war, Lewis attended his local Anglican church as usual for Communion. Holy Trinity Church was a comfortable walk away from The Kilns, on the north-east fringe of Oxford. The Friday evening before, his friend Dr Humphrey Havard had come around, and they listened on the radio to a speech by Hitler for which the BBC provided a running translation. It had dawned on Lewis, listening intently, how plausible the self-styled leader or guide of Germany could seem, even though he knew of course Hitler's claims were patently untrue. In his "final appeal to common sense", Hitler declared: "It never has been my intention to wage war, but rather to build up a State with a new social order and the finest possible standard of culture."[2]

The emotive voice of Hitler's preaching may have still rung in Lewis's mind in the quiet haven of his church that Sunday 21 July 1940. The England he loved and had adopted was in grave danger of invasion by Hitler's forces, efficient like a machine. The Battle of Britain had started – that day alone, nearly 200 patrols were dispatched by the RAF in response to enemy air activity. In any case, Lewis's thoughts turned to the master of evil, whom the strutting dictator resembled in some respects – not least in his egotism and arch narcissism. Maybe a war-orientated bureaucracy was a more fitting contemporary image of hell than the poet John Milton's famous depiction of Pandemonium in *Paradise Lost*? Like Hitler's determined attempts to occupy and control European countries, Satan was systematically bent on invading all parts of human life, aiming at utter suppression.

If Lewis's thoughts had turned to his map of the human soul, sketched out in his first prose fiction nine years before, it would have been appropriate. There, in *The Pilgrim's Regress,* military railways from hell threatened the soul from north and south. We do know that Lewis's thoughts in 1940 were often on John Milton, as he was working on his epic poem, *Paradise Lost,* for a series of lectures.

Warnie had been evacuated just a few weeks before with thousands of other soldiers from the desperate beaches and jetties of Dunkirk, and was still on active service, despite his age (he was now in his mid-forties). That afternoon, Lewis reported to Warnie in a letter what turned out to be the origins of *The Screwtape Letters*, in which an important figure in Hell's "lowerarchy" would speak plausibly and eloquently about Satanic strategies for winning over human beings, or keeping them secure in the grip of his "Father Below". Screwtape in fact would brilliantly emulate his master, the "father of lies".

For Lewis, the conflict of good and evil fitted exactly into the imagery of modern warfare, with its terror, apocalyptic weapons, and global reach. Though he was most shaped by his experiences of the First World War, some of Lewis's most popular writings on the nature of evil and goodness, and the forces lying behind evil, were penned during the Second World War, and also shortly before, when war with Hitler became increasingly inevitable, and immediately afterwards, in the years of social reflection and the rebuilding of a broken Europe.

Hitler's story of a superior race, and the greatness and destiny of a particular nation, had seemed plausible to millions of modern people, despite being a concoction of lies. What did his compelling and deceptive story tell about the nature of evil? Why was his egoism and self-absorption so attractive to a supposedly enlightened modern world? What did war itself, swollen to modern proportions, reveal about the battle for the human soul? In Lewis's modest church in Headington Quarry, in a quiet suburb of a beautiful city visibly unscarred by war, the talk was, as it had been for hundreds of years, of a cosmic battle against the world, the flesh, and the devil. This tradition of talk resonated with Lewis as he stood, sat, and kneeled during the church service.

It was perhaps natural for a book such as *The Screwtape Letters* to be born during an apocalyptic war, a total war, using state-of-the-art modern weapons. What is surprising is that Lewis would be able to approach his subject with humour and with sure-footed satire, without trivializing the horror of evil and human suffering.

"My memories of the last war haunted my dreams for years," Lewis had disclosed in a letter written on 8 May 1939. In an essay, "Learning in Wartime", written soon after September 1939, he pointed out: "War creates no absolutely new situation; it simply aggravates the permanent human situation so that we can no longer ignore it." During the years of the First World War and immediately after it, Lewis's experience was first, for him, a materialistic view of the war of nature and spirit, and then, later, it became a Christian vision of cosmic battle between good and evil.

Meetings of the Inklings throughout the war years were gilded by the presence of Charles Williams, who was evacuated to Oxford along with the London office of Oxford University Press at the outbreak of war. He was never to return to London: he died suddenly a few days after Germany surrendered. Because of visits to the group after he and Lewis became acquainted back in 1936, he was already known to the Inklings, and quickly became a regular attendee. He also met frequently with Lewis and Tolkien outside of the Inklings gatherings.

Charles Williams spoke with a marked East London accent, which was unusual to the ears of the mostly private school-educated Oxford academics. (Tolkien was an important exception, having been educated at a grammar school in Birmingham.) The Londoner brought a freshness to the lives of Lewis and his friends. He had a brilliant though quirky mind and imagination and, like Lewis and Tolkien, was an orthodox but not tame man of faith. His poetry has, to this day, still to be fully appreciated, especially his reworking of the stories of King Arthur.

Charles Williams's move to Oxford, and his admittance into the Inklings, helped to exert a deep and lasting influence on Lewis. When he looked back to this time after many years, Tolkien described Lewis as being captivated by Williams's "spell", feeling that Lewis was too impressionable a person. He would refer to the Inklings as Lewis's "séance". This was an allusion to Williams's fascination with the occult. Without doubt, Williams's interest in witchcraft and the supernatural was conducive to Lewis's inspiration to write about Screwtape and devilry.

Wartime conditions became a creative matrix of not only Lewis's writings at that time, but also books and other writings by fellow Inklings that explored devilry and its effects on human beings. Most famously, the output of the group included *The Screwtape Letters* and *The Lord of the Rings,* but also the less known novel of Charles Williams's, *All Hallows Eve,* admired by T.S. Eliot (who knew Williams of old). Eliot also published Williams's study, *Witchcraft*, during these years, commissioned by him for Faber and Faber. Eliot once remarked of Williams: "He could have joked with the devil and turned the joke against him."[3] The war was also reflected in the conversations of the Inklings as many of these works in progress were read to the club.

A rather iconic session of the Inklings had taken place on 9 November 1939, less than two months after Charles Williams arrived on the scene, a meeting that illustrates the atmosphere of wartime Inklings sessions, at least the overtly literary ones.

Warnie was at that stage of the war away from Oxford in France. His absence did mean that his brother corresponded with him, which meant that there were references to meetings of the Inklings in the letters. In a long letter to him dated 11 November 1939, Lewis recorded his week and included a scene in his college rooms, after a meal in the nearby Eastgate Hotel:

On Thursday we had a meeting of the Inklings – you and
Coghill both absented unfortunately.... I have never in my life
seen Dyson so exuberant – "a roaring cataract of nonsense".
The bill of fare afterwards [in Lewis's college rooms] consisted
of a section of the new Hobbit book from Tolkien, a nativity
play from Williams (unusually intelligible for him, and
approved by all) and a chapter out of the book on the Problem
of Pain from me. It so happened – it would take too long to
explain why – that the subject matter of the three readings
formed almost a logical sequence, and produced a really first
rate evening's talk of the usual wide-ranging kind – "from
grave to gay, from lively to severe".[4] I wished very much we
could have had you with us.[5]

The piece read by Tolkien would have been the latest draft of a
section of Book One of what became the two-book *The Fellowship
of the Ring* – he was making momentous changes relating, among
other things, to the demonic nature of the one Ring and the
question of Aragorn's identity. The piece most probably touched
upon the nature of evil as the likely common theme of the three
readings mentioned by Lewis, which had "formed almost a logical
sequence". His own chapter probably explored this theme, given
that he read from *The Problem of Pain,* and Charles Williams's play
The House by the Stable, concerned the battle to win the human soul
over to evil. In it, Williams very effectively presented the skewed,
inverse perspective of hell. Lewis's *The Problem of Pain,* of course,
raised an issue central to the experience of war, with its suffering
and terror.

Lewis's brief description of a momentous Inklings meeting draws
attention to the ever-talkative Hugo Dyson. Dyson's exuberance
did not distract in any way from the sobering common theme that
emerged from his reading, or those by Tolkien or Williams.

Charles Williams's contribution to the evening, *The House by
the Stable*, was a short Christmas play, completed on 26 October,
just a few days before. In it, two allegorical figures, Pride, in the

form of a pretty woman, and Hell, her brother, seek to elicit the precious jewel of the soul from the breast of Man. The proceedings are interrupted by the figures of Joseph and the pregnant Mary, seeking shelter for the night. In them, God had intervened in human history.

The twisted perspective that marks all devilry is evident from the beginning of the play. Pride, for Williams, like Milton, and like his friend Lewis, was the heart and motivator of sin. Here the allegorical figure of Pride seductively says to Man (clearly Everyman):

> You are Man, the lord of this great house Earth,
> Or (as its name is called in my country) Sin;
> You are its god and mine; since you first smiled
> And stretched your hand to me and brought me in,
> Since our tenderness began, I have loved you, Man,
> And will – do not doubt; kiss me again.

After Man responds in terms of adoration, speaking of her "dove's eyes" and how she stops him feeling alone in his "greatness", she says:

> So this wonderful house where moon and sun
> Run with lights, and all kinds of creatures crawl
> To be your servants, and your only business is to take
> Delight in your own might – it is yours and mine,
> A shrine for your godhead, and for me because I am yours.[6]

In his point of view, focused upon Pride and Hell and the battle for Man's very soul, Williams works an orthodox view of evil as perversion of good, not something that exists in itself, into a contemporary form. In portraying the love of Man for Pride, he is not saying that love itself is an evil, but that Pride is a perversion of something good. His picture of Man's soul as a lost jewel has a simple and evocative beauty.

By the summer of the next year, after hearing Williams read this play (which would have linked in Lewis's mind with Milton's exploration of pride in *Paradise Lost*), Lewis had had the idea for *The Screwtape Letters*. He took up the imaginative possibilities of the topsy-turvy perspective of hell much further than Williams had. While the play may not have directly influenced the birth of Screwtape, its reading had its part in reinforcing what Owen Barfield called the *Weltanschauung* or worldview that was part of at least those who were at the core of the Inklings, Barfield included.

It may have been around this time in November 1939 that having heard a chapter or more from *The Problem of Pain*, Charles Williams remarked (as Lewis remembered) that God had not been displeased with the complaining and impatient Job in the Bible.

> The weight of the divine displeasure had been reserved for the "comforters", the self-appointed advocates on God's side, the people who tried to show that all was well – "the sort of people", he said, immeasurably dropping his lower jaw and fixing me with his eyes –"the sort of people who wrote books on the Problem of Pain".[7]

They were words that, though meant in jest, were likely to trouble Lewis, who was essentially a humble person. He constantly examined his increasing role as a Christian apologist – a defender of the faith in an age of growing unbelief. "I have been," he once quipped, "a converted Pagan living among apostate Puritans."[8]

Lewis published seven books in wartime, or just after, that in part or whole concerned devilry, the problem of evil, and damnation or salvation in the moral choices of human beings. *The Problem of Pain* was published in 1940. Two years later, his study of and introduction to Milton's *Paradise Lost* appeared – a Christian epic that has influenced contemporary writers as diverse as Lewis and the atheist Philip Pullman. As well as a brilliant defence of the poem, building on Charles Williams's insights on Milton, Lewis expounds on the nature of hierarchy, the devil, and angelic beings.

Lewis's imaginative counterpart to this study of Milton was his second science fiction novel, *Perelandra (Voyage to Venus),* which would appear in the next year. Here the story of Adam and Eve is enacted on another planet, in which a surprising hero, the Tolkien-like philologist, Dr Elwin ("Elf-friend") Ransom, is carried to Venus from earth to intervene in helping to thwart the devilry. This is the same Ransom who featured in the preceding story, *Out of the Silent Planet*. Some of the prose in the novel is so poetic that Ruth Pitter turned parts of it into poetic stanzas.[9]

The best-selling *The Screwtape Letters* appeared in 1942 – the correspondence of a senior devil to a junior demon newly graduated from the Tempters' Training College in a bureaucratic hell. The letters had already appeared as a series in a Christian weekly called *The Guardian*, with one reader, a "country clergyman", cancelling his subscription, according to Lewis, on the grounds that "much of the advice given in these letters seemed to him not only erroneous but positively diabolical".[10]

The following year, the year *Perelandra* was published, Lewis's philosophical tract *The Abolition of Man* appeared. This book also had an imaginative counterpart, the third and final volume of science fiction, called *That Hideous Strength*. The influence of Charles Williams on it was obvious to Lewis's friends. Though the story is a mixture of this-worldly setting with some realistic characters and extraordinary supernatural happenings, the book has a number of affinities with *The Screwtape Letters*. In this case, the diabolic intention is not simply to damn individual humans but to place society itself under demonic rule, through the use of bureaucracy and technology in the hands of materialistic scientists who have become the new magicians and, ironically, are supping with the devil.

In a contemporary review, George Orwell judged:

> There is nothing outrageously improbable in such a
> conspiracy. Indeed, at a moment when a single atomic bomb

– of a type already pronounced "obsolete" – has just blown probably three hundred thousand people to fragments, it sounds all too topical. Plenty of people in our age do entertain the monstrous dreams of power that Mr. Lewis attributes to his characters, and we are within sight of the time when such dreams will be realisable.[11]

As his friendship with Lewis continued to deepen, Charles Williams read regularly to the Inklings, including extracts from his Arthurian cycle of poetry and certainly his final novel, *All Hallows Eve*. The latter is set in wartime London, with two of the leading characters killed before the novel opens. In the words of the poet and novelist John Wain, who was a fledgling member of the Inklings in the period immediately after the war and a student during it, Charles Williams "gave himself to Oxford as unreservedly as Oxford gave itself to him". When Lewis and Tolkien arranged for him to lecture in the university on Milton and other topics, his talks were performed superbly, and proved enormously popular. Wain tells how

His lectures were crowded out.... Williams, on the platform, enjoyed himself so much that even the most obstinate sceptics in the audience finally capitulated and shared his enjoyment. Great poetry was something to be revelled in, to be rejoiced over, and Williams revelled and rejoiced up there before our eyes.[12]

The joy of friendship and the company of the Inklings contrasted sharply with the realities of war, which made many demands and required sacrifice. Warnie had been recalled to military service at the onset of war in 1939, because of his previous career in the army, but Lewis and most of his Inklings friends were deemed too old or physically unfit to serve. Many of them were, like Lewis, scarred by war and felt obliged to make their own war effort. Lewis expressed this in a number of ways, including the subject of much of his writing during that golden period of the Inklings. But the opening of the war gave him an immediate opportunity to do something else. Like Professor Kirke in *The Lion, the Witch and the Wardrobe*, he and Mrs Moore took in evacuees from London, who were in danger from bombing.

It was now nearly ten years since Lewis, Mrs Moore, and her daughter Maureen had moved into The Kilns, the red-brick bungalow-style house on the fringe of Oxford, with its extensive grounds, large flooded quarry, and wooded hill. Even with maids in the house, there was room for several children. (Their general factotum, Fred Paxford, lived in a ramshackle wooden bungalow in the grounds.) Three days before the war started, the evacuation of over 1.5 million children had begun from vulnerable British cities.

The children in the first batch to come to The Kilns, all girls, brought little with them – a gas mask in a large box attached to a shoulder strap, spare clothing, toothbrush, comb, a handkerchief, and a bag of food for the day they travelled. Lewis, whose experience of children up to this time was quite limited, instantly warmed to the evacuees. He wrote to Warnie that the girls seemed "very nice, unaffected creatures and all most flatteringly delighted with their new surroundings". He added that they were fond of animals (as Lewis was himself). One evacuee who turned up later in the war mistook Lewis for the gardener, on account of his habitually shabby attire. The distinguished scholar's response, that child remembered, was to boom with laughter.

The evacuees, coming from cities, had little or no experience of the countryside. The Kilns had come to resemble to some extent a tiny farm, or at least a smallholding, and this resemblance increased as the war progressed. The low, rambling brick house was set in acres of land, with an apple orchard, a pond in the nearby woodland, and many hens. Eggs were on the menu every day. There were coops for hens and cages for rabbits to be cleaned.

The evacuees took to Mrs Moore, by then in her late sixties. She was kind to them. They noticed that Minto made a huge fuss of Lewis – he was the centre of attention. In fact, for her, and thus also for her daughter Maureen, he was the axis around which life revolved. One evacuee, Jill "June" Flewett,[13] who arrived later in the war, remarked: "The running of the house, the cooking, the meals – everything she did – was geared for Jack's happiness and comfort. The whole household revolved on the premise that Jack must be looked after, and Warnie was expected to tag along."[14]

The impact of the evacuees on Lewis carried over into his writing, which was to touch the lives of readers and film audiences around the globe in later years. He started to write a story soon after the first children arrived, which was then abandoned and put in a drawer.

> This book is about four children whose names were Ann, Martin, Rose and Peter. But it is most about Peter who was the youngest. They all had to go away from London suddenly because of Air Raids, and because Father, who was in the Army, had gone off to the War and Mother was doing some kind of war work. They were sent to stay with a kind of relation of Mother's who was a very old Professor who lived all by himself in the country.[15]

Lewis would take up the story again a few years later, in 1949. It became the first story of Narnia, *The Lion, the Witch and the Wardrobe,* in which evacuee children enter another, magical, world through an old wardrobe. The wardrobe was like one the real evacuee children would have come across in The Kilns, which had been carved by Lewis's grandfather. The story connected the events of wartime England with a battle against an ancient evil in Narnia, as the evacuee children in the story help loyal Narnian talking beasts to overcome the power of the White Witch, who has placed their lush valley country under a curse of perpetual winter.

Lewis, like many of his age, served during the Second World War in the Local Defence Volunteers, later renamed the Home Guard, or "Dad's Army" as it was nicknamed. It fulfilled a variety of duties. The Volunteers were formed when the threat of invasion, including paratroopers from the skies, was acute. Tolkien served in a different role, on firewatch duties. When Warnie was eventually discharged from military service, he also served with the Home Guard, utilizing his boat, *The Bosphorus,* to patrol Oxford's waterways.

Lewis refers several times in his letters to his patrols, which were largely uneventful. Commenting on his unintentionally comic platoon members, he laconically observed in a letter to the absent Warnie: "Provided always that we don't meet any Germans I anticipate some considerable enjoyment from this brotherhood in arms."[16]

One night, as his duties did not start until 1:30 a.m., he invited Hugo Dyson and Dr Humphrey Havard to dine with him in college, to be joined by other Inklings later. He considered it was no use going to bed, to be woken after such a brief while; it was better "to make a 'wake' of it in the original sense". They had a "good Inklings", finishing at around 12:50 a.m. On his way to his rendezvous with the patrol members, Lewis ate his sandwiches – unable to provide sandwiches for them all, he could not face eating his in front of them.[17] Because of these duties, the Inklings got into the habit, for a time, of meeting on Friday evenings rather than the usual Thursdays.

Although there was little to record of interest in the patrols, other than observations about carrying a heavy rifle once more and other memories evoked from the last war, Lewis was often inspired by the experience of walking through Oxford in the quiet hours of the night. "The High [Street]", Lewis wrote to Warnie,

> seen in coolness and emptiness was exquisite…. One
> excellent thing about this job is that it gives you, once a week,
> the chance of a walk at the only time in the 24 hours when it
> is really pleasant for walking in summer. Indeed "pleasant" is
> too weak a word for the actual patrol – which with owls and

bats and night smells and moonlight reflected from water, and the sort of dreamlike receptivity one gets from being rather tired – it was ravishing.[18]

Lewis also found that the patrolling could lead to debate that touched on issues that went beyond the horizons of the world. He recounted such an occasion in a letter to a fellow churchman, the Anglican monk Brother George Every SSM:

> In the small hours of this morning I succeeded in making my L.D.V.[19] fellow sentry realise for the first time in his life that "nature" can't have "purposes" unless it is a rational substance, and if it is you'd much better call it God, or the gods, or a god, or the devil. The fact that he'd never seen this before is, I suppose, an example of just what you mean about style – the great fog of nonsense spread over all nations.[20]

For Lewis, there was another major change in his routines to adjust to. The war years marked his establishment as an outstanding popular communicator of the Christian faith. His efforts to communicate Christianity clearly, concisely, and imaginatively were driven by the reality of the war. From very early on in the war he gave talks to RAF personnel, many of whom were unlikely to survive a quota of bombing missions or defensive action against enemy forces. Humphrey Stuart Babbage, a Royal Air Force chaplain, invited Lewis to speak to a heavy-bombing squadron in Norfolk. "Our casualties," he remembered,

> had been heavy: we were, at the time, engaged in massive night bombings against some of the most heavily fortified targets in Germany and occupied Europe. A tour of duty consisted of thirty or more operations against enemy targets: after that, a man was taken off for a period of rest before being scheduled for another tour. The grim fact was that, on the average, a man only completed thirteen raids before being

killed or posted missing. These men (in the glory of their budding manhood) knew, statistically speaking, that there was little chance of their completing even one tour.[21]

The talks were given by Lewis under his conviction that an even greater and far more important conflict was raging – the battle for the individual human soul. The experience of speaking to men who had a very realistic view of their likelihood of survival brought it home to Lewis how necessary it was to avoid jargon, or even precise concepts that had become unfamiliar in a post-Christian milieu. His very first talk, at RAF Abingdon near Oxford, he considered an abject failure. After it he worked hard to be more successful in his speaking to non-academic listeners.

Among a heavy commitment to these RAF duties, and his academic load, Lewis wrote with astonishing productivity. His popularity following the best-selling appearance of *The Screwtape Letters* was immensely boosted by the four series of talks he gave on BBC radio in 1941, 1942, and 1944. The talks were straightforward and lucid, providing an outstanding example of early media evangelism. They survive today in the collection published as *Mere Christianity*, which continues to be a compelling and unmatched, even though dated, presentation of basic Christian belief in the twenty-first century, over seventy years after the talks were transmitted by the BBC.

The British Broadcasting Corporation had invited Lewis to give these hugely popular talks early in 1941, when war had already made people generally more thoughtful about ultimate issues. Lewis more and more regarded England as a post-Christian country. He decided that many people thought that they had left Christianity behind, when in fact they had never been true believers in the first place, or even had a proper introduction to it.

His feelings about the first set of talks were captured in a letter. The broadcasts, he revealed, were preparation for the gospel rather than evangelism – their aim was to persuade modern people that there is a moral law, that we are guilty of disobeying it. The existence of a lawgiver was quite likely to follow from the reality of the moral law. Unless the Christian doctrine of the atonement (what Christ accomplished in his death and resurrection) was added to this bleak analysis, he concluded, it yielded despair rather than any consolation.

Just one of those BBC recordings on "Mere Christianity" has survived, "The New Man" – listening to it, one can imagine Lewis's rich voice, edged by static, filling living rooms and public places throughout Britain.

Lewis's powerful tones also dominated smoky rooms in favoured pubs, or his college rooms, when the Inklings met. Though there was joking, stories, and deep laughter, the underlying content was as momentous as the broadcast talks. Remembering the fellowship of the literary group and Lewis's reading of instalments of *The Screwtape Letters*, Dr Humphrey Havard wrote:

The usual procedure, after drinks and gossip had been exchanged, was to settle into armchairs and then for someone to be invited to read a recent manuscript. The rest then commented, led nearly always by Lewis. Criticism was frank but friendly. Coming from a highly literate audience, it was often profuse and detailed. The universal complaint from the speaker actually holding the floor was that everyone else spoke so much that it was barely possible to get his own ideas in edgeways. True enough, the informality of the group led occasionally to several trying to speak at once. As the only non-literary and nonteaching member, my chief contribution was to listen. The talk was good, witty, learned, high hearted, and very stimulating. We all felt the itch to join in.

It was in this way that the early *Screwtape Letters* first saw daylight. They were greeted hilariously. We heard several of Lewis's poems... and chapters from the *Problem of Pain* and *Miracles*.[22]

War with Germany ended in May 1945. The exaltation and boisterousness of Lewis and his friends was tempered by the sudden loss of Charles Williams within days of the announcement, after an unsuccessful operation. At the end of 1945 a few of the friends gamely gathered and celebrated what was to have been a long "Victory Inklings". They based themselves at a pub called The Bull at Fairford, in the Cotswold hills of Gloucestershire. The celebration lasted four days (Tuesday 11 to Friday 14 December), days that were snatched from their responsibilities and commitments. The party included Lewis and Warnie, Tolkien, and, some of the time, Dr Havard. The depleted group made the best of the jaunt. The first day Warnie spent walking with Tolkien before the others arrived.

Warnie recorded events in his diary, including the walks, quiet reading, conversation, and moments of transcendence. They were able to dream of the future, so much more hopeful without war. In The Bull he writes:

> We were very cosy in our own lounge in the evening where I read Lewis Carroll's *Life* by [Stuart Dodgson] Collingwood, and Tollers my Dr. J.[ohn] Brown's *Letters*. J[ack] arrived, without [Owen] Barfield who was ill, by 9.35 on Wednesday, and Humphrey [Havard] turned up to lunch by car; after which we had one of the best winter walks I ever took... On Thursday... [i]n the afternoon we walked through Horcott and Whelford... Whelford, a mere Hamlet, has a simple little Church where we all felt that God dwells; nothing to "see" in it. There, to my surprise and pleasure, Tollers said a prayer. Down on the river was a perfect mill house where we amused ourselves by dreaming of it as a home for the Inklings...[23]

A season of fruitfulness lay ahead now war was over. Lewis and his companions had mellowed. This post-war period would see the publication of *The Chronicles of Narnia* (1950–56) and *The Lord of the Rings* (1954–55). Those mature writings either originated in, or were mostly written within, the period of war or impending war. In them, the theme of devilry so central to their writers was particularly successful. Though Tolkien was taken aback and indeed baffled by the fact, it is not really so odd or surprising that *The Screwtape Letters* had been dedicated to him by Lewis.

The wartime period, in fact, had been something of a golden age for the Inklings. There were two important magical ingredients in the mix that created this uplift. One had been the arrival of Charles Williams in Oxford on the heels of the outbreak of war. The other ingredient was magic in its darkest form – the global war itself, fought with the most terrifying weapons modern technology could devise, devouring entire cities. The vitality of this period continued for several years more, until the demise, probably in autumn 1949, of the Inklings as a reading group made up of a least a core of writers. There was an evening when, for the very first time, no one turned up. By natural inclination and presumably tacit agreement, the informal group continued as a weekly and usually lively conversation group, meeting in pubs up to Lewis's death.

John Wain vividly recalled this period of the Inklings and the meetings in Lewis's rooms at Magdalen College. Though he joined the club after the war, the setting would have been very much the same:

> I can see that room so clearly now, the electric fire pumping heat into the dank air, the faded screen that broke some of the keener draughts, the enamel beer jug on the table, the well-worn sofa and armchairs, and the men drifting in (those from distant colleges would be later), leaving overcoats and hats in any corner and coming over to warm their hands before finding a chair. There was no fixed etiquette, but the rudimentary honours would be done partly by Lewis and partly by his brother, W.H. Lewis, a man who stays in my memory as the most courteous I have ever met – not with mere politeness, but with a genial, self-forgetting

considerateness that was as instinctive to him as breathing. Sometimes, when the less vital members of the circle were in a big majority, the evening would fall flat; but the best of them were as good as anything I shall live to see.[24]

Lewis needed a group of like-minded friends around him. In those wartime years, it was the perfect place for him and his friends to explore devilry and other more joyous themes. The Inklings listened, sometimes with laughter, to readings from *The Screwtape Letters,* the "new Hobbit," *All Hallows Eve, The Great Divorce*, and other pieces featuring diabolical goings-on, heaven, unfallen planets, purgatorial suffering, fellowship, love, and the renunciation of power. Lewis grieved the loss of Charles Williams, and borrowed from his central themes in his future writings in loving tribute, just as his debt to Tolkien was to be evident in the world of Narnia and his 1956 novel, *Till We Have Faces,* one of his best pieces of writing.

12

A New Era and a Change of Strategy: The Narnia Factor

If success had been what Lewis was after, he had it all. His broadcast talks during the war, and the publication in particular of *The Screwtape Letters,* had made him perhaps the highest profile Christian communicator of his time in Britain. His fame was soon going to spread to the USA. A reporter from *Time* magazine had been in Oxford in 1944 researching a feature on him, interviewing, among others of his friends, Charles Williams. That story eventually appeared as a cover feature on 8 September 1947, taking as its angle *The Screwtape Letters,* and entitled "Don v. Devil". The writer was unable to fathom the mystery of Lewis's domestic situation with Mrs Moore, no doubt because of the silence of his friends. From that point, Lewis's popularity in the United States took off, and has been higher there than in his own country ever since.

Lewis had long ago left behind his ambition to be a great poet, but was very aware of the effectiveness of his books in helping to communicate Christian faith to modern readers. The broadcast talks and his visits to RAF stations in wartime had helped him also to gauge what he could do as a popular rather than academic lecturer. But an experiment that was much closer to his heart, allowing him to directly engage with those who did not believe, was the Oxford University Socratic Club, which had begun in the war years and which he continued to support with gusto when the war was over. His experiences with the club helped him to continue to develop as a Christian communicator, honing his skills, but also enabled him to take a different course in his writing outside of his literary studies (he was still slowly and relentlessly making his way through the unfolding chapters of his magisterial *English Literature in the Sixteenth Century, Excluding Drama*). The club had a greatly different scale to the large audiences of his BBC and RAF talks, which was very much to his liking. It gave him the chance to interact much more personally with both his opponents and his supporters.

The Socratic Club was started in 1941 by Estelle "Stella" Aldwinkle, a pastoral worker among students, and was attached to St Aldate's Church in Oxford. The Greek philosopher Socrates had in ancient times taught the principle of following the argument wherever it led you, and Stella Aldwinkle created the club to apply Socrates' principle, in Lewis's words, to the "*pros* and *cons* of the Christian religion". Chaired by Aldwinkle, the club discussed questions about Christian faith raised by atheists, agnostics, and those disillusioned about religion. Lewis served as president, at her request, until he took up a professorship at Cambridge in late 1954. Its committee would scrutinize the pages of *Who's Who* to find intelligent atheists who might have the time or the zeal to come and present their creed. A.J. Ayer, Antony Flew, and Gilbert Ryle (a don at Lewis's college, Magdalen) were among outstanding philosophers who addressed the club.

One meeting early on the club's life was recalled by Helen Tyrrell Wheeler, a wartime student of Lewis's:

> I have a strong visual memory of these evenings, always associated with lamplight inside and total blackout without, of a big sprawling comfortable room with as many people sitting on the floor as in the old-fashioned immense armchairs and

C.S. Lewis hurrying over Magdalen Bridge from his rooms to preside. He always established an immense, though rather impersonal, geniality and with his bright eyes and ruddy farmer's cheeks looked not unlike a medieval illustration of a fiery seraphim, though dressed in decent academic black.[1]

Ian Davie also remembered Lewis from the Socratic Club as being like a "jolly farmer... a ruddy, back-slapping type".[2]

The Socratic Club met every week when term was running. Usually there were two speakers, one to read a paper and the other to respond, followed by open discussion. Very often it was Lewis who responded to the opening speaker. He also contributed the lead paper from time to time. Charles Williams, Dr Humphrey Havard, and other friends of Lewis gave papers that were sufficiently controversial to draw a crowd, such as Williams on free love. When he spoke on "Are There Any Valid Objections to Free Love?" to the club on 2 March 1942, the lecture hall was full. Lewis in the chair stated, after the ensuing discussion wandered here and there, that the meeting had to make up its mind whether it wanted to discuss the habits of bees or those of humans.

Afterwards, as was his custom, he invited several of his students and two or three others, back to his college rooms for conversation and a drink. This time Derek Brewer, a current student, was invited with others to meet Charles Williams. Williams, Brewer noted, was wearing an elderly blue suit and, while he was talking with vigour, flicked cigarette ash all over his waistcoat. During the conversation, Lewis and Williams were in agreement that one can no more avoid pleasure than pain in this life. Lewis then, with pleasure, pulled out his copy of Williams's *Taliessin Through Logres* from his shelves and encouraged the poet to read from it. Williams performed this request with zest.[3]

During the Socratic Club meetings, Lewis's wit was always ready. On one occasion, when as usual he was in the chair, someone very much taken up with the new analytical philosophy asked, during the discussion time, "How can you prove anything? I mean, how can you prove there is not a blue cow sitting on that piano?" Lewis responded, "In what sense blue?"

A debate that Lewis had with Cambridge philosopher Elizabeth Anscombe, who had studied under the influential philosopher Ludwig Wittgenstein, is often interpreted as being responsible for a defeat that led Lewis into serious doubt about his whole approach to the intellectual defence of Christian faith. Anscombe's paper, however, simply aimed to clarify and to bring out some confusion in an argument Lewis had used in chapter 3 of his book *Miracles*. There, he had held that a naturalist (materialist) position was self-refuting. Lewis did acknowledge afterwards that he was unclear in his argument, but neither he nor Anscombe regarded it as anything less than essentially robust.

In response to the debate, Lewis rewrote the chapter, clarifying it for a later edition. Philosophers over the years since that debate have worked over Lewis's basic and rather elegant argument and found that it had considerable staying power.[4]

Rather than destroying Lewis's confidence, and forcing him to turn away from an intellectual defence of Christianity, what he did eventually acknowledge was that philosophy had become increasingly specialized and analytical. He did not object to such analysis, but felt that if he tried to continue in that more and more rarefied world, he would only be communicating with a smaller and smaller audience. He increasingly felt that his calling was to a broader readership.

After this realization, he took a much more indirect approach to Christian communication. He followed in the spirit, even if not in the letter, of his friend Tolkien, who was content to write *The Lord of the Rings* without a single mention of God. Yet the book is shot through with divine providence and other theological elements. This allusiveness applied to further works of lay theology that Lewis wrote, such as *The Four Loves* (1960) and even more so, *Letters to Malcolm: Chiefly on Prayer* (1964).

It is true that for a while at the end of the forties, Lewis expected his books to fall into a quiet obscurity, as he explained to a generous American called Dr Warfield M. Firor, who supplied him with food parcels during the years of post-war austerity: "I am going to be (if I live long enough) one of those men who *was* a famous writer in his forties and dies unknown – like Christian going down into the green valley of humiliation."[5]

This quiet humbling was not required for very long. With burgeoning interest in the USA in his writings, and the success of his annually appearing stories of Narnia for children, he realized that he had an important opportunity to seize. The course he decided to take had its seeds in the coin-tossing many years before with Tolkien, when they had agreed that the world needed more of the kind of books they liked to read. Later, Lewis had reckoned that, in his make-up, what he called the "imaginative man" was the most basic part of him.[6]

Lewis expressed his sense of a calling to a new direction in his writing in a letter. One of the most gifted and intelligent evangelicals after the war, Carl F.H. Henry, wrote to Lewis in 1955 asking him to contribute to a new monthly magazine he was setting up as editor, called *Christianity Today,* and aiming to provide thoughtful theological comment on society and culture, with a strong literary quality.

Lewis, who would soon meet and like the evangelist Billy Graham, when he ran a university mission in Cambridge in November that year, replied thoughtfully and respectfully:

My thought and talent (such as they are) now flow in different, though I think not less Christian, channels, and I do not think I am at all likely to write more *directly* theological pieces.... If I am now good for anything it is for catching the reader unawares – thro' fiction and symbol. I have done what I could in the way of frontal attacks, but now feel quite sure those days are over.[7]

Perhaps another seed for this momentous decision by Lewis had been planted nearly ten years before when he and Warnie, the year after the war, had travelled to the University of St Andrews on the east coast of Scotland. There Lewis was made a Doctor of Divinity on 28 June 1946, a rare honour for a layman. As their train crossed into Scotland, Warnie recorded later in his diary, after "miserable, hungry England" here they have "real porridge, of which I had almost forgotten the taste, plenty of butter, edible sausages, toast, marmalade, coffee!"[8] But it was some words expressed at the degree ceremony by Professor D.M. Baillie, Dean of the Faculty of Divinity, that were truly remarkable:

> With his pen and with his voice on the radio Mr Lewis has succeeded in capturing the attention of many who will not readily listen to professional theologians, and has taught them many lessons concerning the deep things of God.... In recent years Mr Lewis has arranged a new kind of marriage between theological reflection and poetic imagination, and this fruitful union is now producing works which are difficult to classify in any literary genre: it can only be said in respectful admiration that he pursues "things unattempted yet in prose or rhyme".[9]

Even if not a seed, these words may have helped Lewis to clarify thoughts he was already harbouring about future ventures.

The visit to St Andrews with Warnie had been one of a few bright spots in the years after the war. This period was marked by the steady decline of Mrs Moore, both physical and mental, which meant many curtailments of their activities. One casualty was the annual walking tour, which was an event both looked forward to. It was difficult for Lewis, in fact, to find any respite from the rising level of care that Minto required, leaving him increasingly exhausted. Immediately after the war, food rationing was still severe, and there were fuel shortages. Indeed, Lewis was forced at times in college to wear a dressing gown over his indoor clothes to keep warm. Yet, despite the pressures, he continued writing literary scholarship, popular theology, and fiction.

Maureen (now Mrs Maureen Blake) came to the rescue with brief respites, when she could, by offering her expansive house in Malvern to Lewis and Warnie while she and her husband stayed in The Kilns to care for her mother. Maureen's husband, Leonard, taught music at Malvern College and the setting of their home, 4 The Lees, was familiar to Lewis and his brother from their schooldays. Sometimes Tolkien and other friends such as Hugo Dyson would join the brothers in Malvern, and walk, as well as enjoy favourite local pubs, including the Unicorn. They might be joined by George Sayer, a friend and former student of Lewis's, who was teaching English at Malvern.

On the domestic front, 1947 was a difficult year for Lewis, as life at The Kilns became more and more fraught. It became difficult, if not impossible, to retain maids under Mrs Moore's increasingly unreasonable rule. From one day to the next, Lewis wrote, he did not know when he could pull back from his duties "as a nurse and a domestic servant". He explained in that same letter that "there are psychological as well as material difficulties in my home".[10]

An additional burden were Warnie's increasing bouts of drinking, a symptom of his creeping alcoholism, a condition that distressed Lewis considerably. In June that year, Lewis was forced to leave Mrs Moore and travel to Drogheda, in the Irish Republic, where his brother had been taken seriously ill through alcohol misuse.

A further burden was the aging family dog, Bruce, to which Mrs Moore clung tenaciously. It was a relief to the brothers when he died in his dotage early in 1950. In his diary, Warnie recalled some of the dog's worse traits. Bruce would sometimes bark incessantly all night, and then, while he dozed during the day, Mrs Moore would order the "boys" (Lewis and Warnie) to make no noise in case they woke him. The elderly dog also suffered from incontinence, relieving himself in her "overheated" bedroom, stinking out the house. It was an ordeal to walk near the room because of the overpowering stench.

Three months later, the crisis in The Kilns household escalated. Mrs Moore had been semi-paralyzed for some time, requiring her to be watched almost permanently. Then, one night, she fell out of bed three times. There was no option but for Minto to be admitted to a nursing home.

At Restholme, in Oxford's Woodstock Road, first reports within hours from a Sister Haydon complained of Mrs Moore's "very strong language". Minto demanded to know when she would be able to get out of her hellish prison. Lewis was a frequent visitor for the next eight months until Mrs Moore died, on Friday 12 January 1951.

A couple of days after her burial in the parish church the Lewis brothers attended — Holy Trinity, Headington Quarry — Warnie bitterly wrote in his diary: "And so ends the mysterious self imposed slavery in which J[ack] has lived for at least thirty years."[11]

Release from his obligations to his adopted mother was a further element of change for Lewis at this period. His shift of direction towards more indirect and allusive communication of Christian theology was no more evident than in his starting to write the first of *The Chronicles of Narnia*. This was just two years after the publication of one of the best of his overtly theological books, *Miracles,* in 1947. Even that was not couched in the specialist language of theology or philosophy, though it had much to contribute to both disciplines. The book was directly aimed at thoughtful lay people for whom the question of miracles was real. It compared the very different perspectives of a materialist (or naturalist) view and one that was supernaturalist. This prepared the ground, Lewis argued, for properly considering the New Testament miracles.

The Lion, the Witch and the Wardrobe, Lewis's first Narnian story, began with a vivid mental picture of a faun in a snowy wood carrying a parcel — the image that had first come to him when he was a young man. A further ingredient in the soup of his sources was the landscapes of his childhood. These included the Mourne Mountains of County Down, the green countryside at their north-eastern feet and beyond, with its drumlins and undulating fields and woods, and the wild, bleak moors and rugged coastline of

County Antrim. These were Narnia and its environs. Significantly, on an occasion when he longed to visit Northern Ireland, but was confined by the declining health of Mrs Moore, he spoke in a letter of Ulster as his "ain countrie", thinking of the hills of County Down and the coastline of County Antrim.

In the summer of 1948, Lewis had remarked vaguely to a visiting American writer, Chad Walsh, about "completing a children's book he has begun 'in the tradition of E. Nesbit'". Walsh was researching for a book on C.S. Lewis. [12] At some point, Aslan, the creator-lion, had come bounding into the fledgling story, transforming it. Soon after Walsh's visit, Lewis read several chapters of the new story to Tolkien. To his intense disappointment, his friend did not like it. Lewis's imagination was very different from Tolkien's, which was more tightly focused. Lewis was eclectic in his storytelling, picking up elements from here and there in ancient mythology, and always willing to borrow from modern or any other symbolism. With his consistent mind, Tolkien felt it an error to have dryads and nymphs in the same story as Father Christmas. In any case, the latter was a Christian element, and the other magical creatures belonged to pre-Christian paganism.

Lewis had befriended a former student and writer, Roger Lancelyn Green, who had prepared a thesis under the direction of Tolkien on Andrew Lang, the scholar and storyteller, later published. Lewis decided to show him some chapters from his work in progress on *The Lion, the Witch and the Wardrobe*. He had recognized Green's already formidable knowledge of children's literature. It had partly been through reading Green's story "The Wood that Time Forgot" (never published) that Lewis had been inspired to start writing a Narnia story.

By this time, the reading sessions of the Inklings had floundered, but the Tuesday morning pub sessions were still alive and well. Green attended these when he could, and Lewis was in the habit of meeting him in his college rooms at Magdalen, or elsewhere. When Green was told about the children's book Lewis was writing, he was also informed about how Tolkien had disliked it.

Lewis said he wasn't sure if it was any good, and asked Green if he could read some of it to him.

In his rooms at Magdalen College, Lewis read to him the first three chapters. As the young man listened, a feeling of awe possessed him; he believed he was listening for the first time to one of the great children's books. He had read such books widely for his thesis and for a study he had published, *Tellers of Tales,* about the tradition of children's literature, a book admired by Lewis. It was rather like hearing a book such as *The Wind in the Willows* read to him by its author for the first time.

When Lewis asked Green's verdict, he replied that he must go on with it. Shortly after that meeting, Lewis handed Green a manuscript, the first of the series of Narnian stories he was to read in that form. Green would give both positive and negative criticism, to which Lewis responded. He also came up with the generic title, *The Chronicles of Narnia,* but was unable to get Lewis to remove Father Christmas from the story; he agreed with Tolkien on this. Lewis has proved to be right in retaining him, however. Michael Ward, for instance, has powerfully pointed out the logic of including him.[13]

One of Tolkien's main objections to Lewis's Narnian stories was that they were too allegorical: that is, too literally representative of Christian doctrine. Though Lewis did insert many Christian pointers in the stories, his intention was not to write allegory. In fact, he did not expect the pointers to be registered by readers unless they already knew the Christian story, and had flashes of recognition.

His working assumption was, in fact, that his contemporaries, especially children, had a poor knowledge of even basic Christian teaching. Instead of being didactic, he saw the Narnian stories as arising out of what he called a "supposal" – his "supposal" was a world of talking animals – that set the frame of the stories. *What if* there was a world created by a talking animal, the king of the beasts, who was also divine? What would this world be like? What might happen in it? He explained his reasoning in a letter shortly before his death:

The Narnian series is not exactly allegory. I'm not saying "Let us represent in terms of Märchen [fairy tale] the *actual* story of this world." Rather "Supposing the Narnian world, let us guess what form the activities of the Second Person or Creator, Redeemer, and Judge might take there." This, you see, overlaps with allegory but is not quite the same.[14]

When Lewis had written *The Lion, the Witch and the Wardrobe* he began a "prequel" to it, which was eventually titled *The Magician's Nephew*. Its writing, however, did not come easily. Lewis needed to explore and, to some extent, explain his "supposal" of a land of talking animals, ruled by a divine king of the beasts, into which humans (Sons of Adam and Daughters of Eve) could come through portals, or be called from their world. What was the origin of Narnia? How was it that there was a lantern in the woods to the far west?

The Magician's Nephew was in fact eventually to be the sixth, not the second, Narnian tale that he wrote, because of the difficulties that he experienced. The immediate predecessor to *The Lion, the Witch and the Wardrobe* that he had started had to be abandoned. The fragment survived in one of Lewis's notebooks, instead of being thrown into a bin. Roger Lancelyn Green, his sympathetic critic, had helped him to see the flaws in its conception.

One reason "The Le Fay Fragment", as it has since been called by scholars, was soon abandoned is that the magic at work in it was in this rather than in another world. It is an intriguing fragment, hauntingly evoking the original fall of humanity.

In it, Digory has the gift of understanding the speech of trees and animals, but loses it forever when he cuts off a branch of his favourite oak tree to impress Polly. Digory is bereft when he discovers the truth:

> The only life he had ever known was a life in which you could talk to animals and trees. If that was to come to an end the world would be so different for him that he would be a complete stranger in it.

Lewis finally alluded to the fall of human beings in what became *The Magician's Nephew*, where the nephew, Digory, stubbornly fails to resist striking a bell in the world of Charn, with terrible consequences for the new world of Narnia.

The Lion, the Witch and the Wardrobe appeared in 1950. Lewis had completed the writing of *Prince Caspian* by the end of 1949, *The Voyage of the "Dawn Treader"* soon after, and *The Horse and His Boy* by summer the next year. Within a few months, he had written most of *The Silver Chair*. He then returned to the origins of Narnia, completing about three-quarters of *The Magician's Nephew*. Roger Lancelyn Green, to whom Lewis was showing all the writing, pointed out a structural problem, and Lewis set aside the writing for a while. In the meantime, he was taken up with work on his huge volume *English Literature in the Sixteenth Century*, a period that he particularly loved and that he drew upon in creating the world of Narnia.

The task of writing that academic study was so great that he was forced to take a year's sabbatical to work on it. His college granted him leave from his duties and teaching, extending from October 1951 to October 1952. He then turned to writing *The Last Battle*, leaving aside the problems of *The Magician's Nephew* for the time being, finishing it in the spring of 1953. After this, Lewis completed *The Magician's Nephew*, which Green heartily endorsed in February 1954, noting in his diary: "It seems the best of the lot.... It's a single unity now, and irresistibly gripping and compelling."

The Last Battle was scheduled as the final book to be published, appearing in 1956. It won the prestigious literary award the Carnegie Medal, in recognition of the whole series. Lewis's change of strategy, turning to imaginative writing, firmly underpinned by orthodox Christian belief, was paying off. The books were being received by a very wide readership. Lewis's postbag was getting larger and larger, as child readers wrote to him, along with numerous adult readers of other books, such as *The Screwtape Letters*.

Though the Narnia stories were by then a great success, he had no idea how their readership would continue to rise and rise in the ensuing years. It is estimated that total sales of books in *The Chronicles of Narnia* are at least 120 million.[15] Sales of *The Lion, the Witch and the Wardrobe* alone are estimated at more than 85 million.[16]

The seven stories that make up *The Chronicles of Narnia* take place over about the first half of the twentieth century, and over two and a half millennia of Narnian history from its creation to its final days. Because of anomalies in time, the children who are drawn into Narnia on a number of occasions find themselves at various points in its history, and thus we get a picture of the entire history of Narnia from its creation to its unmaking and the new creation of all worlds.

In order of Narnian chronology, the titles are: *The Magician's Nephew*; *The Lion, the Witch and the Wardrobe*; *The Horse and His Boy*; *Prince Caspian: The Return to Narnia*; *The Voyage of the "Dawn Treader"*; *The Silver Chair*; and *The Last Battle*. Many readers prefer to start with *The Lion, the Witch and the Wardrobe* because of its simplicity, magical power, and for the way it sets up the basic "supposals" from which Lewis created all the stories and the world of Narnia.

Narnia's original creation is described in *The Magician's Nephew*. Digory Kirke and Polly Plummer, after entering the old and dying world of Charn through a pool in the Wood between the Worlds, find their way, seemingly by chance, into a land of Nothing. Here, gradually, Narnia is created before their eyes by the song of Aslan, the talking lion and ruler of Narnia.

Unfortunately, Digory brings evil into that paradise world in the form of Jadis, destroyer of Charn, whom he had previously awakened. Jadis goes off to the fringes of Narnia, but reappears in later ages as the White Witch who puts a spell over Narnia of a winter that never comes to Christmas. The arrival of four evacuee children – Peter, Susan, Edmund, and Lucy Pevensie – through the Wardrobe (told in *The Lion, the Witch and the Wardrobe*) coincides with the return of Aslan and the beginning of the end of the witch's curse. Aslan's death on behalf of Edmund, and his return to life by a deeper law than the one by which Jadis operates her magic, leads to her defeat and death. Narnia's Golden Age follows.

With the return of the Pevensie children to our world, Narnia slowly falls into disorder. The Telmarines, humans led by Caspian the First, occupy the land and silence the talking beasts and trees. (The Telmarines had stumbled by accident into Narnia through a portal from our world.) "Old Narnia" only survives under cover as those faithful to Aslan keep the faith alive that he will return. Prince Caspian (his story is told in the book of that name) has been brought up by his wicked Uncle Miraz and Aunt Prunaprismia, who have deposed his father, Caspian the Ninth. The young prince learns of the myth of Old Narnia and longs for it to be true. He escapes a plot to kill him and joins forces with the Old Narnians. In the nick of time, help comes from the four Pevensie children drawn back into Narnia. With the death of Uncle Miraz, the prince becomes Caspian the Tenth.

Caspian's adventures at sea are recounted in *The Voyage of the "Dawn Treader"*. After these adventures, he returns to Narnia. In time, his son, Prince Rilian, is kidnapped and held in servitude in an underworld for ten years by a witch of the line of Jadis. She plots to take over Narnia using him as a puppet king. As told in the story of *The Silver Chair*, he is rescued by a cousin of the Pevensie children, Eustace Scrubb, and his friend, Jill Pole, who are brought into Narnia for this task.

After many ages the last king of Narnia, Tirian, and indeed Narnia itself, are threatened by a devilish plot that uses a counterfeit Aslan, who links up with the Calormene forces (southerners who are a constant threat to Narnia's security). This is Narnia's darkest hour. As told in *The Last Battle*, Tirian prays for help from the Sons of Adam and Daughters of Eve, and Aslan brings Eustace and Jill to his aid. Aslan himself finally intervenes and dissolves the whole world. This turns out to be a beginning rather than an end as the new Narnia is revealed.

Aslan (Turkish for "lion") is the unifying symbol of all the stories. Aslan is intended to represent Christ, but not as an allegorical figure. In Narnia he appears not as a man but, appropriately, as a Narnian talking lion. The symbol of the lion (a traditional image of authority), as we saw, perhaps owes something to Charles Williams's novel *The Place of the Lion*. In his *The Problem of Pain*, Lewis wrote: "I think the lion, when he has ceased to be dangerous, will still be awful."

Avoiding religious language, and specific reference to biblical history, Lewis in the Narnian stories demonstrates the distinctive and real nature of God in the magical figure of Aslan, who is elusive yet definite, wild, surprising, and always shaping events his way, even when all seems dark and lost. Lewis balances Aslan's wildness and terrifying nature perfectly with his approachability, beauty, and gentleness. In *The Lion, the Witch and the Wardrobe*, Lucy and Susan do something that they never would have dared to do without his permission. They sink their cold hands into the sea of his beautiful mane to comfort him. After he returns to life, he dances with them, and afterwards Lucy can't make up her mind whether it was like playing with a thunderstorm or with a kitten.

13

The Surprising American:
Mrs Joy Davidman Gresham

On Tuesday 10 January 1950, Lewis received a letter from Mrs
Helen Joy Davidman Gresham. She was a 34-year-old novelist and
poet who had won an impressive literary award and wrote under
her maiden name of Joy Davidman. It was thus, in that day's usual
large pile of unsolicited letters, that Joy entered Lewis's life. Nearly
six years later, Warnie noted in his diary that, before that day:

> neither of us had ever heard of her, then she appeared in
> the mail as just another American fan, Mrs W.L. Gresham
> from the neighbourhood of New York. With, however, the
> difference that she stood out from the ruck by her amusing
> and well-written letters, and soon J[ack] and she had become
> "pen-friends".[1]

On that day, Lewis, like his brother, was a confirmed bachelor still
living with and caring for Mrs Moore.

A little over two weeks after that letter dropped through the
letterbox at The Kilns, Joy wrote to her friend Chad Walsh (the
same Chad Walsh who had visited Lewis in England, and written
the first study of him):

> Just got a letter from Lewis in the mail. I think I told you
> I'd raised an argument or two on some points? Lord, he
> knocked my props out from under me unerringly; one shot to
> a pigeon. I haven't a scrap of my case left. And, what's more,
> I've seldom enjoyed anything more....[2]

In Lewis's adolescence, his friendship with Arthur Greeves was of dominant importance. It could be said that there was a similar importance to his friendship with Barfield, particularly in the 1920s, to J.R.R. Tolkien, especially in the late twenties and the thirties, and to Charles Williams in the Second World War years. Lewis's friendship with Joy Davidman was certainly of comparable importance to his life in the 1950s, up to her early death in July 1960 and beyond. In the case of the others, he continued to meet up with Barfield, Tolkien, and Arthur; his friendships with them continuing throughout his life, and Williams, though gone, remained, like Barfield and Tolkien, a strong influence on his thought and some of his writings.

Joy was not only to be an iconoclast in his life, but also to be a significant influence on his writings, from the point their friendship was established and then deepened into marriage. The story of their relationship has, of course, famously been told in the BBC television film *Shadowlands* (1985), scripted by William Nicholson and directed by Norman Stone, and then in a worldwide version of the same, directed by Sir Richard Attenborough (1993). It was also adapted for the stage (1989).[3]

Joy Davidman was a New Yorker and Jewish, but grew up in an agnostic household (her father was an atheist and her mother remained a nominal Jew). She was of medium height, with alert brown eyes, dark hair, and an arresting complexion. Ideas were more important to her than social niceties. After seeing a starving young woman throw herself off a building in the despairing days of the Great Depression, she became politically aware and turned to the Communist Party. There she was a devout member, involved in the publication of the Communist periodical *New Masses*. She later described her worldview as: "Life is only an electrochemical reaction. Love, art, and altruism are only sex. The universe is only matter. Matter is only energy. I forget what I said energy is only." She married another writer, Bill Gresham, a Gentile whom she genuinely loved. From before she met him, Bill was fighting to make ends meet, and supplemented his meagre earning from writing by folk singing in Greenwich Village. He wrote both novels and screenplays. Bill had been married before, and had fought against Franco in the Spanish Civil War.

After giving birth to two sons, David in 1944 and Douglas in 1945, Joy found herself struggling not only with motherhood but also over Bill's unstable drinking and compulsive unfaithfulness. As a young child, Douglas remembered his father as warm and affectionate, but also, on one occasion, breaking a bottle over his head in a drunken rage.

Joy slowly learned to protect her fundamental shyness behind an often abrasive outward persona. She eventually converted from Marxism to Christianity, in which reading Lewis's books played an important part. However, her ultimate turning point was a strange experience, at a time of extreme crisis in early spring 1946. In later years, she shared the experience with Lewis, whose own gradual conversion from atheism to theism to Christianity had been accompanied by similar mystical theophanies, though not as direct as Joy's:

> There was a Person with me in that room, directly present
> to my consciousness – a Person so real that all my precious
> life was by comparison a mere shadow play. And I myself was
> more alive than I had ever been...[4]

Lewis's attraction to Joy was at first merely intellectual. The letter received on 10 January was the first of many, for they began to correspond regularly. Lewis, then in his early fifties, met her for the first time during the autumn of 1952; Joy had come for a visit to England, in part to recover from a serious illness, but expressly with the purpose of meeting the writer and, in effect, spiritual guide to whom she felt she owed so much. Warnie was present at a second meeting soon after in Magdalen College, and both brothers were taken with her. Warnie particularly enjoyed her uninhibited New York manner. He records in his diary that she turned to him, in the presence of three or four men, and "asked in the most natural tone in the world, 'Is there anywhere in this monastic establishment where a lady can relieve herself?'"[5]

After a period back in New York State, and with her marriage falling apart, Joy Davidman came to live in London with her sons, firstly in pleasant Swiss Cottage, near Hampstead Heath, and eventually in Oxford, near Lewis. She and Bill Gresham had by then agreed a trial separation, after he had struck up an intense relationship with Joy's cousin, Renée Rodriguez, following an abandoned attempt to live soberly and to practice a newfound Christian faith. On 5 August 1954, after a quick divorce, Bill Gresham married Renée.

Douglas and David were soon familiar with The Kilns and its extensive grounds. Lewis was amazed at the energy of the young American boys, and Douglas was astonished at the mismatch between his mental picture of the author of Narnia and the actuality. He was eight and his brother David nine when they arrived at The Kilns for a four-day stay.

Douglas heard a booming voice, which his mother indicated belonged to Jack Lewis, and then was presented with "a slightly stooped, round-shouldered, balding gentleman whose full smiling mouth revealed long, prominent teeth, yellowed, like those of some large rodent, by tobacco staining". His clothing, too, surprised Douglas. He was not wearing shining armour, like a knight of old, as befitted the maker of the Narnia stories, but a shabby tweed jacket, baggy flannel trousers, and a shirt that was clean but had once been white. The boy, however, was taken by Jack's face. "His florid and rather large face was lit as if from within with the warmth of his interest and his welcome. I never knew a man whose face was more expressive of the vitality of his person."[6]

As Joy Davidman and her sons were getting to know Lewis by travelling from London to Oxford to see him, his attention became focused upon a new Chair of Medieval and Renaissance literature being offered in Cambridge, over eighty miles to the east of Oxford. After almost thirty years teaching at Magdalen College, he had had no promotion. Though he was one of the most popular lecturers in Oxford, and outstanding even among his peers, he had been passed over for professorships at Oxford several times. This frustrated Tolkien, who wished him to have an Oxford English chair. Tolkien, however, was one of the electors to the new Cambridge chair, and eventually persuaded Lewis to accept the post.[7]

Lewis is most commonly associated in people's minds with Oxford – he was an undergraduate of University College, he was a fellow of Magdalen College for nearly thirty years; together with Tolkien he helped shape the curriculum of the Oxford Final Honours English School, most of his academic publications were written there, and he was the life and soul of the Oxford Inklings. He was, however, to be closely associated with Cambridge University for nearly eight years, from late 1954 until his early retirement due to ill health in 1963.

During those years he resided in his Cambridge college – also named after Mary Magdalen – part of the week during termtime, while continuing to live at The Kilns. He would publish several important books at Cambridge – *Studies in Words* (1960), *An Experiment in Criticism* (1961), and *The Discarded Image* (1964). Also of significance are the Cambridge publications *Studies in Medieval and Renaissance Literature* (1966), *Selected Literary Essays* (1969), and *Spenser's Images of Life* (1967) – the latter reconstructed from Lewis's extensive lecture notes.

For the critic and novelist David Lodge, Lewis's literary criticism

shows a remarkable range of interest and expertise...
C.S. Lewis in many ways represented the "Oxford" tradition of literary criticism at its best: relaxed, knowledgeable,

enthusiastic, conservative.... It is clear that he regarded the study of literature as primarily a historical one, and its justification as the conservation of the past. *De Descriptione Temporum* [Lewis's inaugural lecture at Cambridge] expresses eloquently, learnedly and wittily this conception of the subject and Lewis's doubts about its viability in the future.[8]

However, Lewis was not simply a literary historian. His historical work mainly had a double purpose: to shed light on the textual meaning of old works of literature, and to value such books as remarkable windows into a previous world of understanding. His primary focus was always the individual text, his secondary focus the historical context.

Lewis's inaugural lecture on 29 November 1954 – his fifty-sixth birthday – gave him a platform on which to set out a defence of "Old Western values" that he had championed in his work. It was a rip-roaring start to his Cambridge career; in contrast, his later Cambridge publications would be more low-key, though powerfully reinforcing the values he championed in his boisterous lecture.

The lecture revealed Lewis's sympathies with an earlier age. He recognized that his assumptions and ideas were distasteful to many modern people. He argued that he was in fact a relic of the Old Western Man, a museum piece, if you like; that even if one disagreed with his ideas, one must take account of them as being from a rare (and therefore valuable) specimen of an older world.

In the lecture, Lewis argued that the greatest change in the history of the West took place early in the nineteenth century, and ushered in a characteristically modern mentality.[9] Because of this, Christians and ancient pagans have more in common with each other than either has with the intellectual climate of the modern world. The change can be observed in the areas of politics, the arts, religion, and the birth of the machines. The machine, argued Lewis, had in fact been absorbed into the inner life of modern people as an archetype. Just as older machines are replaced by new and better ones, so too (believes the modern) are ideas, beliefs, and values. This notion that newer is better, the myth of progress, owes much the "the myth of universal evolutionism", which in fact predated Darwin.

The theme of this lecture is actually illustrated in his earlier books, the long essay *The Abolition of Man* (1943), and the science fiction story *That Hideous Strength* (1945).

Joy Davidman was in Cambridge for the occasion. Her presence at that historic lecture was a further indication of her desire to be close to Lewis. She described Lewis's talk to Chad Walsh, in a letter, as

> ... brilliant, intellectually exciting, unexpected, and funny as hell – as you can imagine. The hall was crowded, and there were so many capped and gowned dons in the front rows that they looked like a rookery. Instead of talking in the usual professorial way about the continuity of culture, the value of traditions, etc., he announced that "Old Western Culture", as he called it, was practically dead, leaving only a few scattered survivors like himself... How that man loves being in a minority, even a lost-cause minority! Athanasius contra mundum, or Don Quixote against the windmills. He talked blandly of "post-Christian Europe", which I thought rather previous of him. I sometimes wonder what he would do if Christianity really did triumph everywhere; I suppose he would have to invent a new heresy.[10]

The lecture is full of the flavour of Lewis's bold rhetoric, as when he provocatively claimed:

> Roughly speaking we may say that whereas all history was for our ancestors divided into two periods, the pre-Christian and the Christian, and two only, for us it falls into three – the pre-Christian, the Christian, and what may reasonably be called the post-Christian....[11]

The change, he said, altered the very position of human beings in nature.

Many in Cambridge, not surprisingly, did not like the lecture, or the new professor. They interpreted Lewis's words as a reactionary attempt to restore a lost Christendom, and responded immediately. An entire issue of *Twentieth Century*, in February 1955, focused upon the disastrous developments at Cambridge, heralded by Lewis's lecture. The editorial proclaimed that its twelve contributors, from a variety of disciplines, agreed "on the importance of free liberal, humane inquiry, which they conceive to be proper not only to a university community but to any group that claims to be civilized".

Novelist E.M. Forster, one of the contributors, saw humanism threatened and religion on the march. Humanism's "stronghold in history, the Renaissance, is alleged not to have existed". Now that Lewis had blown the trumpet, they feared, the walls of humanism might fall. Such fears of a crusade against humanism and the Enlightenment were reinforced later in the year with a prominent visit of evangelist Billy Graham to the Cambridge University mission run by the CICCU (Cambridge Inter-Collegiate Christian Union). Graham and Lewis met, and found that they liked each other very much.

Between Friday 18 and Sunday 20 March 1955, Joy spent the weekend at The Kilns with Lewis and Warnie, while David and Douglas were away at boarding school. While there, she had a significant impact on the development of *Till We Have Faces,* a story that Lewis had started many times before and got stuck in the telling.

Upon her arrival, she found Lewis "lamenting that he couldn't get a good idea for a book". The three friends sank into comfortable chairs and kicked "a few ideas around" until one emerged. They then had "another whisky each" and bounced the story concept back and forth. The very next day Lewis wrote the first chapter, and passed it to Joy to comment on. Lewis then worked over it and moved on to a second chapter. He admitted to Joy that he found her help on it indispensable. She in turn felt that though she could not write "one-tenth as well as Jack", she could "tell him how to write more like himself".[12]

Just as much of Lewis's last science fiction volume in the Ransom trilogy, *That Hideous Strength,* was influenced particularly by Charles Williams, it could be said that *Till We Have Faces* clearly bears the impression of Joy Davidman. She was a skilful novelist, author of *Anya* (1940) and *Weeping Bay* (1950). Lewis, likely enough, owed his confidence in writing the story from a female perspective to Joy. Like Orual in the novel, Joy, too, had an epiphany that turned her view of the world upside down.

On first reading, it hardly seems like a work by Lewis at all, though subsequent readings show it is full of his themes. It is also the work of Lewis's with most affinity with his friend Tolkien, and his tales of Middle-earth. This is because of its setting in a pre-Christian, pagan world, where it explores anticipations of the Christian story in ancient myth. Thus, in one book, which Lewis regarded as a work of his maturity, there is a debt to several close friends. It is quite easy to go further, and to see the underlying influence of Owen Barfield as well, with his emphasis upon knowledge of reality coming through the play of imagination.

Lewis, in both his life and his writings, was very much concerned with the problem of self-centredness. He saw the choice of self over others and over God as at the root of what is wrong with the world. He saw affection as very basic to what holds humans together, and felt that affection gone wrong can be a particularly painful example of self-centredness. He constantly explored the virtues and dangers of affection in his fiction, as well as elsewhere, as in his broadcast talks and book *The Four Loves*. In *The Great Divorce*, for example, the ghost of a mother still desires to possess her son after death. In the novel *Till We Have Faces*, the deep affection Queen Orual feels for her sister, Psyche, turns into a destructive possessiveness that she cannot distinguish from love.

Till We Have Faces: A Myth Retold was published in 1956, the year of Lewis's civil wedding with Joy. The book, fittingly, is dedicated

"To Joy Davidman". In it he retells an old classical myth, that of Cupid and Psyche, one that had haunted him for very many years.

Lewis took the myth from Apuleius's second-century *The Golden Ass*. In Apuleius's story, Psyche is so beautiful that Venus becomes jealous of her. Cupid, sent by Venus to make Psyche fall in love with an ugly creature, falls in love with her himself. After bringing her to a palace, he only visits her in the dark, and forbids her to see his face. Out of jealousy, Psyche's sisters tell her that her lover is a monster who will devour her. She takes a lamp one night and looks at Cupid's face, but he wakes up. In anger, the god leaves her. Psyche seeks her lover throughout the world. Venus sets her various impossible tasks, all of which she accomplishes except the last, when curiosity makes her open a deadly casket from the underworld. At last, however, she is allowed to marry Cupid.

Lewis essentially follows the classical myth, but retells it through the eyes of Orual, Psyche's half-sister, who seeks to defend her protective actions to the gods as being the result of deep love for Psyche, not jealousy. He makes some subtle and effective changes to the classical story, an important one being Orual's fleeting glimpse of Psyche's palace in the mists of a high mountain. He also makes much of the idea of Psyche as a sacrificial victim given to the god of the mountain. Lewis casts the myth in the setting of a historical novel, several hundred years BC.

Till We Have Faces is unlike Lewis's other fiction, and is consequently less easy to interpret. It in fact repays several readings. One key to the novel (it has several rich layers of meaning) is the theme of love. Orual's crippling self-centredness takes the form of possessive love, distorting what it should have been. Only as she steps out of the prison of her selfish obsessions is Orual able to be truly herself, and able to love her sister. She is also able to see past distorted images to the beauty of God, the vision Psyche had followed.

In a letter to Clyde S. Kilby, Lewis explained that Psyche represents a Christ-likeness, though she is not intended as a figure of Christ. Psyche is able to see a glimpse of the true God, in all his beauty, and in his legitimate demand for a perfect sacrifice. Princess Psyche in Lewis's story is prepared to die for the sake of the people of Glome. Lewis explained in a letter to Clyde S. Kilby that Psyche was intended as an example of the *anima naturaliter Christiana* (that is, "a soul that is naturally Christian").[13] Psyche made the best of the limitations of the pagan religion of her upbringing. The pagan insights guided her towards the true God – but within the restrictions of her own imagination, and that of her culture.

The moment of sudden recognition for Orual in Lewis's story results in a new perception of events, and perhaps even of reality itself. This recognition is what Lewis called "undeception". This is a theme that runs through his writings. The shattering of Orual's self-centredness, and the change from possessive to wholesome love, is perhaps Lewis's most sustained treatment of deception and its removal. In his stories, the road out of the self almost always requires such recognition of deception. His hope is that in some way the reader will undergo some change of perception for the better.

After the weekend at The Kilns, when Joy had been able to help Lewis with ideas for *Till We Have Faces,* Joy and he were soon very much closer, both in their developing relationship and geographically. She and the boys moved to Headington, with Lewis's financial assistance. After the move, he and Joy were before long meeting daily. Joy's rented house, 10 Old High Street, was only about a mile from The Kilns. Within weeks of the move, Lewis told Arthur Greeves while holidaying with him in Ireland in September that he was thinking of marrying Joy in a civil ceremony only.[14]

They married the following year, at the Oxford Registry Office on 23 April 1956 solely with the purpose of giving Joy British nationality, to prevent her having to leave the country. It was to be a civil marriage only, to meet the requirements of the law for living in the UK. It would mean citizenship and security for Joy and her sons. They had been in England two and a half years, and it was now their home.

At least this is how Lewis understood the situation of the civil wedding. His head did not know his heart at this stage. Or could it be that his heart was carefully protected against a full commitment to Joy, so soon after his obligations to Mrs Moore had ended? His friends, those who knew about the arrangement, could see the obvious more clearly. Warnie experienced no illusions, and started to wonder how soon he ought to leave The Kilns and live independently of his brother. Despite the traumas he had experienced there under the rule of Mrs Moore, he had had a certain stability and settled happiness in living with his brother.

One of Lewis's friends who did not know of the arrangement with Joy was Tolkien. Lewis was very aware of his strong feelings, as a devout Roman Catholic, about remarriage and the separation of civil and church marriage. When Tolkien did eventually find out, it was to intensify the strain on their already cooling friendship (though that was never broken).

In the autumn of 1956, the year of the civil wedding, Lewis and Joy learned not only that she had cancer, but that it was inoperable. It was news without hint or warning, and Lewis was deeply shocked. Cancer was, of course, an old acquaintance. He had lost both parents, other relations, and friends to it. Joy's two boys were then about the same age as the Lewis brothers had been when their mother died; the parallels were haunting. With Thanatos a rival for Joy (as he put it), Lewis's affection for her deepened into exclusive love. In retrospect, Lewis wrote in tribute after her death:

> Her mind was lithe and quick and muscular as a leopard. Passion, tenderness and pain were all equally unable to disarm it. It scented the first whiff of cant or slush; then sprang, and knocked you over before you knew what was happening.[15]

On 14 December that year, Lewis publicly announced the fact of the wedding in *The Times,* and Joy and her sons moved into The Kilns. There was no question in Joy's or Lewis's minds that

Warnie should stay as an integral member of the household. The two decided to have a second, Christian, wedding, but Lewis's request for one was turned down by the Bishop of Oxford, on the grounds that Joy was a divorcee. Not knowing where to turn, Lewis desperately asked Peter Bide, a former student and Anglican minister in another diocese, if he would conduct the service. He had first asked Bide to pray for Joy's healing, which he had done. On 21 March 1957 a bedside Christian wedding ceremony took place in the hospital where Joy was being treated. After that, Joy came back home to The Kilns to die.

At this stage, Tolkien remained unaware of what was going on with his friend. The very day of the Christian wedding ceremony, he wrote to Kathleen Farrer, a close friend of Joy's, expressing his belief that Kathleen had been very much taken up with "the troubles of poor Jack Lewis". He confessed that he knew little of these, beyond "cautious hints" from Dr Humphrey Havard (who, when treating Joy as her GP, had failed to diagnose her cancer). Whenever Tolkien met up with Lewis, his friend took refuge in talk about books, for which Tolkien had never known any anxiety or grief temper his enthusiasm.

After the prayer for healing, Joy had an unexpected reprieve. Her diseased bones rejuvenated against all medical expectations, and by July 1957 she was well enough to get out and about. Douglas Gresham remembered:

> As mother became more and more a healthy, active woman, she became more and more a wife. Now The Kilns became a happy home, filled with the riches of life.... Guests began to come ever more frequently... and discussion at our dinner table was full of life, jollity, fierce debate and profound philosophy.[16]

On one occasion, Joy gave a lecture on Charles Williams in Pusey House, just down the road from the Eagle and Child pub where he had often met with fellow Inklings during the war years. She wrote to Bill Gresham, her ex-husband:

I was a little nervous about addressing an audience of Oxford undergraduates, expecting them to be hypercritical, but I needn't have worried. I never had such a good audience, light as Viennese pastry, in contrast to those lumps of soggy dough I used to handle in New York. They got all my jokes, even the hints of jokes, instantly, and roared aloud… [17]

Debra Winger, who starred as Joy in the film *Shadowlands,* wrote of her "keen spirit, mind, and wit".[18] These qualities were brightly evident at that lecture on Charles Williams.

Throughout this period, Lewis continued his work in Cambridge on weekdays during termtime. David and Douglas were away at boarding school. The next year, Joy and Lewis had a fortnight's vacation in Ireland. The remission was the beginning of the happiest few years of both of their lives. Lewis confessed to fellow Inkling Nevill Coghill: "I never expected to have, in my sixties, the happiness that passed me by in my twenties."[19]

According to Warnie, the marriage fulfilled "a whole dimension to his nature that had previously been starved and thwarted". It also, for Lewis, put paid to any doubts he had had as a bachelor that God was an invented substitute for love. "For those few years [Joy] and I feasted on love," he recalled in *A Grief Observed,* "every mode of it – solemn and merry, romantic and realistic, sometimes as dramatic as a thunderstorm, sometimes as comfortable and unemphatic as putting on your soft slippers." In that book he recorded in raw meditational form the stages of his profound grief at her death.

The cancer eventually returned, but the Lewises were able to take a trip to Greece in the spring of 1960, a journey both of them very much wanted to make. They were accompanied by Roger and June Lancelyn Green. Joy underwent cancer surgery on 20 May 1960 and then returned once again to The Kilns to die. She slipped away on 13 July 1960, two months after the Greek holiday. Just before she died, with Lewis at her bedside, she said, "I am at peace with God."

14

Leaving the Shadowlands

Lewis began his account of losing Joy Davidman, *A Grief Observed,*
with the words: "No one ever told me that grief felt so like fear." His
observance of that grief was a shadow in his remaining years, weeks,
and days, although he had finished jotting down his meditations just
months after Joy's death. When Roger Lancelyn Green visited him
in September, he showed him the exercise books in which he had
written them, and discussed with him the thought of publication.

Initially, it was published under a pen name adapted from one he
used when bringing out poems, "N. W. Clerk",[1] and the book did
not appear under his own name until after his death. He began to
decline physically quite soon without Joy, but continued resolutely
to carry out his university duties at Cambridge, to work on books,
to keep up his still voluminous correspondence, and to meet with
the Inklings on Monday lunchtimes once a week in the Eagle and
Child public house, and later the Lamb and Flag across the road in
St Giles, before leaving for Cambridge.

The truth was that Lewis never really got over the loss of Joy.
Some weeks after her death, on 5 August, however, he affirmed
his Christian hope in the resurrection of the body in a letter to
a correspondent. He confessed, though, that he found the state
until the resurrection of those who have died unimaginable. He
wondered if Joy was in the same time as those left alive; if she was

not, it made no sense to wonder where she was now. His grief was compounded by constant worry about his unassuming brother's alcoholism and increasingly frequent binges.

As usual, Lewis had continued his regular correspondence with Arthur, sharing Joy's last days and moments with him. A bright occasion for him in the next year was a two-day holiday they had together in Oxford in June. Lewis had arranged to go in a hired car (with a driver) to pick up Arthur from London. The idea was to have a pleasant drive back to Oxford through the Chiltern Hills and the Thames Valley.

Later, in a letter, Lewis told Arthur that the brief holiday had been a happy time for him; one of the best he had had for a considerable while. In the same letter, he mentioned that he needed surgery for an enlarged prostate gland. It turned out that the poor state of his kidneys prevented surgery for a while. He would be troubled with his "waterworks" for the remainder of his days.

Warnie (whom Lewis described as his "Nurse and Secretary" at one point) took over much of his correspondence when he had periods of illness, for which he needed blood transfusions. These periods also sometimes affected his ability to work on his Cambridge duties during termtime. Warnie continued to battle against his alcoholism, recording in his diary, on 20 October 1961, that he had been a teetotaller for 355 days for the year to that date. In the following 365 days, he managed to avoid drinking for 298 days.

During the next year, 1962, Lewis was forced to spend much time at The Kilns because of illness. His friends rallied to help him. On Wednesday evenings, his local parish minister, Ronald Head, served him Communion at home. Others would take him out to the Lamb and Flag for a beer, and then onto the Trout at Godstow for a meal afterwards. There were many visits from friends, including Inklings, former students, and colleagues. These included Owen Barfield, Cecil Harwood, Roger Lancelyn Green, George Sayer, John Wain, and Ken Tynan. Douglas, his stepson, was still part of the household, and pursuing his studies. News of the suicide of Douglas's father, Bill Gresham, saddened them all at The Kilns. He had taken an overdose in September 1962, after being diagnosed with cancer of the throat and tongue, with the likelihood of losing his sight.

That Christmas, Lewis replied to a letter from Tolkien, confessing, "All my philosophy of history hangs upon a sentence of your own, 'Deeds were done which were not *wholly* in vain.'" The sentence he quoted was remembered from *The Fellowship of the Ring*, which had been read to Lewis long ago: "There was sorrow then too, and gathering dark, but great valour, and great deeds that were not wholly vain." Tolkien must have found consolation in the fact that his suffering friend had drawn comfort from his words.

The winter of 1963 was one of the worst in living memory. The bitter conditions meant that Lewis was unable to attend his local parish church for many weeks after Christmas 1962. It meant that there was an additional factor, as well as illness, confining him to his home, still empty with the absence of Joy.

Lewis was determined to make an effort, writing to Arthur to arrange a holiday in Ireland, on which Douglas was to accompany him as his porter, because of Lewis's increasing difficulties with mobility. Douglas looked forward to the prospect of Ireland with relish. For one thing, it would take him away from The Kilns, which appeared increasingly oppressive. Life there seemed under a dark cloud. Despite his infirmities, Lewis was still spending part of termtime weeks in Cambridge, lecturing, and overseeing the occasional research student.

The Inklings still met up on Monday mornings. The club would not survive the passing of Lewis, but one meeting was noted in the diary of his faithful friend, Roger Lancelyn Green. His entry for 17 June 1963 recorded: "To 'Lamb and Flag' about 12, there joined CSL. Several others – Gervase Mathew, Humphrey Havard, Colin Hardie, and a young American, Walter Hooper, who is writing some sort of book or thesis about Jack."[2]

Walter Hooper was to give Lewis much appreciated assistance with some of his correspondence during the summer (while Warnie had absented himself), before returning to temporary lecturing duties in Kentucky. Lewis had invited him to come back to Oxford as "some sort of secretary", in Douglas's words.[3] Walter Hooper would return to Oxford a few months later, despite the death of his mentor, and help to oversee the publication or reissue of many of C.S. Lewis's books that otherwise might have been lost from view, or languished. He would painstakingly edit many of these books.

A month after the Inklings meeting attended by Green, Lewis had a heart attack while at Acland Nursing Home for a blood transfusion, and fell into a coma. He was given Extreme Unction, in high Anglican manner, but surprised everyone by emerging from unconsciousness and asking for a cup of tea. The planned Irish holiday had to be abandoned. Soon after, Lewis gave in to the inevitable and decided to resign as Professor of Medieval and Renaissance literature at Cambridge. The university responded by electing him an honorary fellow of Magdalene College. Lewis now faced the dilemma of what to do with all his books located in his college rooms. Walter Hooper, eager to help, came to his rescue. He and Douglas spent a week in Cambridge boxing up and despatching his books and various papers.

Warnie's absence during that summer of 1963 had been a long one. He simply had not been able to face the situation at The Kilns. Warnie revealed his deepest feelings in his diary. On Tuesday, 5 September 1963,[4] for instance, while away in Ireland, he complained of the "discomforts of Kilns's life" without Joy's steering hand. He also was racked by "constant anxiety about J.[ack], overworked". The discomfort was affecting his sleep: "There have been nights this summer when I woke suddenly in sheer terror, telling myself that I was trapped without hope in this hell hole wh. I wd. never leave again until I do so in a hearse."

Warnie, too, had been heartbroken over the loss of Joy. To him, she was a close friend and a much-loved sister-in-law. He could not face the loss of his brother, if he was to die before him. While in Ireland, he had "drunk himself into hospital", as Lewis put it in a letter to Arthur Greeves.

After his sustained alcoholic bout in Ireland, Warnie returned to The Kilns in September. So it was that the two brothers were together once again during Lewis's final months, throughout which he remained lucid, despite his bodily system gradually failing and his bloodstream filling with toxins. It was like the old days when, as boys, they skilfully savoured the holidays after the school term had ended.

During those twilight days, his visitors, now necessarily fewer, included Tolkien and his eldest son, John, a Roman Catholic priest. John Tolkien remembered: "We drove over to The Kilns for what turned out to be a very excellent time together for about an hour. I remember the conversation was very much about the *Morte d'Arthur* and whether trees died."[5]

Friday 22 November 1963 began much as any day at The Kilns at that time. Lewis and Warnie breakfasted together, tackled the inevitable correspondence, and afterwards settled with a sigh to a newspaper crossword. After lunch, Lewis nodded off in his chair. Warnie suggested that he would be better off in bed, and so he made his way to his nearby room. (Since his long illness, he had moved downstairs to sleep, with Douglas taking over his bedroom.)

At four in the afternoon, as usual, Warnie prepared a pot of tea. Opening the door, he found his brother comfortable and drowsy. The few words that they exchanged were to be the last. An hour and a half later, Warnie heard a crash. He was instantly on his feet and into his brother's room. Jack Lewis was lying slumped by the foot of his bed. After just three or four minutes, his breathing ceased. He was gone. In that realization, the thought shocked Warnie that, whatever happened to him in the future, it could be nothing worse than this. It was one week before Jack's sixty-fifth birthday.

About an hour after Lewis died, President John F. Kennedy was assassinated. That same day, Aldous Huxley, author of *Brave New World* and other novels, also died. The news of Lewis's death was overshadowed by the President's shooting.

In a letter to his daughter, Priscilla, after Lewis's funeral, on Tuesday 26 November, Tolkien wrote:

> So far I have felt the normal feelings of a man of my age – like an old tree that is losing all its leaves one by one: this feels like an axe-blow near the roots. Very sad that we should have been so separated in the last years; but our time of close communion endured in memory for both of us. I had a mass said this morning, and was there, and served....

Warnie Lewis survived his brother by nearly ten years, grieving for him and battling against his alcoholism. The pages of his diary continued to fill. On Monday 9 April 1973, he died while reading a book in the quietness of The Kilns. He was buried with his brother in the churchyard of Holy Trinity Church, Headington Quarry, where the two had worshipped. On a single flat stone covering the grave their names are engraved, with an inscription: "Men must endure their going hence." This was the quotation carefully preserved by Warren Hamilton Lewis and Clive Staples Lewis, which had been displayed on their father's Shakespearean calendar the day their mother died in 1908.

A Brief Chronology

1862 18 May: Birth of Florence (Flora) Augusta Hamilton, mother of
C.S. Lewis, in Queenstown, County Cork, in the south of Ireland.

1863 23 August: Birth of Albert J. Lewis, father of C.S. Lewis, in Cork, in the
south of Ireland.

1872 28 March: Birth of Janie King Askins (later, Mrs Moore, "Minto").

1886 20 September: Birth of Charles Williams.

1892 3 January: John Ronald Reuel Tolkien born in Bloemfontein,
South Africa.

1894 29 August: Albert Lewis and Flora Hamilton married in St Mark's
Church, Dundela, Belfast.

1895 16 June: Birth of C.S. Lewis's brother, Warren Hamilton Lewis,
in Belfast.

1895 Birth of Arthur Greeves.

1898 29 November: Clive Staples Lewis born in Belfast.

1898 Births of Owen Barfield and Cecil Harwood.

1901 About this time, Warnie Lewis brings the lid of a biscuit tin into the
nursery of the infant Jack.

1905 Lewis family moves to their new home, Little Lea, on the outskirts
of Belfast.

1906 Birth of Maureen Moore, daughter of Mrs Janie King Moore.

1908 15 February: Flora Hamilton Lewis has major surgery for cancer.

1908 23 August: Flora Hamilton Lewis dies of cancer, on her husband's
birthday.

1908 September: Lewis is sent to Wynyard School in Watford, near London.

1910 Autumn: Lewis attends Campbell College near his Belfast home for
half a term. Tolkien succeeds in Oxford Entrance Examination, and is
offered an Open Classical Exhibition to Exeter College.

1911 Lewis is sent to Malvern, England, for preparatory study. It is during
this time that he abandons his childhood Christian faith.

1913 September: Lewis enters Malvern College, after gaining a classical
scholarship.

1914 February: Warnie enters the Royal Military Academy at Sandhurst.

1914 April: Lewis starts a lifelong friendship with Arthur Greeves in Belfast.

1914 4 August: Britain declares war on Germany.

1914 19 September: Lewis begins private study with W.T. Kirkpatrick, the Great Knock, in Bookham, Surrey, with whom he remains until March 1917.

1915 Reading George MacDonald's *Phantastes*. Looking back, he said the dream story "baptized" his imagination.

1915 18 April: Birth in New York of Helen Joy Davidman (later Helen Joy Davidman Gresham Lewis, wife of C.S. Lewis).

1916 December: Lewis sits for a classical scholarship and is elected to University College, Oxford.

1917 From 26 April until September, Lewis is nominally a student at University College, Oxford, undergoing officer training for war. He meets Paddy Moore.

1917 September: Lewis is commissioned as a junior officer (second lieutenant) in the Somerset Light Infantry.

1917 November: Lewis reaches the front line in France.

1918 End of January or early February: Lewis is hospitalized in the British Red Cross hospital at Le Tréport, ill with trench fever.

1918 15 April: Lewis is wounded in battle. The same month, Edward Francis Courtenay "Paddy" Moore is killed in another part of the battle. He is awarded the Military Cross on 2 December "for conspicuous gallantry and initiative".

1918 22 May: Lewis is transferred to a comfortable hospital in London.

1918 11 November: End of First World War.

1919 January: Lewis resumes his studies at University College, Oxford.

1919 March: Lewis's *Spirits in Bondage: A Cycle of Lyrics* published under the name Clive Hamilton by Heinemann.

1920 He achieves a First Class in the first part of Classical Honour Moderations (Greek and Latin literature).

1920 Lewis establishes a house in Oxford for Mrs Moore and her daughter, Maureen. Lewis lives with the Moores, probably from 1920.

1921 Death of W.T. Kirkpatrick, the Great Knock.

1922 He gains a First Class in Greats, the final part of Honour Moderations (philosophy and ancient history).

1923 He is awarded a First Class in English.

1923 Lewis begins composing *Dymer*.

1924 October: Lewis begins teaching philosophy at University College, standing in for E.F. Carritt, for one year.

1925 20 May: Lewis elected a fellow of Magdalen College, Oxford, where, from October, he serves as Tutor in English language and literature for nearly thirty years until leaving for Magdalene College, Cambridge, in 1955.

1925 October: Tolkien is appointed Rawlinson and Bosworth Professor of Anglo-Saxon at Oxford.

1926 11 May: The first recorded meeting between J.R.R. Tolkien and C.S. Lewis.

1926 Publication of long narrative poem, *Dymer*, again under the name Clive Hamilton.

1928 2 May: Albert Lewis retires with an annual pension from his position as Belfast Corporation County Solicitor.

1928 Owen Barfield publishes his Oxford B.Litt as the influential *Poetic Diction*.

1929 According to Lewis, he becomes a theist in Trinity Term.

1929 25 September: Albert Lewis dies of cancer in Belfast.

Late 1929 Tolkien gives "Lay of Leithian" to Lewis to read, and draws up his "Sketch of The Mythology" to fill out its background. Lewis reads it the night of 6 December.

1930 May: Warnie Lewis decides to edit and arrange the Lewis family papers.

1930 October: Mrs Moore, Lewis, and Warnie purchase The Kilns near Oxford.

1930? Tolkien begins to write *The Hobbit*.

1931 Tolkien's reformed English School syllabus, drawn up with C.S. Lewis, is accepted, bringing together language and literature.

1931 19–20 September: After a long night's conversation on Addison's Walk in Oxford with Tolkien and Hugo Dyson, Lewis becomes convinced of the truth of Christian faith.

1931 28 September: Lewis returns to Christian faith while riding to Whipsnade Zoo in the sidecar of his brother's motorbike.

1931 Christmas Day: Lewis starts to take communion in church, after a gap of many years.

Late 1932 Lewis reads the incomplete draft of *The Hobbit*.

1933 25 May: Lewis's semi-autobiographical fiction, *The Pilgrim's Regress: An Allegorical Apology for Christianity, Reason and Romanticism*, is published.

1933 The autumn term may have marked the beginning of Lewis's convening of a circle of friends named the Inklings.

1934 Dr "Humphrey" Havard takes over a medical practice with surgeries in St Giles and Headington, and becomes C.S. Lewis's GP.

1936 11 March: Charles Williams receives his first letter from Lewis, in appreciation of his novel *The Place of the Lion*.

1936 Spring: Lewis proposes he and Tolkien write stories of time and space. A coin toss gives Lewis space travel and Tolkien the challenge of writing on time travel.

1936 Publication of Lewis's greatly lauded *The Allegory of Love: A Study in Medieval Tradition*.

1937 December: Tolkien begins writing *The Lord of the Rings*; much of it will be read to the Inklings, and some of it to Lewis alone.

1938 Publication of Lewis's first science fiction book, *Out of the Silent Planet*.

1939 2 September: Evacuee children arrive at The Kilns. Around this time, Lewis begins a story, soon abandoned, about some evacuees who stay with an old professor.

1939 4 September: Warnie Lewis recalled to active service the day after Britain declares war on Germany.

1939 7 September: Charles Williams moves with the London branch of Oxford University Press to Oxford.

1940 Lewis begins lecturing on Christianity for the Royal Air Force, which he continues to do until 1941.

1940 27 August: Maureen Moore marries Leonard J. Blake, then director of music at Worksop College, Nottinghamshire.

1940 14 October: Lewis's *The Problem of Pain* is published. It is dedicated to the Inklings.

1941 The Oxford University Socratic Club is formed shortly after Christmas, and Lewis becomes president.

1941 6 August: Lewis broadcasts the first of twenty-five talks on BBC radio.

1942 Charles Williams's *The Forgiveness of Sins* is published, dedicated to the Inklings.

1942 Lewis publishes the enormously popular *The Screwtape Letters*, dedicated to J.R.R. Tolkien.

1943 18 February: An honorary Oxford MA is awarded to Charles Williams.

1943 Lewis publishes *Perelandra (Voyage to Venus)*, the second of his science fiction books. Some of its rich poetic prose was later turned into poems by Ruth Pitter.

1944 5 January: Williams tells Michal, his wife, about a *Time* magazine journalist writing on Lewis. The cover story eventually appears in 1947 and helps to ensure Lewis's popularity in the United States.

1944 Lewis lectures at Cambridge – the Clark Lectures. These lectures become the important chapter "New Learning and New Ignorance" in his volume for *The Oxford History of English Literature*.

1945 Germany surrenders on 8 May, Japan on 2 September. End of Second World War.

1945 15 May: Warnie Lewis records in his diary the sudden, unexpected death of Charles Williams. "And so vanishes one of the best and nicest men it has ever been my good fortune to meet. May God receive him into His everlasting happiness."

1945 Lewis publishes his third science fiction story, *That Hideous Strength: A Modern Fairy-Tale for Grown-Ups*, greatly influenced by Charles Williams. This same year he brings out his dream story, *The Great*

Divorce: A Dream, about a bus trip from hell to the borderlands of heaven.

1945 Birth of Douglas Gresham.

1946 Award of Doctor of Divinity by St Andrews University, Scotland.

1947 Lewis publishes his study *Miracles: A Preliminary Study*, philosophical theology for the lay person.

1948 2 February: Philosopher Elizabeth Anscombe gives a paper to the Oxford Socratic Club, replying to C.S. Lewis's argument in his book *Miracles* that naturalism is self-refuting, and seeking clarification.

1949 With his mother's death, Arthur Greeves moves from Strandtown, Belfast, to Crawfordsburn, County Down.

1949 20 October: The last Thursday night Inklings literary meeting is recorded in Warnie's diary. "No one turned up" the following week. The group continues to meet informally until Lewis's death.

1950 10 January: Lewis receives a letter from a 34-year-old American writer Helen Joy Davidman Gresham.

1950 Publication of *The Lion, the Witch and the Wardrobe*.

1951 12 January: Mrs Moore dies. Since the previous April, she had been confined to a nursing home in Oxford.

1951 Publication of *Prince Caspian: The Return to Narnia*.

1952 Publication of *The Voyage of the "Dawn Treader"*.

1952 Publication of Lewis's *Mere Christianity,* collecting his wartime BBC radio broadcasts.

1952 September: Lewis meets Joy Davidman for the first time.

1953 Publication of *The Silver Chair*.

1954 Lewis is persuaded by Tolkien to accept the Chair of Medieval and Renaissance literature at Cambridge. He gives his inaugural lecture, *De Descriptione Temporum*, on his 56th birthday, 29 November.

1954 Publication of *The Horse and His Boy*.

1954 Publication of the first two volumes of *The Lord of the Rings*. Tolkien dedicates this first edition to the Inklings.

1954 Lewis publishes *English Literature in the Sixteenth Century, Excluding Drama*.

1955 Publication of Lewis's *Surprised by Joy: The Shape of My Early Life*.

1956 23 April: Lewis enters into a civil marriage with Joy Davidman at the Oxford Registry Office, in order for her to gain British citizenship.

1955 Publication of *The Magician's Nephew*.

1956 Lewis publishes *The Last Battle*, which is awarded the Carnegie Medal, a prestigious award for children's books. His *Till We Have Faces: A Myth Retold* is also published this year.

1957 21 March: Lewis's Christian marriage with Joy Davidman takes place while she is in hospital.

1957 September: Joy Davidman's health is improving; by 10 December she is walking again.

1957 December: Death of Dorothy L. Sayers, friend of C.S. Lewis.

1958 Publishes *Reflections on the Psalms,* a literary study for the lay person that is an important contribution to biblical theology.

1957 Publication of Owen Barfield's groundbreaking *Saving the Appearances.*

1959 October: X-ray shows return of Joy's cancer.

1959 Owen Barfield retires as a solicitor, freeing him to write many more books, and to lecture, particularly in the United States.

1959 Death in Strandtown of Jane McNeill, Belfast friend of C.S. Lewis and Warnie Lewis, and also scholar Helen Waddell.

1960 May: Joy Davidman and Edith Tolkien are in hospital together.

1960 13 July: Joy dies at the age of 45, not long after the couple risk a Greek holiday.

1960 *The Four Loves* is published, exploring affection, friendship, erotic love, and *agape* (charity, or divine love).

1961 Under the pen name N.W. Clerk, Lewis publishes *A Grief Observed.*

1961 Lewis brings out *An Experiment in Criticism*, a lucid and inspiring distillation of a lifetime's response to books.

1963 15 June: Lewis has a heart attack while under treatment for poor health at Acland Nursing Home.

1963 September: Warnie returns to The Kilns after having been in Ireland for several months.

1963 Friday 22 November: Lewis dies at home, one week before his 65th birthday.

1964 Publication of *Letters to Malcolm: Chiefly on Prayer*, prepared by Lewis for publication before his death.

1966 Warnie Lewis publishes *Letters of C.S. Lewis.*

1966 Death of Arthur Greeves.

1973 9 April: Warren Hamilton Lewis dies, still mourning his beloved brother.

1973 Sunday 2 September: Tolkien dies in Bournemouth.

1975 Deaths of Henry "Hugo" Victor Dyson Dyson and Cecil Harwood.

1980 Death of Nevill Coghill.

1985 Death of Dr Robert Emlyn "Humphrey" Havard.

1987 Death of Roger Lancelyn Green.

1997 15 February: Death of Maureen Blake (née Moore, titled by inheritance, Dame Maureen Dunbar of Hempriggs).

1997 14 December: Owen Barfield dies, just short of his 100th birthday.

1998 Conferences are held in Belfast and worldwide to commemorate the centenary of C.S. Lewis's birth.

Notes

1. A Northern Irish Childhood

1. Later Mrs Claire Clapperton; see Clyde S. Kilby and Marjorie Lamp Meade (eds.), *Brothers and Friends: The Diaries of Major Warren Hamilton Lewis* (San Francisco: Harper & Row, 1982), p. 81.

2. Flora Lewis, letters 3 and 8 May 1900, W.H. Lewis (ed.), *The Lewis Papers: Memoirs of the Lewis Family, 1850–1930* (unpublished collection deposited at The Marion E. Wade Center, Wheaton College, IL).

3. C.S. Lewis, *Surprised by Joy: The Shape of My Early Life* (London: Geoffrey Bles, 1955), chapter 1.

4. From an unpublished memoir willed by W.H. Lewis to The Marion E. Wade Center, Wheaton College; copy in the Bodleian Library, Oxford.

5. C.S. Lewis, *The Voyage of the "Dawn Treader"* (London: Geoffrey Bles, 1952), chapter 16.

6. While studying English and philosophy at Ulster University in the seventies, I had digs in the station house at Castlerock for a term, at the time when I was becoming increasingly aware of C.S. Lewis's strong association with the north Irish coast.

7. Flora Lewis, letter 10 July 1901, W.H. Lewis (ed.), *The Lewis Papers.*

8. Flora Lewis, letter 14 July 1901, *ibid.*

9. See C.S. Lewis, *Surprised by Joy*, chapter 1.

10. Agnes Romilly White, *Gape Row* (London: Selwyn & Blount, 1934), page reference unknown. Passage quoted in unpublished diary entry, 20 October 1934, by Warren Lewis. Also quoted in Patricia Craig (ed.) *The Ulster Anthology* (Belfast: Blackstaff Press, 2006), p. 66.

11. C.S. Lewis, *Surprised by Joy,* chapter 3.

12. "The Sailor: A Study" in Walter Hooper (ed.), *Boxen: The Imaginary World of the Young C.S. Lewis* (London: Collins, 1985), p. 192.

13. Bodleian Library, C.S. Lewis Special Collection, d. 241, fol. 22.

14. *Ibid.*, d. 809–810. The Wordsworth quote is from his ode "Intimations of Immortality".

15. C.S. Lewis, letter 6 June 1916, Walter Hooper (ed.), *C.S. Lewis: Collected Letters Vol. I: Family Letters 1905–1931* (London: HarperCollins, 2000), p. 188.

16. C.S. Lewis, *The Lion, the Witch and the Wardrobe* (London: Geoffrey Bles, 1950), chapter 17.

17. From W.H. Lewis (ed.), *The Lewis Papers,* spelling retained; quoted in Walter Hooper, *C.S. Lewis: A Companion and Guide* (London: HarperCollins, 1996), pp. 5–6.

18. From W.H. Lewis (ed.), *The Lewis Papers*.
19. W.H. Lewis, unpublished memoir, deposited in The Marion E. Wade Center.
20. The letters are quoted from W.H. Lewis (ed.), *The Lewis Papers*.
21. *Ibid.*
22. Early draft of *Surprised by Joy,* the Bodleian Library, C.S. Lewis Special Collection, d. 241, fol. 22.
23. C.S. Lewis, *The Magician's Nephew* (London: Bodley Head, 1955), chapter 15.

2. Schooldays and Arthur Greeves: Watford, Belfast, and Malvern

1. From unpublished diaries of W.H. Lewis, The Marion E. Wade Center, Wheaton College.
2. C.S. Lewis, *Surprised by Joy*, chapter 2.
3. Both letters from W.H. Lewis (ed.), *The Lewis Papers*, Vol. II, p. 146.
4. George Sayer, *Jack: C.S. Lewis and His Times* (London: Macmillan, 1988), pp. 30–31.
5. Henry W. Longfellow's translation of Esaias Tegnér's Swedish poem *Drapa*.
6. C.S. Lewis, *Mere Christianity* (London: Geoffrey Bles, 1952), Book II, chapter 10.
7. A selection has been published; the entire diaries are held at The Marion E. Wade Center, bequeathed there by him. Warren Lewis was a natural historian, his abilities evidenced later in life in his books on seventeenth-century French social history.
8. Memoir of C.S. Lewis, in W.H. Lewis (ed.), *Letters of C.S. Lewis* (London: Geoffrey Bles, 1966); revised edition, Walter Hooper (ed.) (1988), p. 25.
9. Oral history interview with Dr Havard, 26 July 1984, The Marion E. Wade Center, Wheaton College.
10. W.H. Lewis, unpublished memoir, The Marion E. Wade Center, Wheaton College.
11. Quoted in Roger Lancelyn Green and Walter Hooper, *C.S. Lewis: A Biography* (London: HarperCollins, 2nd edition, 2002), p. 20.
12. W.H. Lewis (ed.), *The Lewis Papers*, Vol. IV, p.160.
13. G.B. Tennyson (ed.), *Owen Barfield on C.S. Lewis* (San Raphael, CA: The Barfield Press, 1989), p. 126.
14. C.S. Lewis, *Surprised by Joy*, chapter 8.
15. Sir Ivan Neill, in David Bleakley, *C.S. Lewis at Home in Ireland: A Centenary Biography* (Belfast: Strandtown Press, 1998), p. 137.
16. A.N. Wilson, *C.S. Lewis: A Biography* (London: Collins, 1990), p. 38.
17. Quoted in Roger Lancelyn Green and Walter Hooper, *C.S. Lewis: A Biography* (London: Collins, 1974), p. 98.

3. "The Great Knock": Bookham, Surrey

1. Kirkpatrick made his mark on C.S. Lewis's fiction, to be seen in some characteristics of the learned Professor Digory Kirke in the Narnian Chronicles and in the sceptical Ulsterman Andrew MacPhee in *That Hideous Strength*.
2. C.S. Lewis, Walter Hooper (ed.), *Of Other Worlds: Essays and Stories* (London: Geoffrey Bles, 1966), p. 79.
3. C.S. Lewis, *Surprised by Joy,* chapter 10.
4. Letter 7 January 1915, in W.H. Lewis (ed.), *The Lewis Papers,* Vol. IV, p. 279.
5. See letter to Arthur Greeves, 1 October 1931, in Walter Hooper (ed.), *C.S. Lewis: Collected Letters Vol. I: Family Letters 1905–1931*, p. 973.
6. In early November 1917.
7. This kind of effect can be seen in verse and paintings of the Romantic Movement, which transformed the way people saw the English Lake District.
8. Walter Hooper (ed.), *C.S. Lewis: Collected Letters Vol. I: Family Letters 1905–1931 (*London: HarperCollins, 2000), p. 104. For more information on damage by submarine activity see: http://www.mareud.com/Timelines/1914-1918.htm (accessed 7 February 2013).
9. *Ibid.*, pp. 111–112.
10. Lewis set out his typical day at Bookham in a letter to Arthur dated 13 October 1914 in Walter Hooper (ed.), *C.S. Lewis: Collected Letters Vol. I: Family Letters 1905–1931*, p. 79.
11. See for example Lewis's letter to Arthur Greeves, 4 July 1916, in Walter Hooper (ed.) *C.S. Lewis: Collected Letters Vol. I: Family Letters 1905–1931*, p. 205.
12. Oxford University is a federation of colleges within the city, rather than a single campus.

4. Oxford and France: "This is What War is Like…"

1. Walter Hooper (ed.), *C.S. Lewis: Collected Letters Vol. I: Family Letters 1905–1931 (*London: HarperCollins, 2000), p. 299.
2. Letter to Arthur Greeves, 20 February 1917 in Walter Hooper (ed.), *They Stand Together: The Letters of C.S. Lewis to Arthur Greeves (1914–1963)* (London: Collins, 1979) and Walter Hooper (ed.), *C.S. Lewis: Collected Letters Vol. I: Family Letters 1905–1931* (London: HarperCollins, 2000).
3. Letter to Arthur Greeves, 3 June 1917 in *ibid.*
4. The Marion E. Wade Center Oral History interview. Mrs Moore also mentioned this fact in a later letter to Albert Lewis, *The Lewis Papers*, Vol. VI, p. 44–45.
5. Letter to Albert Lewis from Mrs Janie Moore 1917, in W.H. Lewis (ed.), *The Lewis Papers*, Vol. V, p. 239.

6. K.J. Gilchrist, *A Morning After War: C.S. Lewis & WWI* (New York: Peter Lang, 2005), p. 125.
7. Walter Hooper (ed.), *C.S. Lewis: Collected Letters Vol. I: Family Letters 1905–1931*, p. 341. Lewis warmly reminisces about Johnson in *Surprised by Joy,* chapter 12.
8. Walter Hooper (ed.), *Ibid.*, p. 342.
9. See his poem "French Nocturne" in *Spirits in Bondage: A Cycle of Lyrics* (London: William Heinemann, 1919).
10. K.J. Gilchrist, *A Morning After War: C.S. Lewis & WWI*, p. 76.
11. Walter Hooper (ed.), *C.S. Lewis: Collected Letters Vol. I: Family Letters 1905–1931*, p. 349.
12. Letter to Arthur Greeves, 14 December 1917, in *ibid.*
13. K.J. Gilchrist discusses this sanitizing of the horrors in his *A Morning After War*. For instance, casualties were often described as dying instantly from a head wound, whereas the reality was very different.
14. C.S. Lewis, *Surprised by Joy*, chapter 12.
15. Martin Gilbert, *First World War* (London: Weidenfeld & Nicolson, 1994), pp. 406–407.
16. Second Lieutenant E.F.C. Moore's death would not be confirmed officially until September.
17. W.H. Lewis (ed.), *The Lewis Papers*, Vol. V, p. 308.
18. C.S. Lewis, *Dymer,* Canto VIII, 1, 2, collected in C.S. Lewis, Walter Hooper (ed.), *Narrative Poems* (London: Geoffrey Bles, 1969).
19. Everard Wyrall, *History of the Somerset Light Infantry* (Sussex: Naval & Military Press Ltd., 2006), pp. 293–295. Sergeant Ayres belonged to the "other ranks".
20. Quoted in Roger Lancelyn Green and Walter Hooper, *C.S. Lewis: A Biography* (London: HarperCollins, 2nd edition, 2002), p. 44.
21. For an analysis of his thought and its development at this period, see David C. Downing, *The Most Reluctant Convert: C.S. Lewis's Journey to Faith* (Downers Grove, IL.: IVP, 2002; Leicester: IVP, 2002).
22. For more on the philosopher Arthur Schopenhauer see *ibid.*, pp. 92–93.
23. Walter Hooper (ed.), *C.S. Lewis: Collected Letters Vol. I: Family Letters 1905–1931*, p. 386.
24. W.H. Lewis, "Memoir of C.S. Lewis", in *Letters of C.S. Lewis,* pp. 9–10.
25. W.H. Lewis (ed.), *The Lewis Papers*, Vol. VI, p. 79.

5. Student Days: Oxford, and Mrs Janie Moore

1. K.J. Gilchrist, *A Morning After War: C.S. Lewis & WWI*, p. 218.
2. A.N. Wilson, *C.S. Lewis: A Biography*, pp. 65–66.
3. A number of the rented flats and houses Lewis shared with Mrs Moore and Maureen, however, also had live-in landladies.

4. Green and Hooper say in their biography that Lewis didn't move in with the Moores until June 1921, but Lewis refers in a letter to Arthur as early as May 1920 of the Moores' move to new accommodation in Headington and his living there. See the letter of 3? May 1920 in Walter Hooper (ed.), *They Stand Together: The Letters of C.S. Lewis to Arthur Greeves (1914–1963)* (London: Collins, 1979), p. 275.

5. Clyde S. Kilby and Marjorie Lamp Meade (eds.), *Brothers and Friends: The Diaries of Major Warren Hamilton Lewis*, 14 July 1930, p. 69.

6. C.S. Lewis, *Surprised by Joy*, chapter 13.

7. For example, in letter 12 February 1918, in Walter Hooper (ed.), *They Stand Together*, p. 208.

8. A.N. Wilson, *C.S. Lewis: A Biography*, p. 580.

9. See K.J. Gilchrist, *A Morning After War: C.S. Lewis & WWI*, pp. 112–113.

10. The Marion E. Wade Center Oral History interview with Maureen Moore.

11. W.H. Lewis (ed.), *The Lewis Papers*, Vol. VI, pp. 44–45.

12. 20 May 1919, in W.H. Lewis (ed.), *The Lewis Papers*.

13. Wednesday 6 August 1919, in W.H. Lewis (ed.), *The Lewis Papers*, Vol. VI, p. 161.

14. Letter to Albert Lewis, Sunday 4 April 1920 in Walter Hooper (ed.), *C.S. Lewis: Collected Letters Vol. I: Family Letters 1905–1931* (London: HarperCollins, 2000).

15. A.N. Wilson, *C.S. Lewis: A Biography*, p. 93.

16. To Arthur Greeves, June 1921, in Walter Hooper (ed.), *They Stand Together*, p. 287.

6. The Aspiring Poet and Scholar in Hard Times: The Inspiration of Owen Barfield

1. Letter 2 February 1923 in Walter Hooper (ed.), *All My Road Before Me: The Diary of C.S. Lewis, 1922–1927*.

2. John Carey, "Coghill, Nevill Henry Kendal Aylmer (1899–1980)", *Oxford Dictionary of National Biography* (Oxford University Press, 2004; online edition, May 2008).

3. C.S. Lewis, Walter Hooper (ed.), *Selected Literary Essays* (Cambridge: Cambridge University Press, 1969), p. xi.

4. *Ibid.*, p. xii.

5. Nevill Coghill writing in 1965, in Jocelyn Gibb (ed.), *Light on C.S. Lewis* (London: Geoffrey Bles, 1965), pp. 54–55.

6. *Ibid.*, pp. 54–55.

7. G.B. Tennyson (ed.), *Owen Barfield on C.S. Lewis*, p. 3.

8. C.S. Lewis, *Surprised by Joy*, chapter 13.

9. James T. Como (ed.), *C.S. Lewis at the Breakfast Table and Other Reminiscences* (New York: Macmillan, 1979), p. 4.

10. *Ibid.*, p. 4.

11. G.B. Tennyson (ed.), *Owen Barfield on C.S. Lewis*, pp. 5–6.

12. In *New York Times* obituary, 19 December 1997.

13. *Ibid.*

14. C.S. Lewis, *Surprised by Joy*, chapter 13.

15. W.H. Lewis (ed.), *The Lewis Papers*, Vol. VIII, p. 140.

16. Another Oxford B.Litt student closely associated with C.S. Lewis also published his thesis. Roger Lancelyn Green's *Andrew Lang: A Critical Biography* was published in 1946. One of Green's supervisors for his B.Litt was J.R.R. Tolkien.

17. W.H. Lewis (ed.), *Letters of C.S. Lewis* (London: Geoffrey Bles, 1966), p. 20.

18. C.S. Lewis, Walter Hooper (ed.), *Narrative Poems*.

7. The Young Don: Meeting J.R.R. Tolkien

1. Entry 8 September 1923 in Walter Hooper (ed.), *All My Road Before Me: The Diary of C.S. Lewis, 1922–1927* (London: HarperCollins, 1991).

2. C.S. Lewis, *The Discarded Image: An Introduction to Medieval and Renaissance Literature* (Cambridge: Cambridge University Press, 1964), pp. vii–viii.

3. I am assuming that this is the same conversation recorded in *Surprised by Joy*, which is very likely. See Walter Hooper (ed.) *All My Road Before Me: The Diary of C.S. Lewis, 1922–1927*, p. 379, and C.S. Lewis, *Surprised by Joy*, chapter 14.

4. Entry Tuesday 11 May 1926 in Walter Hooper (ed.), *All My Road Before Me*.

5. Alistair Fowler, "C.S. Lewis: Supervisor" in *Yale Review*, Vol. 91, No. 4 (October 2003), pp. 64–80.

6. Entry Wednesday 12 May 1926 in Walter Hooper (ed.), *All My Road Before Me*.

7. Helen Gardner, "Clive Staples Lewis 1898–1963", in *Proc. British Academy 51* (1965), pp. 417–428.

8. Homer, *The Odyssey*, quoted in K. J. Gilchrist, *A Morning After War: C.S. Lewis & WWI*, p. vii, from Robert Fagles's translation, *The Odyssey* (New York: Penguin, 1997).

9. J.R.R. Tolkien retold some of the stories in poetry modelled upon the *Poetic Edda,* published after his death in *The Legend of Sigurd and Gudrún* (London: HarperCollins, 2009).

10. C.S. Lewis, *Surprised by Joy*, chapter 14.

11. A phrase of Lewis's from *Miracles: A Preliminary Study* (London: Geoffrey Bles, 1947), p. 17.

12. J.R.R. Tolkien, Humphrey Carpenter (ed.), *Letters of J.R.R. Tolkien* (London: George Allen and Unwin, 1981), letter 276.

13. Letter to Roger Lancelyn Green, 17 July 1971. Quoted in Roger Lancelyn Green and Walter Hooper, *C.S. Lewis: A Biography* (London: HarperCollins, 3rd edition, 2002), p. 210.

14. C.S. Lewis letter, 7 December 1929, quoted in J.R.R. Tolkien, Christopher Tolkien (ed.), *The Lays of Beleriand* (London: George Allen and Unwin, 1985), p. 151.

8. The Most Reluctant Convert

1. C.S. Lewis, *Surprised by Joy*, chapter 13.
2. *Ibid.*, chapter 14.
3. *Ibid.*, chapter 14.
4. To Owen Barfield, conjectured date of 3 February 1930, in Walter Hooper (ed.), *C.S. Lewis: Collected Letters Vol. I: Family Letters 1905–1931*.
5. One is the letter to Owen Barfield, conjectured date of 3 February 1930, and the other is to A.K. Hamilton Jenkin, 21 March 1930. Both letters are in Walter Hooper (ed.), *C.S. Lewis: Collected Letters Vol. I: Family Letters 1905–1931*.
6. Letter to Sister Penelope CSMV, 9 August 1939, in Walter Hooper (ed.), *C.S. Lewis: Collected Letters Vol. II: Books, Broadcasts and the War 1931–1949*.
7. In prepublication information about his intellectual biography, *C.S. Lewis: A Life: The Story of the Man Who Created Narnia* (London: Hodder & Stoughton, to be published 2013), author Alister McGrath reveals that he has found evidence that points to 1930 as the year of Lewis's conversion to theism.
8. C.S. Lewis, *Surprised by Joy*, chapter 14.
9. C.S. Lewis, Walter Hooper (ed.), *Christian Reflections* (London: Geoffrey Bles, 1967), chapter 14.
10. See G. B. Tennyson (ed.), *Owen Barfield on C.S. Lewis*, pp. 98–103. I have explored Lewis's later more wholistic and developed view of imagination, and the question of the knowledge it may capture, in "Myth, Fact and Incarnation", in Eduardo Segura and Thomas Honegger (eds.), *Myth and Magic: Art according to the Inklings* (Zollikofen, Switzerland: Walking Tree, 2007), pp. 71–98.
11. C.S. Lewis, *Dymer,* new edition (London: J.M. Dent, 1950), p. xi.
12. Letter Sunday 5 January 1930, in Walter Hooper (ed.), *C.S. Lewis: Collected Letters Vol. I: Family Letters 1905–1931*, p. 858.
13. Roger Lancelyn Green and Walter Hooper, *C.S. Lewis: A Biography* (London: Collins, 1974). See also Lewis's letter to Arthur Greeves, 22 December 1929, in Hooper (ed.), *C.S. Lewis: Collected Letters Vol. I*.
14. C.S. Lewis, *Surprised by Joy*, chapter 14.
15. Entry for Monday 7 July 1930, in Clyde S. Kilby and Marjorie Lamp Meade (eds.), *Brothers and Friends: The Diaries of Major Warren Hamilton Lewis*.
16. Author's note: The "mess" is the officer's mess, i.e. the place where they ate, drank, and socialized.
17. Entry for Sunday 25 May 1930, in Clyde S. Kilby and Marjorie Lamp Meade (eds.), *Brothers and Friends: The Diaries of Major Warren Hamilton Lewis*.

18. Oral History interview with Maureen Moore, then Lady Dunbar, made by The Marion E. Wade Center, Wheaton College, 1984.

19. After his brother's death, they were bequeathed by Warren Lewis to The Marion E. Wade Center, Wheaton, along with other invaluable material. This was as a result of his friendship with pioneering C.S. Lewis and J.R.R. Tolkien scholar Clyde S. Kilby.

20. John Lawlor, *C.S. Lewis: Memories and Reflections* (Dallas: Spence Publishing Company, 1998), p. 20.

21. Quoted in Humphrey Carpenter, *The Inklings: C.S. Lewis, J.R.R. Tolkien, Charles Williams and Their Friends* (London: George Allen and Unwin, 1978), p. 42.

22. Letter 18 October 1931 in Walter Hooper (ed.), *C.S. Lewis: Collected Letters Vol. I: Family Letters 1905–1931*.

23. C. S. Lewis, Walter Hooper (ed.), *God in the Dock: Essays on Theology and Ethics* (Grand Rapids, MI: Eerdmans, 1970), p. 67.

24. Lewis examined this theme more fully in his book *Miracles*.

25. Letter to Dom Bede Griffiths OSB, 21 December 1941, in Walter Hooper (ed.), *C.S. Lewis: Collected Letters Volume II: Books, Broadcasts and War, 1931–1949*.

26. Quoted in Roger Lancelyn Green and Walter Hooper, *C.S. Lewis: A Biography* (London: Collins, 1974), p. 113. A copy of the document is housed in The Marion E. Wade Centre, Wheaton College, Illinois.

27. Letter to Arthur Greeves, Sunday 26 January 1930, in Walter Hooper (ed.), *C.S. Lewis: Collected Letters Vol. I: Family Letters 1905–1931*.

28. C.S. Lewis, *Surprised by Joy*, chapter 15.

9. The Company of Friends

1. James Boswell – companion of Dr Samuel Johnson, and author of his extensive biography.

2. From his unpublished memoir of C.S. Lewis, held at The Marion E. Wade Center, Wheaton College.

3. Entry for Wednesday 26 July 1933, in Clyde S. Kilby and Marjorie Lamp Meade (eds.), *Brothers and Friends: The Diaries of Major Warren Hamilton Lewis*.

4. i.e. Alexander Pope's poem, "The Rape of the Lock".

5. Entry for Saturday 18 February 1933, in Clyde S. Kilby and Marjorie Lamp Meade (eds.), *Brothers and Friends: The Diaries of Major Warren Hamilton Lewis*.

6. Letter to Warnie, 22 November 1931, in Walter Hooper (ed.), *C.S. Lewis: Collected Letters Vol. II: Books, Broadcasts and the War 1931–1949*; see also Lewis's letter to Arthur Greeves, 29 July 1930, in Walter Hooper (ed.), *C.S. Lewis: Collected Letters Vol. I: Family Letters 1905–1931*.

7. Letter from J.R.R. Tolkien, 11 September 1967. The letter was reproduced in William L. White's *The Image of Man in C.S. Lewis* (London: Hodder, 1970, pp. 221–222), complete with Tolkien's home phone

number! Tolkien gives a very similar account in a letter to Donald Swann earlier, on 14 October 1966 (see my *J.R.R. Tolkien: The Making of a Legend* (Oxford: Lion, 2012), p. 171). Having two such similar accounts drawn from memory but nearly a year apart suggests the accuracy of the record.

8. C.S. Lewis, *The Four Loves* (London: Geoffrey Bles, 1960), chapter 4.

9. Letter to Oxford University Press, 18 September 1935, in Roger Lancelyn Green and Walter Hooper, *C.S. Lewis: A Biography,* (London: HarperCollins, new edition, 2002), p. 135.

10. Letter to Arthur Greeves, 25 March 1933, in Walter Hooper (ed.), *C.S. Lewis: Collected Letters Vol. II: Books, Broadcasts and the War 1931–1949.*

11. Letter to Belle Allen, 19 January 1953, in Walter Hooper (ed.), *C.S. Lewis: Collected Letters Vol. III: Narnia, Cambridge and Joy 1950–1963* (London: HarperCollins, 2006).

12. Letter to Arthur Greeves, 25 March 1933 in Walter Hooper (ed.), *C.S. Lewis: Collected Letters Vol. II: Books, Broadcasts and the War 1931–1949.*

13. Warnie disguised Mrs Moore's name in his diaries, employing another of her names, King.

14. See entry for 2 October 1933 in Clyde S. Kilby and Marjorie Lamp Meade (eds.), *Brothers and Friends: The Diaries of Major Warren Hamilton Lewis.*

15. Corrections were made on long columns of paper before the text was divided into page lengths, as correcting was expensive and time-consuming, and involved remoulding the metal block that made up a line of text on the page.

16. Clyde S. Kilby and Marjorie Lamp Meade (eds.), *Brothers and Friends: The Diaries of Major Warren Hamilton Lewis*, pp. 102–103.

17. *Ibid.*, p. 64.

18. William Griffin, *Clive Staples Lewis: A Dramatic Life* (New York: Harper & Row, 1986), p. 176.

19. Entry for Thursday 21 December 1933 in Clyde S. Kilby and Marjorie Lamp Meade (eds.), *Brothers and Friends: The Diaries of Major Warren Hamilton Lewis.*

20. Entry for 6 November 1933, diary of W.H. Lewis, The Marion E. Wade Center.

21. *Ibid.*

10. Storytelling and Reflections: Through the Changing Thirties with Tolkien

1. Letter to Arthur Greeves, 4 February 1933 in Walter Hooper (ed.), *They Stand Together: The Letters of C.S. Lewis to Arthur Greeves (1914–1963)* (London: Collins, 1979) and Walter Hooper (ed.), *C.S. Lewis: Collected Letters Vol. I: Family Letters 1905–1931* (London: HarperCollins, 2000).

2. Harry Blamires, "Against the Stream: C.S. Lewis and the Literary Scene", in Journal of the Irish Christian Study Centre 1 (1983), p. 15.

3. This suggests Havard joined the group before Lewis's well-received *Out of the Silent Planet* was published in 1938, and perhaps even before the publication of Tolkien's *The Hobbit* in September 1937.

4. Edmund Crispin, *Swan Song* (London: Gollancz, 1947), pp. 59–60.

5. David L. Russell, "C.S. Lewis", in *British Children's Writers*, Vol. 160 of *Dictionary of Literary Biography* (Detroit: Bruccoli Clark Layman, 1996), pp. 134–149.

6. Letter to Charles Williams, 11 March 1936, in Walter Hooper (ed.), *C.S. Lewis: Collected Letters Vol. II: Books, Broadcasts and the War 1931–1949.*

7. Charles Williams, letter to C.S. Lewis, 12 March 1936. Bodleian Library, MS.Eng. c.6825, fol. 48, quoted in Roger Lancelyn Green and Walter Hooper, *C.S. Lewis: A Biography* (fully revised and expanded edition; London: HarperCollins, 2002), p. 137.

8. C.S. Lewis (ed.), *Essays Presented to Charles Williams* (London: Oxford University Press, 1947), p. viii.

9. See J.R.R. Tolkien, letter to Christopher Tolkien, 31 July 1944, in Humphrey Carpenter (ed.), *Letters of J.R.R. Tolkien*, letter 77.

10. Letter to Sister Penelope CSMV, 9 July (or August) 1939, in Walter Hooper (ed.), *C.S. Lewis: Collected Letters Vol. II: Books, Broadcasts and the War 1931–1949.*

11. Marjorie Hope Nicolson, *Voyages to the Moon* (New York: Macmillan Co., 1948).

11. The Wartime Years and After: Enter Charles Williams

1. John D. Mabbott, *Oxford Memories* (Oxford: Thorntons of Oxford, 1986), p. 91.

2. *The Times,* 20 July 1940, p. 4, quoted by Walter Hooper in W. Hooper (ed.), *C.S. Lewis: Collected Letters Vol. II: Books, Broadcasts and the War 1931–1949,* p. 425.

3. T.S. Eliot, "Introduction", in Charles Williams, *All Hallows Eve* (New York: Farrar, Straus and Giroux, 1977), p. xiv.

4. Quotation from Alexander Pope, *Essay on Man*, iv., 1. 385.

5. Letter to Warnie, Saturday 11 November 1939, in Walter Hooper (ed.), *C.S. Lewis: Collected Letters Vol. II: Books, Broadcasts and the War 1931–1949.*

6. Charles Williams, *Seed of Adam and Other Plays* (London: Oxford University Press, 1948), pp. 45–46.

7. C.S. Lewis, "Introduction", in C.S. Lewis (ed.), *Essays Presented to Charles Williams*, p. xiii.

8. C.S. Lewis, *Surprised by Joy*, chapter 4.

9. See Don W. King, *C.S. Lewis, Poet: The Legacy of His Poetic Impulse* (Kent, Ohio: The Kent State University Press, 2001), especially Appendix 1.

10. C.S. Lewis, "Preface" to *The Screwtape Letters and Screwtape Proposes a Toast* (London: Geoffrey Bles, 1961).

11. George Orwell, "The Scientist Takes Over", review of C.S. Lewis,

That Hideous Strength (1945), *Manchester Evening News*, 16 August 1945. Reprinted as No. 2720 (first half) in *The Complete Works of George Orwell*, edited by Peter Davison, Vol. XVII (1998), pp. 250–251.

12. John Wain, "Oxford", in *Sprightly Running: Part of an Autobiography* (London: Macmillan, 1965), p. 149.

13. Jill Flewett (Lady Freud) was later an actress who married Sir Clement Freud, grandson of the psychoanalyst Sigmund Freud and brother of the artist Lucian Freud.

14. In Stephen Schofield (ed.), *In Search of C.S. Lewis* (New Jersey: Bridge, 1984), p. 58.

15. Quoted in Roger Lancelyn Green and Walter Hooper, *C.S. Lewis: A Biography* (fully revised and expanded edition; London: HarperCollins, 2002), p. 303.

16. Letter to Warnie, Saturday 20 July 1940, in Walter Hooper (ed.), *C.S. Lewis: Collected Letters Vol. II: Books, Broadcasts and the War 1931–1949*.

17. Letter to Warnie, Sunday 11 August 1940, in *ibid*.

18. Letter to Warnie, Saturday 17 August 1940, in *ibid*.

19. Local Defence Volunteer (later renamed the Home Guard).

20. Letter to Br George Avery, Saturday 12 October 1940, in Walter Hooper (ed.), *C.S. Lewis: Collected Letters Vol. II: Books, Broadcasts and the War 1931–1949*.

21. Carolyn Keefe (ed.), *C.S. Lewis: Speaker and Teacher* (London: Hodder, 1974), pp. 87–88.

22. Robert E. Havard, "Philia: Jack at Ease", in James T. Como (ed.), *C.S. Lewis at the Breakfast Table and Other Reminiscences*, p. 217.

23. Clyde S. Kilby and Marjorie Lamp Mead (eds.), *Brothers and Friends: The Diaries of Major Warren Hamilton Lewis*, pp. 184–185.

24. John Wain, "Oxford", in *Sprightly Running*, p. 184.

12. A New Era and a Change of Strategy: The Narnia Factor

1. David Graham (ed.), *We Remember C.S. Lewis: Essays & Memoirs* (Nashville, TN: Broadman & Holman, 2001), p. 51.

2. Oral History interview with Ian Davie, The Marion E. Wade Center, Wheaton College, 1991.

3. Derek Brewer, "The Tutor: A Portrait", in James T. Como (ed.), *C.S. Lewis at the Breakfast Table and Other Reminiscences*, p. 57.

4. See "A Reply to Mr C.S. Lewis's Argument that 'Naturalism' is Self-Refuting", in G. E. M. Anscombe, *Collected Philosophical Papers Vol. II: Metaphysics and the Philosophy of Mind* (Minneapolis, MN: University of Minnesota Press, 1981), pp. 224–232. See also *Journal of Inklings Studies*, Vol. 1, No. 2 (October 2011), where the whole issue is devoted to the Lewis-Anscombe debate.

5. Letter to Dr Warfield M. Firor, Thursday 20 December 1951, in Walter Hooper (ed.), *C.S. Lewis: Collected Letters Vol. III: Narnia, Cambridge and Joy 1950–1963*.

6. See his expression of the fundamental "imaginative man" in a later letter to the Milton Society of America in 1954 – undated letter, probably October 1954, in Walter Hooper (ed.), *C.S. Lewis: Collected Letters Vol. III: Narnia, Cambridge and Joy 1950–1963*.

7. Letter to Carl F.H. Henry, 28 September 1955, in Walter Hooper (ed.), *C.S. Lewis: Collected Letters Vol. III: Narnia, Cambridge and Joy 1950–1963*.

8. Diary entry 27 June 1946, in Clyde S. Kilby and Marjorie Lamp Meade (eds.), *Brothers and Friends: The Diaries of Major Warren Hamilton Lewis*.

9. From *St Andrews Citizen*, 29 June 1946. The very apt quotation of "things unattempted yet in prose or rhyme" is from John Milton's prayer for help and inspiration in his new venture in the opening lines of *Paradise Lost*.

10. Letter to Lord Salisbury, 9 March 1947, in Walter Hooper (ed.), *C.S. Lewis: Collected Letters Vol. II: Books, Broadcasts and the War 1931–1949*.

11. Entry for Wednesday 17 January 1951, in Clyde S. Kilby and Marjorie Lamp Meade (eds.), *Brothers and Friends: The Diaries of Major Warren Hamilton Lewis*.

12. Published as Chad Walsh, *C.S. Lewis: Apostle to the Skeptics* (New York: Macmillan, 1949).

13. See Michael Ward, *Planet Narnia: The Seven Heavens in the Imagination of C.S. Lewis* (New York: Oxford University Press, 2008).

14. Letter to Mr Anderson, 23 September 1963, in Walter Hooper (ed.), *C.S. Lewis Collected Letters Vol. II: Narnia, Cambridge and Joy 1950–1963*.

15. "Hollywood's liberal losses", 20 November 2005, by Brian C. Anderson, *Chicago Sun-Times*, http://www.manhattan-institute.org/html/miarticle.htm?id=3855#.URwbSo45gyE (accessed 7 February 2013).

16. *The Telegraph*, 3 April 2010, http://www.telegraph.co.uk/culture/books/books-life/7545438/The-20-greatest-childrens-books-ever.html (accessed 7 February 2013).

13. The Surprising American: Mrs Joy Davidman Gresham

1. Entry for Monday 5 November 1956, in Clyde S. Kilby, and Marjorie Lamp Meade (eds), *Brothers and Friends: The Diaries of Major Warren Hamilton Lewis* (New York: Harper & Row, 1982).

2. Lyle W. Dorsett, *And God Came In* (New York: Macmillan, 1983), p. 70.

3. See the biographies *Shadowlands,* by Brian Sibley (who researched the BBC film), *And God Came In*, by Lyle Dorsett, and *Lenten Lands: My Childhood with Joy Davidman and C.S. Lewis,* by Douglas Gresham, younger son of Joy Davidman and stepson of C.S. Lewis.

4. Joy Davidman, "The Longest Way Round", in Don W. King (ed.), *Out of My Bone: The Letters of Joy Davidman* (Grand Rapids, MI: Eerdmans, 2009), p. 94.

5. Warnie Lewis, entry for Monday 5 November 1956, in Clyde S. Kilby, and Marjorie Lamp Meade (eds.), *Brothers and Friends: The Diaries of Major Warren Hamilton Lewis*.

6. Douglas Gresham, *Lenten Lands: My Childhood with Joy Davidman and C.S. Lewis* (London: Collins, 1989), p. 55.

7. For a full account of the events leading up to Lewis's move to Cambridge, and Tolkien's crucial role in it, see my *J.R.R. Tolkien and C.S. Lewis: The Story of a Friendship* (Stroud: Sutton Publishing, 2003), chapter 10, p. 146 ff.

8. Quoted in Colin Duriez, *J.R.R. Tolkien and C.S. Lewis: The Story of a Friendship*, p. 147.

9. There are some parallels with Francis Schaeffer's small book *Escape From Reason* (Leicester: IVP, 1968), which also posits a cataclysmic divide between modern and older thought starting around that time.

10. Letter 13 December 1954 in Don W. King (ed.), *Out of My Bone: The Letters of Joy Davidman*, pp. 227–228.

11. "*De Descriptione Temporum*" (1955), in *C.S. Lewis: Selected Literary Essays*, pp. 1–14.

12. Walter Hooper, *C.S. Lewis: A Companion and Guide* (London: HarperCollins, 1996), p. 247; Roger Lancelyn Green and Walter Hooper, *C.S. Lewis: A Biography* (fully revised and expanded edition; London: HarperCollins, 2002), p. 353; Joy Davidman, letter to Bill Gresham, 29 April 1955, in Don W. King (ed.), *Out of My Bone: The Letters of Joy Davidman*, p. 246.

13. Lewis is quoting Tertullian, in reference to the Latin poet Virgil, who appeared to be anticipating the coming of Christ.

14. See Walter Hooper's comment in Walter Hooper (ed.), *C.S. Lewis: Collected Letters Vol. III: Narnia, Cambridge and Joy 1950–1963*, p. 643.

15. C.S. Lewis, *A Grief Observed*, published under the pseudonym N.W. Clerk (London: Faber and Faber, 1961), p. 8.

16. Douglas Gresham, *Lenten Lands,* pp. 87–88.

17. Don W. King (ed.), *Out of My Bone: The Letters of Joy Davidman*, p. 280.

18. Back jacket endorsement on *ibid*.

19. Jocelyn Gibb (ed.), *Light on C.S. Lewis*, p. 63.

14. Leaving the Shadowlands

1. N.W. stands for Nat Whilk, Old English for "I know not whom", and Clerk is Middle English for "scholar".

2. Roger Lancelyn Green and Walter Hooper, *C.S. Lewis: A Biography* (London: Collins, 1974), p. 159.

3. Douglas Gresham, *Lenten Lands,* p. 154.

4. Clyde S. Kilby and Marjorie Lamp Meade (eds.), *Brothers and Friends: The Diaries of Major Warren Hamilton Lewis*.

5. Roger Lancelyn Green and Walter Hooper, *C.S. Lewis: A Biography* (fully revised and expanded edition; London: HarperCollins, 2002), p. 430.

Select Bibliography

Writings of C.S. Lewis

Spirits in Bondage: A Cycle of Lyrics (London: William Heinemann, 1919).

Dymer (London: J. M. Dent, 1926; new edition 1950).

The Pilgrim's Regress: An Allegorical Apology for Christianity, Reason and Romanticism (London: J. M. Dent, 1933; new edition 1943).

The Allegory of Love: A Study in Medieval Tradition (Oxford: Clarendon Press, 1936).

Out of the Silent Planet (London: John Lane, 1938).

Rehabilitations and Other Essays (London: Oxford University Press, 1939).

The Personal Heresy: A Controversy, with E. M. W. Tillyard (London: Oxford University Press, 1939).

The Problem of Pain (London: Geoffrey Bles, 1940).

Broadcast Talks (London: Geoffrey Bles, 1942).

A Preface to Paradise Lost (London: Oxford University Press, 1942).

The Screwtape Letters (London: Geoffrey Bles, 1942). Reprinted with an additional letter as *The Screwtape Letters and Screwtape Proposes a Toast* (London: Geoffrey Bles, 1961). Further new material in *The Screwtape Letters with Screwtape Proposes a Toast* (New York: Macmillan, 1982).

The Weight of Glory (London: SPCK, Little Books on Religion No. 189, 1942).

Christian Behaviour: A Further Series of Broadcast Talks (London: Geoffrey Bles, London, 1943).

Perelandra (London: John Lane, 1943). Reprinted in paperback as *Voyage to Venus* (Pan Books: London, 1953).

The Abolition of Man: Reflections on Education with Special Reference to the Teaching of English in the Upper Forms of Schools, Riddell Memorial Lectures, fifteenth series (London: Oxford University Press: 1943).

Beyond Personality: The Christian Idea of God (London: Geoffrey Bles, 1944).

That Hideous Strength: A Modern Fairy-Tale for Grown-Ups (London: John Lane, 1945). A version abridged by the author was published as *The Tortured Planet* (New York: Avon Books, 1946) and as *That Hideous Strength* (Pan Books: London, 1955).

The Great Divorce: A Dream (London: Geoffrey Bles, 1946). Originally published as a series in *The Guardian*. Bles inaccurately dated the book as 1945.

George MacDonald: An Anthology, compiled by, and with an introduction by, C.S. Lewis (London: Geoffrey Bles, 1946).

Essays Presented to Charles Williams edited by, and with an introduction by, C.S. Lewis (London: Oxford University Press, 1947).

Miracles: A Preliminary Study (London: Geoffrey Bles, 1947; reprinted, with an expanded version of chapter 3, London: Collins Fontana Books, 1960).

Arthurian Torso: Containing the Posthumous Fragment of the Figure of Arthur by Charles Williams and A Commentary on the Arthurian Poems of Charles Williams by C.S. Lewis (London: Oxford University Press, 1948).

Transposition and Other Addresses (London: Geoffrey Bles, 1949), published in the United States as *The Weight of Glory and Other Addresses* (New York: Macmillan, 1949).

The Lion, the Witch and the Wardrobe (London: Geoffrey Bles, 1950).

Prince Caspian: The Return to Narnia (London: Geoffrey Bles, 1951).

Mere Christianity (London: Geoffrey Bles, 1952). A revised and expanded version of *Broadcast Talks, Christian Behaviour* and *Beyond Personality.*

The Voyage of the "Dawn Treader" (London: Geoffrey Bles, 1952).

The Silver Chair (London: Geoffrey Bles, 1953).

The Horse and His Boy (London: Geoffrey Bles, 1954).

English Literature in the Sixteenth Century, Excluding Drama. Volume III of *The Oxford History of English Literature* (Oxford: Clarendon Press, 1954). In 1990 the series was renumbered and Lewis's volume was reissued as Volume IV, *Poetry and Prose in the Sixteenth Century.*

The Magician's Nephew (London: Bodley Head, 1955).

Surprised by Joy: The Shape of My Early Life (London: Geoffrey Bles, 1955).

The Last Battle (London: Bodley Head, 1956).

Till We Have Faces: A Myth Retold (London: Geoffrey Bles, 1956).

Reflections on the Psalms (London: Geoffrey Bles, 1958).

The Four Loves (London: Geoffrey Bles, 1960).

Studies in Words (Cambridge: Cambridge University Press, 1960).

The World's Last Night and Other Essays (New York: Harcourt, Brace & Co., 1960).

A Grief Observed (published under the pseudonym N.W. Clerk) (London: Faber and Faber, 1961).

An Experiment in Criticism (Cambridge: Cambridge University Press, 1961).

They Asked for a Paper: Papers and Addresses (London: Geoffrey Bles, 1962).

Posthumous writings and collections

Letters to Malcolm: Chiefly on Prayer (London: Geoffrey Bles, 1964).

The Discarded Image: An Introduction to Medieval and Renaissance Literature (Cambridge: Cambridge University Press, 1964).

Poems, Walter Hooper (ed.) (London: Geoffrey Bles, 1964).

Studies in Medieval and Renaissance Literature, Walter Hooper (ed.) (Cambridge: Cambridge University Press, 1966).

Letters of C.S. Lewis, W.H. Lewis (ed. and with a memoir by him) (London: Geoffrey Bles, 1966). Revised edition, Walter Hooper (ed.) (1988).

Of Other Worlds: Essays and Stories, Walter Hooper (ed.) (London: Geoffrey Bles, 1966).

Christian Reflections, Walter Hooper (ed.) (London: Geoffrey Bles, 1967).

Spenser's Images of Life, Alistair Fowler (ed.) (Cambridge: Cambridge University Press, 1967).

Letters to an American Lady, Clyde S. Kilby (ed.) (Grand Rapids, MI: Eerdmans, 1967; London: Hodder & Stoughton, 1969).

A Mind Awake: An Anthology of C.S. Lewis, Clyde S. Kilby (ed.) (London: Geoffrey Bles, 1968).

Narrative Poems, Walter Hooper (ed. and preface) (London: Geoffrey Bles, 1969).

Selected Literary Essays, Walter Hooper (ed. and preface) (Cambridge: Cambridge University Press, 1969).

God in the Dock: Essays on Theology and Ethics, Walter Hooper (ed. and preface) (Grand Rapids, MI: Eerdmans, 1970). A paperback edition of part of it was published as *God in the Dock: Essays on Theology* (London: Collins Fontana Books, 1979) and as *Undeceptions: Essays on Theology and Ethics* (London: Geoffrey Bles, 1971).

Fern Seeds and Elephants and Other Essays on Christianity, Walter Hooper (ed. and preface) (London: Collins Fontana Books, 1975).

The Dark Tower and Other Stories, Walter Hooper (ed. and preface) (London: Collins, 1977).

The Joyful Christian: Readings from C.S. Lewis, William Griffin (ed.) (New York: Macmillan, 1977).

They Stand Together: The Letters of C.S. Lewis to Arthur Greeves (1914–1963), Walter Hooper (ed.) (London: Collins, 1979).

Of This and Other Worlds, Walter Hooper (ed.) (London: Collins Fount, 1982).

The Business of Heaven, Daily Readings from C.S. Lewis, Walter Hooper (ed.) (London: Collins Fount, 1984).

Boxen: The Imaginary World of the Young C.S. Lewis, Walter Hooper (ed.) (London: Collins, 1985).

Letters to Children, Lyle W. Dorsett and Marjorie Lamp Mead (eds.) (New York: Collins; London, 1985).

First and Second Things: Essays on Theology and Ethics, Walter Hooper (ed. and preface) (Glasgow: Collins Fount, 1985).

Present Concerns, Walter Hooper (ed.) (London: Collins Fount, 1986).

Timeless at Heart, Walter Hooper (ed.) (London: Collins Fount, 1987).

Letters: C.S. Lewis and Don Giovanni Calabria: A Study in Friendship, Martin Moynihan (ed. and introduction) (Glasgow: Collins, 1988); includes Latin text. First issued as *The Latin Letters of C.S. Lewis* (Westchester, IL: Crossway Books, 1987); paperback edition, without Latin text.

All My Road Before Me: The Diary of C.S. Lewis, 1922–1927, Walter Hooper (ed.) (London: HarperCollins, 1991).

The Collected Poems of C .S. Lewis, Walter Hooper (ed.) (London: HarperCollins, 1994).

C.S. Lewis: Essay Collection and Other Short Pieces, Lesley Walmsley (ed.) (London: HarperCollins, 2000).

C.S. Lewis: Collected Letters Vol. I: Family Letters 1905–1931, Walter Hooper (ed.) (London: HarperCollins, 2000).

C.S. Lewis: Collected Letters Vol. II: Books, Broadcasts and the War 1931–1949, Walter Hooper (ed.) (London: HarperCollins, 2004).

C.S. Lewis: Collected Letters Vol. III: Narnia, Cambridge and Joy 1950–1963, Walter Hooper (ed.) (London: HarperCollins, 2006).

Select list of books relating to C.S. Lewis

Adey, Lionel, *C.S. Lewis: Writer, Dreamer and Mentor* (Grand Rapids, MI; Cambridge: Eerdmans, 1998).

———, *C.S. Lewis's "Great War" with Owen Barfield* (Victoria, BC: University of Victoria Press, 1978).

Arnott, Anne, *The Secret Country of C.S. Lewis* (London: Hodder & Stoughton, 1974).

Blaxland de Lange, Simon, *Owen Barfield: Romanticism Come of Age, A Biography* (Forest Row: Temple Lodge, 2006).

Bleakley, David, *C.S. Lewis at Home in Ireland: A Centenary Biography* (Belfast: Strandtown Press, 1998).

Carnell, Corbin S., *Bright Shadows of Reality* (Grand Rapids, MI: Eerdmans, 1974).

Carpenter, Humphrey, *The Inklings: C.S. Lewis, J.R.R. Tolkien, Charles Williams and Their Friends* (London: George Allen and Unwin, 1978).

Carpenter, Humphrey and Marie Prichard, *The Oxford Companion to Children's Literature* (Oxford: Oxford University Press, 1984).

Como, James T., (ed.), *C.S. Lewis at the Breakfast Table and Other Reminiscences* (New York: Macmillan, 1979).

Dorsett, Lyle, *Joy and C.S. Lewis* (London: HarperCollins, 1988).

Downing, David C., *The Most Reluctant Convert: C.S. Lewis's Journey to Faith* (Downers Grove, IL: IVP, 2002).

Duncan, John Ryan, *The Magic Never Ends: The Life and Work of C.S. Lewis* (Nashville, TN: Thomas Nelson, 2002; British edition, Milton Keynes: Authentic, 2002).

Duriez, Colin, *The C.S. Lewis Encyclopedia* (Wheaton, IL: Crossway; London: SPCK, 2000).

————, *Tolkien and C.S. Lewis: The Gift of Friendship* (Mahwah, NJ: The Paulist Press, 2003).

————, *A Field Guide to Narnia* (Downers Grove, IL: IVP, 2004).

————, *The C.S. Lewis Chronicles: The Indispensable Biography of the Creator of Narnia Full of Little-Known Facts, Events and Miscellany* (New York: BlueBridge, 2005).

————, *J.R.R. Tolkien: The Making of a Legend* (Oxford: Lion, 2012).

Edwards, Bruce L. (ed.), *C.S. Lewis: Life, Works and Legacy*, 4 Vols (Westport, CT: Praeger Publishing, 2007).

Ford, Paul F., *Companion to Narnia* (San Francisco, CA: Harper & Row, 1994).

Fuller, Edmund, *Books with Men Behind Them* (New York: Random House, 1962).

Gibb, Jocelyn, (ed.), *Light on C.S. Lewis* (London: Geoffrey Bles, 1965).

Gilchrist, K.J., *A Morning After War: C.S. Lewis & WWI.* (New York: Peter Lang, 2005).

Graham, David (ed.), *We Remember C.S. Lewis: Essays & Memoirs* (Nashville, TN: Broadman & Holman, 2001).

Green, Roger Lancelyn and Walter Hooper, *C.S. Lewis: A Biography* (London: Collins, 1974); Roger Lancelyn Green and Walter Hooper, *C.S. Lewis: A Biography* (fully revised and expanded edition; London: HarperCollins, 2002).

Gresham, Douglas, *Lenten Lands: My Childhood with Joy Davidman and C.S. Lewis* (London: Collins, 1989).

————, *Jack's Life: The Life Story of C.S. Lewis* (Nashville, TN: Broadman & Holman Publishers, 2005).

Griffin, William, *Clive Staples Lewis: A Dramatic Life* (New York: Harper & Row, 1986). Published in the UK as *C.S. Lewis: The Authentic Voice* (Tring: Lion, 1988).

Harwood, Laurence, *C.S. Lewis, My Godfather: Letters, Photos and Recollections* (Downers Grove, IL: IVP, 2007).

Hooper, Walter, *C.S. Lewis: A Companion and Guide* (London: HarperCollins, 1996).

————, *Past Watchful Dragons* (London: Collins Fount, 1980).

Howard, Thomas, *The Achievement of C.S. Lewis: A Reading of His Fiction* (Wheaton, IL: Shaw, 1980).

Jacobs, Alan, *The Narnian* (London: SPCK, 2005).

Keefe, Carolyn (ed.), *C.S. Lewis: Speaker and Teacher* (London: Hodder, 1974).

Kilby, Clyde S., *The Christian World of C.S. Lewis* (Grand Rapids, MI: Eerdmans, 1965).

————, *Images of Salvation in the Fiction of C.S. Lewis* (Wheaton, IL: Shaw, 1978).

Kilby, Clyde S. and Douglas Gilbert, *C.S. Lewis: Images of His World* (Grand Rapids, MI: Eerdmans, 1973).

Kilby, Clyde S. and Marjorie Lamp Meade (eds.), *Brothers and Friends: The Diaries of Major Warren Hamilton Lewis* (San Francisco, CA: Harper & Row, 1982).

King, Don W., *C.S. Lewis, Poet: The Legacy of His Poetic Impulse* (Kent, Ohio: The Kent State University Press, 2001).

King, Don W., (ed.), *Out of My Bone: The Letters of Joy Davidman* (Grand Rapids, MI: Eerdmans, 2009).

Lawlor, John, *C.S. Lewis: Memories and Reflections* (Dallas: Spence Publishing Company, 1998), p. 20.

Lewis, Warren Hamilton, (ed.), *The Lewis Papers: Memoirs of the Lewis Family, 1850–1930*. Unpublished papers bequeathed to The Marion E. Wade Center, Wheaton College, IL, USA.

Lindskoog, Kathryn, *C.S. Lewis: Mere Christian* (Glendale, CA: Gospel Light, 1973).

————, *The Lion of Judah in Never-Never Land: God, Man and Nature in C.S. Lewis's Narnia Tales* (Grand Rapids, MI: Eerdmans, 1973).

Mabbott, John D., *Oxford Memories* (Oxford: Thorntons of Oxford, 1986).

Manlove, C.N., *Christian Fantasy: From 1200 to the Present* (Basingstoke; London: Macmillan, 1992).

Martin, Thomas L., (ed.), *Reading the Classics with C.S. Lewis* (Grand Rapids, MI: Baker Academic; Carlisle, UK: Paternoster, 2000).

Mills, David, (ed.), *The Pilgrim's Guide: C.S. Lewis and the Art of Witness* (Grand Rapids, MI: Eerdmans, 1998).

Myers, Doris, *C.S. Lewis in Context* (Kent, Ohio: The Kent State University Press, 1994).

Phillips, Justin, *C.S. Lewis at the BBC* (London: HarperCollins, 2002).

Reilly, Robert J., *Romantic Religion: A Study of Barfield, Lewis, Williams and Tolkien* (Athens, GA: University of Georgia Press, 1971).

Sayer, George, *Jack: C.S. Lewis and His Times* (London: Macmillan, 1988).

Schakel, Peter J., *Reading with the Heart: The Way Into Narnia* (Grand Rapids, MI: Eerdmans, 1979).

————, *Reason and Imagination in C.S. Lewis: A Study of Till We Have Faces* (Exeter: Paternoster, 1984).

Schofield, Stephen, (ed.), *In Search of C.S. Lewis* (New Jersey: Bridge, 1984).

Schultz, Jeffrey D. and John G. West Jr., (eds.), *The C.S. Lewis Readers' Encyclopedia* (Grand Rapids, MI: Zondervan, 1998).

Sibley, Brian, *The Land of Narnia*, illustrated by Pauline Baynes (London: Collins, 1989).

————, *Shadowlands* (London: Hodder, 1985).

Schmidt, Gary D. and Donald R. Hettinga, (eds.), *British Children's Writers*, Vol. 160 of *Dictionary of Literary Biography* (Detroit: Bruccoli Clark Layman, 1996).

Tennyson, G.B. (ed.), *Owen Barfield on C.S. Lewis* (San Raphael, CA: The Barfield Press, 1989).

Tolkien, J.R.R., Humphrey Carpenter (ed.), *Letters of J.R.R. Tolkien* (London: George Allen and Unwin, 1981).

Walsh, Chad, *C.S. Lewis: Apostle to the Skeptics* (New York: Macmillan, 1949).

————, *The Literary Legacy of C.S. Lewis* (New York: Harcourt Brace Jovanovich, 1979).

Wain, John, *Sprightly Running: Part of an Autobiography* (London: Macmillan, 1965).

Ward, Michael, *Planet Narnia: The Seven Heavens in the Imagination of C.S. Lewis* (New York: Oxford University Press, 2008).

White, William L., *The Image of Man in C.S. Lewis* (London: Hodder, 1970).

Wilson, A.N., *C.S. Lewis: A Biography* (London: Collins, 1990).

Index